Base Camp Denver

101 Hikes in Colorado's Front Range

IMBRIFEX

Also by Pete KJ

Fiction

Mermelada

The Coins

The Maple Leaf

The Rooster's Hindquarters

Black Volta

Nonfiction

The Year We Roamed:
A Father-and-Son Trip Around the World

Roaming Around:
A Daughter and Father World Journey

Base Camp Denver

101 Hikes in Colorado's Front Range

Pete KJ

IMBRIFEX BOOKS

IMBRIFEX BOOKS
Published by Flattop Productions, Inc.
8275 S. Eastern Avenue, Suite 200
Las Vegas, NV 89123, USA

Base Camp Denver: 101 Hikes in Colorado's Front Range

This publication is provided for informational and educational purposes. The information contained in the publication is true to the best of our knowledge, however no representations or warranties are made with respect to its accuracy or safety, and the Publisher and author assume no liability for its use. Outdoor activities are always potentially dangerous. Awareness of local conditions and weather coupled with good decision-making skills and astute judgment will help reduce potential hazards and risks. Preparing yourself with the proper equipment and outdoor skills will lead to an enjoyable experience. The information contained herein is true and complete, however things can change after a guide book is published—trails are rerouted, trailhead signs are removed or damaged, jurisdiction changes in governmental management of an area can affect routes, seasonal impacts, etc. Corrections, updates and suggestions may be sent to the author at petekj@basecampguides.com.

Editor: Nancy Zerbey
Cover and Book Designer: Sue Campbell Book Design
Maps: Chris Erichsen
All interior photos by the author except as noted.
Cover photos: (background) Oleksandr Buzko, iStockphoto; (hikers) Kerkez, iStockphoto
Author Photo: Brooke Warren

Library of Congress Cataloging-in-Publication Data
Names: KJ, Pete, author.
Title: Base camp Denver : 101 hikes in Colorado's Front Range / Pete KJ.
Description: First edition. | Las Vegas, NV : Imbrifex Books, [2019] |
   Includes index.
Identifiers: LCCN 2018042815 (print) | LCCN 2018050253 (ebook) | ISBN
   | ISBN 9781945501135 (alk. paper) | ISBN 9781945501142 (ebook)
Subjects: LCSH: Hiking--Front Range (Colo. and Wyo.)--Guidebooks. |
   Hiking--Colorado--Denver Region--Guidebooks. | Front Range (Colo. and
   Wyo.)--Guidebooks. | Denver (Colo.)--Guidebooks.
Classification: LCC GV199.42.C62 (ebook) | LCC GV199.42.C62 F675 2019 (print)
   | DDC 796.510978--dc23
LC record available at https://lccn.loc.gov/2018042815

First Edition: April 2019
Printed in the Republic of South Korea

IMBRIFEX® is a registered trademark of Flattop Productions, Inc.
BaseCampGuides.com | Imbrifex.com

This book is dedicated to memories of Harvey Manning, Helen Sherman, Bob Spring, and Ira Spring, who created the guidebooks in the 1970s that opened my world up to a lifetime of hiking.

CONTENTS

Before You Hit the Trail

DENVER IS AN AWESOME BASE CAMP FOR DAY HIKERS. YOU CAN CATCH THE SUNRISE FROM a mountaintop and still make it to work in the morning. You can wander remote wilderness by day, and then hit a great restaurant and sleep in a bed at night.

With so much great hiking so close to the city, it can be hard to know where to begin. It's easy to get lost in hiking websites and their pop-up windows before leaving the house, and just as easy to fall into the habit of walking the same handful of beloved trails over and over again. This book bridges the gap, offering 101 carefully chosen hikes near Denver. Whether you are just beginning to explore the Front Range, or are a seasoned hiker looking to expand your route repertoire, this book is a ticket to adventure.

You may think, "Denver, hmm. I think I'll ski in winter and hike in summer." Perish the thought! Abundant hiking beckons all year round. It's true that it takes until June for high peaks and emerald meadows to start losing their snowpack. But you can clamber on foothills amidst startling rock formations in January, tromp butterscotch-scented ponderosa forests in March, and revel in fiery aspen colors in the first week of October. Regardless of time of year, the views are incredible and sunny skies are the norm.

Anyone who can walk can enjoy these trails. No training or experience is necessary, but plenty is gained through hiking. Safety is not a worry as long as you are mindful of the few items discussed below. You also don't need any fancy gear; all you really need are two legs and some decent shoes. And curiosity, because every hike is different, and every hike has stories of history, geology, etymology, or wildlife to tell. It is in the spirit of storytelling that this book was created. Within minutes you can read about some great hikes, choose one, and then go out and write your own story by walking the trail.

Exploring the Front Range on foot is a low-cost and addictive habit, and has the side effect of being incredibly good for you. A few gallons of gas is usually the only cost for the priceless experience of spending time with Mother Nature. The more you go, the more you want to go, and the more your body loves it. Visitors to Denver will do well to pack their hiking boots, and if you live here, you might as well keep them in the car.

Enjoy your time outdoors!

Welcome to the Wall

COLORADO'S FRONT RANGE OF THE ROCKY MOUNTAINS IS ABOUT 150 MILES LONG BY ABOUT 50 miles wide, stretching south from the Wyoming border through north and central Colorado. The Continental Divide is its backbone, and cities from Fort Collins to Pueblo line the plains along its eastern base. Denver sits in the center of this base, and from downtown you can travel just 40 miles west and gain over 8,000 feet.

This magnificent wall is the product of an uplift that began about 60 million years ago, when continental plates collided thousands of miles west. Things finally calmed down about a million years ago, and erosion continued to sculpt the land. Ice ages came and went, assisting with the carving. By the time the most recent frozen period waned, about 11,000 years ago, human beings had taken up residence. Much later, some European humans visited, and in 1859 they found gold, which changed everything. Thousands of folks moved here and settled, and by 1876 Colorado had been admitted to the United States.

The eastern plains are an expansive zone of shortgrass prairie, treeless except for giant cottonwoods and other species that grow near creeks. As the land slopes upward, ponderosas, pinyons, and junipers join the plant mix along with cacti, yuccas, and various shrubs. Between about 6,000 and 8,000 feet there's a transition zone of taller ponderosas and Douglas firs, followed by a cooler and moister zone, up to about 10,000 feet, where aspens thrive, along with evergreens such as Engelmann spruce and lodgepole pines.

Ridge to the top of Mount Bierstadt

As the tree line is approached, at about 11,000 feet (higher in the south), subalpine firs take over along with bristlecone and limber pines. In the cold, windblown upper reaches they form thickets of twisted midget trees collectively known as *krummholz*, a German word for "crooked wood." Above tree line is an Arctic-like zone of hardy, short tundra grasses and tiny wildflowers.

Flowers on the plains bloom in spring, while mountain meadows peak late June through early August. Among the hundreds of vibrant species a few really do stand out: lavender-and-white columbine, pink elephant's head, purple monkshood, and fiery orange Indian paintbrush.

Anyone who hikes the Front Range will see mule deer at some point, and possibly a coyote. Elk and bighorn sheep are common sights as well, at different elevations depending on the season. It is unlikely you will ever see a mountain lion or a bobcat, but you will probably be observed by these elusive creatures at some point. Encounters with black bears are also rare. Moose have made the higher creek bottoms and forests their home in recent decades; several of these hikes almost guarantee a viewing. Frequent fliers include red-tailed hawks, bald and golden eagles, and peregrine falcons. In nearer view, mountain bluebirds flit between the branches and gray jays—also known as "camp robbers"—boldly land to greet you.

You won't be alone above timberline. Marmots are plentiful here; many have lost their fear of humans and will try to rummage through your pack. You might almost step on a ptarmigan as it ambles through the tundra, muttering, looking nonplussed by your presence. Shaggy white mountain goats pose trailside for

photographs. On top of high peaks you may hear a squeak and see a furry gray pika scurry across the rocks. These tiny, big-eared cutie-pies stay awake all winter in their burrows, even on top of Colorado's highest peaks.

When to Hike Where

It's simple: when it's cold, stay lower; when it's hot, go high. All elevations are within a few score miles of Denver, so there's no need to fuss over drive times.

The cliché about Colorado weather—"If you don't like it, wait 10 minutes!"—is misleading. Weather can come from any direction and change quickly, but it is usually predictable. *Spring*, from March to mid-June, is a cool, sunny period free of thunderstorms; mornings start out cold and days warm up quickly. *Summer*, from mid-June through September, is a time of afternoon thunderstorms and great weather otherwise. You'll almost always have a clear hiking window before or after storms (which don't hit everywhere every day). Later afternoons and evenings on long summer days are great for hiking because the lighting effects are beautiful, and solitude abounds. *Autumn* arrives by late September; it is a brief season of cooler weather, beautiful foliage, and few if any thunderstorms. Snow

Fall foliage along Mount Margaret Trail

is possible in autumn, and can be heavy and then melt away. *Winter*, from late October to March, is a time of permanent snowpack in most places above 10,000 feet. This is a good time to bundle up and stick to foothills and prairie. But don't be surprised if you find yourself unbundling on a 70-degree day in January!

From November to March, heavy winds can sometimes blow over the lower lands, and they can happen any time up higher. These winds come over the Continental Divide and descend like a waterfall over the foothills, reaching speeds of 120 mph. You can hike on such windy days, but it might not be much fun. Better to wait a day or two for things to calm down.

A "Best Season" recommendation is given for each of the hikes, and is assigned as follows:

Spring and fall: Medium-altitude hikes (approximately 8,000 to 10,000 feet), which are doable in summer but are more likely to be hot, dry, and crowded then. You'll probably have a better time on these trails during the shoulder months of March to May and/or in foliage season.

Early summer: Higher-altitude hikes (approximately 10,000 to 11,000 feet, and some higher ones with southwestern exposure), which may be largely free of snow by late May or early June. Choose these when you're aching for the higher country that is still caked in white.

Summer: All trails in this book can be hiked in summer, but these months are like precious jewels and their time should be spent wisely. The summer recommendation is therefore reserved for high-altitude hikes (approximately 10,000 to 14,000 feet), where significant snow cover is usually encountered except mid-June through September.

Fall, winter, spring: Hikes below 9,000 feet that can be walked all year, weather permitting. They aren't the best choices for summer because of heat, dryness, and crowds, but mostly because so many options exist for hiking at higher and fresher altitudes at that time.

All year: Hikes below 9,000 feet that are fine all year, thanks to shade-giving foliage, remarkable scenery, and other qualities.

The hikes in this book are numbered north to south, but all regions are varied and interesting. If you have a special interest, for example in waterfalls or hiking with kids, consult the section called "Choose Your Perfect Hike," beginning on page 371.

The 101

I CONSIDERED NEARLY 300 TRAILS AS CANDIDATES FOR THIS BOOK, AND WALKED MORE than 200 of them to whittle the list down to the 101. Coincidentally, 101 turned out to be a perfect number to recommend near Denver. Fewer would not have done the region justice. More could be overwhelming, but more importantly, could point you to trails that might not be worth your time—until you've walked the 101, that is.

What is a day hike in the Front Range? In this book, it's 7 miles long on average, with 1,500 feet of elevation gain. This means it doesn't take all day. You can usually extend the hike, and you can always shorten it. The first mile or two are often great in themselves. The shortest hike in this book is just over 2 miles, and the longest is nearly 16; elevation gains range from negligible to 4,000 feet.

This book doesn't sweat the minutiae. Distances are usually rounded to the nearest half mile, elevations to 100 feet. I feel that greater precision can create a false sense of accuracy, and more importantly, isn't that helpful. The point is to get out there and hike, not to focus on hundredths of miles as read from GPS devices. What is most helpful, to me, is to pay attention to the physical world: to walk, look, and let the mountains speak.

Almost all the hikes are within a two-hour drive from downtown Denver; many are under an hour's drive. A few push the three-hour mark, to reach amazing places west of Fort Collins. One chapter describes hikes in the stunning Gore and Tenmile Ranges of Summit County, which technically are not in the Front Range, but at less than two hours' drive from Denver, how can they be refused?

I arrived at all the trailheads in an ordinary, front-wheel-drive passenger car named Ruby. However, a handful of drives were pretty rough on Ruby, and it would have been better to have a high-clearance, four-wheel-drive vehicle. Those cases are noted. The main car-beaters are Grays Peak (Hike 64) and High Lonesome (Hike 61), two hikes too incredible not to include in this book.

A word on parking. In the driving directions included with each hike, a "small" parking area means space for fewer than a dozen cars. "Large" means room for more than 50. Anything in between is listed simply as "parking." Regardless of lot size, it is important to arrive early in the morning or later in the afternoon to ensure a space, especially in summer. At the end of the driving directions, I have indicated how long it takes to drive to each trailhead from downtown Denver under optimal driving conditions.

About three quarters of the trailheads have no entrance or parking fees. Several are in Colorado state parks, which charged $7 per vehicle in 2018. Several more are on municipal open spaces that levy about the same fee; all cases are noted. It is a good idea to carry some $5 and $1 bills and/or a checkbook to facilitate payment, as cards are not always accepted, and many trailheads have self-pay envelope stations. The highest entrance fee is for Rocky Mountain National Park, which was $25 per day per vehicle in 2018, and was likely to go up.

Hike Ratings

EACH HIKE DESCRIPTION CONTAINS AN "AT A GLANCE" TABLE, IN WHICH RATINGS OF 1 TO 5 are assigned in the following categories:

Difficulty mostly reflects distance and elevation gain, with higher ratings meaning "more difficult." As an average hike is 7 miles with 1,500 feet of gain, a rating of 3 corresponds roughly to that, taking into account Trail Condition.

Trail Condition evaluates a trail with respect to width, continuity, smoothness, and grade. A 3-rated trail has no washouts or vanished portions, requires no tricky stream crossings, and is not overly steep, narrow, rocky, or full of tree roots. The 4- and 5-rated trails are good choices for people with mobility challenges.

Children is a harder rating to assign. Difficulty largely drives it. When the two ratings don't inversely correlate, it is because there are rewarding features early in the hike, after which folks can turn back, and/or wonderful features later on that appeal to children and make it worth the effort. Low-rated hikes tend to be long, with lots of elevation gain and not much in the way of "fun" unless your child is a fitness enthusiast.

Scenery is not all about breathtaking high-mountain vistas or spectacular rock formations. A 3-rated trail might have lovely forests, streams, vales, and meadows but few expansive views. Ratings of 1 and 2 are uncommon; the Front Range is a gorgeous place!

Photography is usually rated the same as Scenery but is sometimes dialed up or down a level. Some great scenery just doesn't photograph all that well, and some modestly scenic hikes have features like curious rock formations, an iconic vista, or waterfalls that make for dynamite photos.

Solitude ratings are fairly evenly distributed between 1 and 4, with only two hikes garnering a 5. One was completely empty on a gorgeous Friday in mid-August (Ute Peak, Hike 69); the other, aptly named High Lonesome (Hike 61), was nearly so, and although it was an epic drive to reach, too amazing not to include. Ratings of 1 and 2 indicate the trail will almost certainly be crowded in summer and on weekends, and may also present parking challenges.

Time to Hike!

ESTIMATED HIKING TIMES ARE JUST THAT: *HIKING* TIMES, NOT "NOT-HIKING" TIMES. REST breaks aren't included since those are entirely up to you. As you use this book, a correlation should emerge between your pace and the *101 Hikes* pace, which is roughly:

- 1 to 2 miles per hour uphill, closer to 1 when the trail is very steep, high-altitude, and/or rocky
- 2 to 2.5 miles per hour for moderate ups and downs on decent-quality trail
- 3 miles per hour on flats and downhill on smooth trail

It feels funny to write about how to walk, but I feel compelled to do it because I see so many people doing it "wrong." Throughout my hiking career I've found great truth in the adage, "To climb a big mountain quickly, you must do it slowly." The most important words here are "do it," meaning you should try to keep moving and minimize rest breaks.

The main problem with rest breaks is that they don't really help you. If you are tired and you stop for a bit, chances are you will feel just as tired within a few minutes of restarting, and want to stop again. A much better strategy is to *slow down* but not stop, even if it means a tortoise pace. Hiking is not a race. Go as slow as you want, but keep going! Find a steady, comfortable slog, one that you can maintain for an hour, two hours, a day.

Another thing about rest breaks, which should be obvious but isn't, is that they bring your progress to a grinding halt. Even if you are going at only a half mile an hour, your projected completion time is within hours. Once you stop, your projected completion time is never.

Other than pace, the most important thing about timing, especially in summer, is to get up early. It's a good idea to arrive at the trailhead at dawn. This gets you out of the city before traffic builds and, more importantly, ensures you a parking space. Arriving late morning on a summer Saturday almost guarantees parking trouble. An early start in summer also gives the treat of clear blue skies almost every day until afternoon, when the clouds build and often burst. If solitude is important to you, arriving early also means you'll have the trail and back-country mostly to yourself. If you get lonely, don't worry, you can greet plenty of folks hiking in as you're on your way out.

If you don't like to get up early, the next best thing to do is get up late, especially during the long days of June through August. The threat of thunderstorms often clears out the trails and parking lots by mid-afternoon, but by 3 or 4 p.m. the storms have usually passed, if they have come at all, giving way to gorgeous sunny late afternoons and evenings when the effects of the slanting light on the mountains can be mesmerizing. Even the three fourteeners in this book (peaks over 14,000 feet) can be hiked after 3 p.m. on long summer days, and though each is wildly popular, you

might find yourself alone on the summit as I did on both Grays (Hike 64) and Quandary (Hike 75).

Clothing and Equipment

YOU DON'T NEED ANY SPECIAL CLOTHES OR EQUIPMENT TO DO THESE HIKES. JUST WALK. Good shoes and good legs are a plus, but you can start with whatever shoes and develop the legs. If you hike more than a little, you'll do well to invest in a pair of

good-quality, lightweight hiking boots, ones made from water-resistant synthetic materials. Or you can buy a cheap pair and see how long the soles last. Trail runners—beefed up running shoes—are fine on dry trails, but not so good in mud, snow, and loose rock.

Other than shoes, the most important items to bring are water and extra clothes—and a pack to carry them in. A good rule for tap water is two liters per person, plus treatment tablets in case you run out and are forced to drink creek or lake water. Of course, you will want to add your favorite trail food to the pack. As for clothes, know that temperatures can swing several dozen degrees during a day. Don't ever go up very high without a hat, gloves, an extra sweater or two, long pants, and a wind/water shell.

Other things to have in the pack are sunscreen, insect repellent, and a first aid kit. A topographic map and compass are highly advised. Bring your

Photo: Takahiro Sakamoto, Unsplash.com

cell phone too (you will often have reception) and a camera if you prefer to use one instead of your phone. Be sure to carry a flashlight; you may be having so much fun that you want to stay out late and need it for the final stretch to the car. I also like to pack a collapsible umbrella. I can't tell you how pleasant it makes hiking in a non-thunderstorm drizzle.

Trekking poles are a personal preference. Some people enjoy the upper body workout, and many swear they need them to protect their knees. Keep in mind that using poles means making four points of contact per walking cycle instead of two, which can complicate the process, especially on rocky and rooty trails.

Maps and Navigation

EACH HIKE DESCRIPTION INCLUDES A DIAGRAM OF THE ROUTE. THE INTENTION IS TO provide a snapshot: something to help you choose the hike, imprint on your brain, and keep in mind while walking. A bold dashed line represents the route described in the text; lighter-weight dashed lines are branching trails and alternative paths. These diagrams are not meant to substitute for actual navigation maps, which you will probably want to buy if you do more than a little hiking. A good topographic map not only helps you avoid getting lost, it adds great pleasure to the hiking experience. You can compare what you see with what's on the map, learn the names of things near and far, get to be on a first-name basis with many mountains, and come to greet them as old friends. You can be more confident in making route deviations, and—best of all—get lots of ideas for your next hike.

My favorite set of topographic maps are in the National Geographic *Trails Illustrated* series. They are accurate and durable, and their size and scale usually give an appropriate level of detail: not too little, not too "zoomed-in." For me it is just as important to track features several dozen miles away as it is to see things that are close.

No matter how careful you are, or how good your map is, you are going to lose your way at some point. Accept it; it's part of the deal. Try to have fun with it, and don't freak out. Stay calm, relaxed, look at the map, look at the features around you, and plan your next move with confidence. Usually the best bet is to retrace your steps until you feel more certain of where you are, even if it means lengthening your trip. Prevention is best, of course. Don't let your confusion build too much before you check the map.

Personal Safety

Hydration
TWO LITERS OF TAP WATER PER PERSON WILL CARRY YOU THROUGH MOST OF THESE HIKES. You should assume that all surface water (lakes and streams) contains the giardia parasite, which can create nasty intestinal trouble.

Drink plenty of fluids before starting out, and spread out your water intake over the hike. Humans can't process more than about a liter per hour; the excess just gets filtered out.

Thunderstorms
PRACTICE HELPS IN READING THE WEATHER AND JUDGING THE LIKELIHOOD OF THUNDER-storms. Cumulus clouds that are spaced apart and fluffy white at the bottoms pose no danger; watch for the very dark ones with an anvil shape at the top. Five seconds between a lightning flash and thunder means the event is a mile away; anything less than 20 seconds signals danger, since lightning can travel ahead of storms. Cold rain and hail are also concerns.

Get off summits and ridges if a storm approaches. Also stay away from depressions, gully bottoms, the bases of rock overhangs, large solitary trees, and standing water. The best place to be is among a group of small, uniformly-sized trees, where you should sit on your pack with your elbows outside your knees to help ball yourself up small. Companions should space out about 50 feet apart.

During a lightning storm, try to stay calm and enjoy yourself. Storms are exceedingly common on summer afternoons, and great times to feel connected with nature's beauty and power. The whole reason for the hazard is that humans are not separate from nature. Rather we are connected, a part of what is going on. Storms usually don't last long, and the lighting effects are gorgeous when the storm passes and the sun reemerges.

Altitude

ALTITUDE SICKNESS IS A BIOLOGICAL DISTURBANCE BROUGHT ON BY INADEQUATE OXYGEN intake. Susceptibility depends on the individual and can be unpredictable. The key is to pay attention to your body and know how it tends to react. Common symptoms include headache, nausea, loss of appetite, and lethargy. You might also experience swelling in your face and hands or feet.

If you are visiting the Front Range from sea level, it's a good idea to spend at least two days at around 8,000 feet before going much higher. Then ascend slowly, stay hydrated, and don't overexert yourself. Above 13,000 feet it is normal to walk in such a way that you can include a brief pause with each step.

A good attitude helps in dealing with altitude. Be relaxed and positive, and try to keep a sense of humor. If you or anyone in your party feels too crappy, just go back down and try again on a different day. The mountains aren't going anywhere.

Sun

YOU CAN GET SUNBURNED, INCLUDING ON YOUR EYEBALLS, ON A CLOUDY DAY. THIS IS especially true at higher altitudes and in snow, which intensify the sun's effects. I speak not proudly from experience, having snow-blinded myself three times during my younger years; two of those times were on cloudy days. You can also get burned in places like the palms of your hands, the roof of your mouth, and beneath your chin. Solution? Bring good sunscreen and good sunglasses on every hike, and use them.

Heat

HEAT EXHAUSTION HAPPENS WHEN THE BODY ABSORBS AND WORKS UP HEAT FASTER than it can dissipate it. Dehydration is the first symptom, followed by cool clammy skin, weakness, nausea, and perhaps fainting. In such cases, find shade and fluids, elevate the feet, and focus on cooling the face and head. Prevention is best: on hot days, hike the high country. It's right there.

Cold

HYPOTHERMIA IS EVIDENCED BY UNCONTROLLABLE SHIVERING, LOSS OF COORDINATION (especially in the hands), fuzzy thinking, drowsiness, and slurred speech. It doesn't have to be terribly cold to occur; many cases occur between 30 and 50 degrees, especially in wet and windy weather. It is best to prevent this condition rather than let it develop, and the solution is to get dry and warm.

Someone going into hypothermia might not be aware it is happening, and even deny it. Reluctant to get up after a rest, they might want to stay back on the trail and wait for you. Don't agree to this. Trust the symptoms and treat them then and there.

General Safety

IF HIKING ALONE, BE SURE TO TELL SOMEONE WHERE you're going and when you'll be back. It's also best to maintain a conservative hiking practice when alone and not go for risky rock scrambles, never push time or weather limits, and so on.

No trail in this book requires crossing waist-deep streams, but there are hundreds of small crossings, many on ad hoc bridges of fallen logs or sequences of rocks. The biggest hazard is usually dunked feet; however, it is important to be mindful of how deep and fast-flowing water can be at different times of year. Don't attempt a crossing if you feel it is "over your head." Better to turn back and try a different route, or return later in the year.

Break in your boots, try to keep your feet dry, and cover trouble spots as soon as they develop with moleskin or tape. If a blister forms, don't pop it as this can invite infection. Instead, cut a circle in the moleskin. If a blister becomes too uncomfortable to continue walking, you can drain it by making a small puncture with a clean needle.

There is no excuse for not having a first aid kit in your backpack. Drugstores sell great ones at very reasonable prices. If you never open it, that's great, but make sure it has bandages (including butterflies), gauze, adhesive tape, antibiotic ointment, blister protection, tweezers, a clean needle, and disinfectant pads.

Wildlife Safety

MOST ANIMALS DON'T WANT TO BE NEAR YOU. To be respectful, it is important to keep your distance. Mountain lions, bears, and bobcats almost always avoid people when they can. Bighorn sheep and mountain goats are more gregarious, but they also need their space. The most troublesome creatures you will likely encounter are mosquitoes, flies, and ticks.

During any potentially contentious wildlife encounter, it is important to stay calm, assume a dominant posture, and maintain a confident demeanor. In the unlikely case that you are attacked, report it to the trail-managing agency and to Colorado Parks & Wildlife.

The main mammals to pay attention to, safety-wise, are moose, which were reintroduced to Colorado in the late 20th century and now number in the thousands. A moose may tolerate your presence nearby, but it is dangerous to get near one. In fact, moose are up there with hippos and rhinos as the most hazardous mammals to humans, worldwide. Most of the time moose seem either oblivious to you or mildly curious. You might even see one grazing by the highway. Other times they can be surly and aggressive, especially in spring, when cows are protective of newborns, and during the fall mating season. At all times, it is critical to control your dog; moose consider dogs to be wolves, their natural predators, and go into fight-or-flight mode around them. At 800 to 1,100 pounds per charging adult moose, you don't want the fight. If a moose approaches, back away slowly and don't throw anything. Speak in a calm, solid voice, and try to hide behind something. Be particularly concerned if it lays its ears back, raises the hairs on its rump, and licks its snout. Leave the moose an escape route, and stay out of its way as it passes.

It's also important to know what to do around a coyote. Coyotes can be fun to watch, and are usually elusive, but closer to urban areas they can lose their fear of people. If you see one, keep your distance

Photo: Nathan Anderson, Unsplash.com

and keep your pet under control. If a coyote does approach, maintain a dominant posture and speak in a loud, confident voice. It's okay to throw rocks or sticks to frighten it away.

Mountain lions avoid humans. Seeing a mountain lion is a rare experience, and attacks are far rarer. It is important, however, to not let small children wander off and to keep pets leashed. If you encounter a mountain lion, stand tall and make yourself look as big as possible, maybe raise your jacket over your head, and back away slowly. Maintain indirect eye contact, speak in a loud voice, and don't run, as this can trigger a predatory response. If you are attacked, fight back. Mountain lions aren't used to anything fighting back, and usually make only one or two brief charges. Don't play dead, as this would give the lion a chance to make a deadly bite.

Black bears, which can vary in color from black to light brown, are shy and nearly always run away from people in the wild. They are omnivores, and can become bold if they think they can get at food scraps or garbage. Rare attacks on humans are defensive in nature and usually regard cubs. If you see a bear, give it space; if it doesn't go away, leave the area. A bear is warning you if it is growling, slapping the ground, and working its jaws; back away slowly and maintain indirect eye contact. If one walks calmly toward you, however, this is an attack and you must fend it off. Don't run! Look large, yell, throw things, and fight back if necessary. Do not play dead.

Rattlesnakes also want to avoid you, but they need time to move away. They are uncommon up high but are at home in the foothills below 7,000 feet or so. Your chances of meeting one increase if you leave the trail in a lower-elevation, rocky area. The rattle is a warning to stay away, not a signal of attack. You aren't in danger unless you are in striking range, and they strike only in self-defense.

Don't throw anything and back away slowly. If bitten, stay calm and walk at a modest pace to the car. Bites are rarely fatal to healthy adults, but small children have a higher risk, as do dogs.

Hiking with Kids

I AM A HIKER TODAY BECAUSE MY PARENTS TOOK ME HIKING WHEN I WAS LITTLE. I HOPE I've done the same favor for my own children. The hikes in this book are for

everyone, including small members of the family. Remember, you don't have to do the whole hike. Rewards often come in the first mile. Do as little or as much as you want, and you may find yourself going hiking more often, and going farther.

I've seen nine-year-olds having a blast five steep miles away from the car. Toddlers can often handle one to four miles round-trip. Older kids sometimes like to run ahead, and it is important to establish rules about not going too far, staying on the trail, and waiting at all junctions.

Things can deteriorate fast for kids when they get tired or uncomfortable. Bring extra clothes, yummy food, and a good sense of humor and adventure. Gently push for forward progress, but be ready to accommodate different agendas, which may not be all about "getting there" but rather about stopping to check things out. Try to keep it moving and keep it fun.

Other Trail Users

I THINK IT IS IMPORTANT TO GREET OTHERS ON THE TRAIL WITH AT LEAST A SMILE. HOWEVER, I don't get offended if people who are grunting their way uphill ignore me, and I make sure to yield them the right-of-way. If someone asks for help, I help; I've probably overdone it on occasion with my unsolicited advice. The fewer people I see, and the farther into the backcountry I go, the weirder it feels to not at least say, "Hi."

Hiking with dogs is popular in Colorado, and many of the trails in this book allow them. On trails where dogs are allowed, they almost always must be on a leash. The exceptions are in some National Forest lands outside of established recreation areas, where off-leash hiking is sometimes allowed. A few localities such as the City of Boulder have a verified voice-control licensing option.

As of this writing, violations of leash rules are rampant. Conditions are ripe

for a backlash, and dogs could become banned in more places if owners keep breaking the rules. Currently, dogs are not allowed on the trails in Rocky Mountain National Park and in a number of state parks and municipal open spaces. If you want to continue to hike with your dog, please abide by the rules.

When on the trail with your dog, be conscious of how invasive she can be of other people's space, and of people's right to hike without being contacted or intimidated by her. Remember, not everyone loves dogs, and some people are afraid of them. Also remember that even if your dog is friendly, she can suddenly behave differently around strangers and unfamiliar dogs on a narrow trail.

Some trails are very popular with mountain bikers, especially in the foothills. Most bikers are considerate and yield to hikers, as they are required to. My experience is that shared use of the trail is generally harmonious, but do watch out for the occasional scary biker.

Hikers must yield to horses, which are less common than bikes although most trails are open to them (it's a

Colorado thing). Horse owners tend to be warm and friendly people, fun to talk to, and will often move out of your way if they can. But horses can be skittish, so it's always a good idea to give them a wide berth, speak calmly, and avoid making sudden movements.

Leave a Trace—On Yourself

PUBLIC LAND IS NOT OWNED BY THE GOVERNMENT. WE OWN IT. IT'S UP TO US TO BE ITS stewards.

Don't build fires. Leave no marks except footprints. Don't cut switchbacks. Pack it out. Leave everything where you found it. Step off the trail to pee, and bury human waste at least 200 feet from trails and water, at least six inches deep. Be considerate of others, keep your distance from and respect wildlife, and control your pets. Travel on durable surfaces, save vegetation from damage, and walk through mud if that's where the trail is. Limit your group size; this has as much to do with being considerate of others as minimizing your impact. And remember, sounds carry.

Sometimes the best part of a hike is getting back to the car, exhausted and exhilarated, and prying those boots off your tired feet. Heaven! Then you get to carry the impact and experience of the delightful day with you back to civilization.

The Denver area is a wonderful place to come back to: a full-service metropolitan area replete with restaurants, breweries, coffeehouses, theaters, museums, an aquarium, a zoo, nightlife, and many trail-loving people to share wilderness stories with. You can soak up the city, enjoy great food and drink, socialize a bit, get some rest—and get ready to hike again.

Enjoy yourself, and enjoy your time outside!

—Pete KJ

Fort Collins

Land of prairies, the Poudre, and snowy peaks

Beautiful and diverse hiking experiences abound in the region near Fort Collins, a lively city just an hour north of Denver. If you're unsure where to go, just start driving up the Cache la Poudre River on CO 14. This gorgeous valley is a conduit to adventure in all seasons. Near its entrance, the slate-colored mound of Greyrock Mountain asks to be climbed even in midwinter. Late spring is a good time to head farther in for a deep-woods walk on Big South, alongside Colorado's designated Wild and Scenic River.

In summer the higher hikes in Poudre Valley can't be beat, from Blue Lake and Twin Crater Lakes in the graceful north-stretching Medicine Bow Range, to Emmaline Lake tucked beneath Comanche Peak on the valley's south side, to the Never Summer Mountains on the northern edge of Rocky Mountain National Park. Contrary to the name, summer does indeed arrive here—and spectacularly. The American Lakes, tucked beneath the incredible Nokhu Crags, might qualify as one of the Earth's most beautiful places. You can view Nokhu from the Diamond Peaks hike or from Iron Mountain (above Trap Park), or take the iconic walk to the lakes themselves. Go in July, and you'll be engulfed in wildflowers.

Outside the Poudre Valley, you can find year-round tromping in the foothills close to town in places like Horsetooth Mountain, where you can climb a famous rock alongside CSU students, and other adventures farther afield at Mount Margaret, Red Feather Lakes, and Soapstone Prairie, near the Wyoming border. For something completely different, drive east into the plains for an otherworldly experience at Pawnee Buttes, in the hike that kicks off this book.

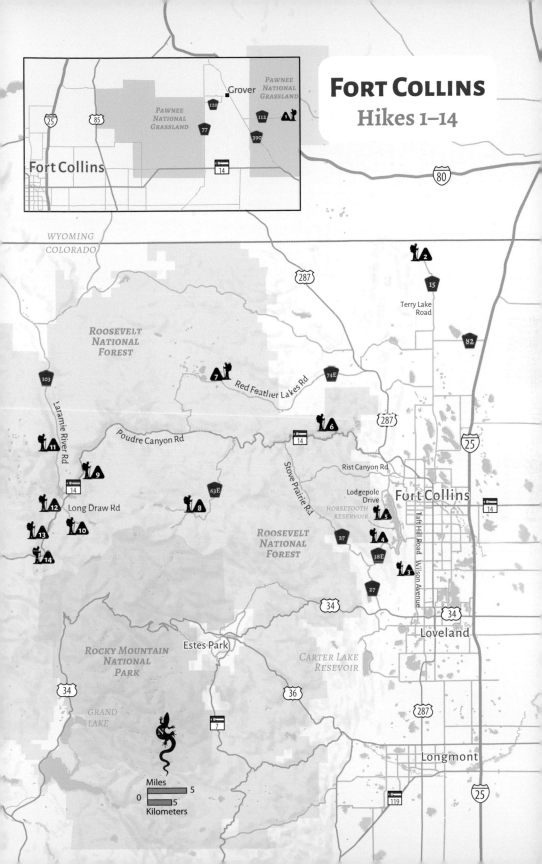

FORT COLLINS
Hikes 1–14

Pawnee National Grassland

Grover

Pawnee National Grassland

Fort Collins

WYOMING
COLORADO

ROOSEVELT NATIONAL FOREST

Red Feather Lakes Rd

Terry Lake Road

Laramie River Rd

Poudre Canyon Rd

Long Draw Rd

Stove Prairie Rd

Rist Canyon Rd

Lodgepole Drive

HORSETOOTH RESERVOIR

Fort Collins

Taft Hill Road

Wilson Avenue

ROOSEVELT NATIONAL FOREST

ROCKY MOUNTAIN NATIONAL PARK

Estes Park

CARTER LAKE RESERVOIR

Loveland

GRAND LAKE

N

Miles
0   5
Kilometers
5

Longmont

Interstate markers: 25, 85, 80, 287, 25, 34, 287, 25

State/road markers: 120, 112, 77, 390, 14, 2, 15, 82, 103, 7, 74E, 6, 11, 9, 14, 63E, 8, 12, 10, 5, 27, 4, 13, 38E, 14, 3, 27, 34, 36, 7, 119

1 Pawnee Buttes

THIS EASY HIKE TO TWO BUTTES IN THE EASTERN PRAIRIE GIVES YOU SPRING FLOWERS, birdsong, windblown solitude, and views stretching off to infinity. It's a journey through time and a blast for everyone, kids included.

At a Glance

DIFFICULTY	🥾	DISTANCE/TIME	4.5 miles/2 hours
TRAIL CONDITIONS	🥾🥾🥾🥾	TRAILHEAD ELEVATION TOTAL HIKING GAIN	5,200 feet 200 feet
CHILDREN	🥾🥾🥾🥾🥾	FEATURES	Eroded landforms, prairie, birds, spring wildflowers
SCENERY	🥾🥾🥾🥾	BEST SEASON	All year
PHOTO	🥾🥾🥾🥾	OTHER USERS	Horses, dogs
SOLITUDE	🥾🥾🥾🥾	NOTES	Toilets at trailhead, very little shade
PROPERTY	Pawnee National Grassland	JURISDICTION	U.S. Forest Service

The drive to this trail near the Wyoming border is crazy circuitous, and things just get weirder at the trailhead, where two buttes appear out on the prairie: startling, boxlike, rising like two gigantic birthday presents. You know you're in for a different kind of treat, no matter how old you are!

Distances are difficult to judge here. The buttes look reachable within minutes, yet the sign says they are two miles away. Begin walking on **Pawnee Buttes Trail** toward some cliffs to their west called The Overlook. A cacophony of birdsong rises over the sounds of breeze and feet scraping trail, especially in mornings during migration seasons. You might see the long ears of a jackrabbit fleeing. A traditional windmill spins to the left; on the horizon churn dozens of modern wind turbines. Several crude oil "grass-hoppers" bob on the plains.

At 0.7 miles, you'll pass through a gated fence and descend into a crater-like valley studded with spiked yucca. In spring there are wildflowers: yellow evening primrose, blue penstemon, purple vetch and phlox. A juniper grove

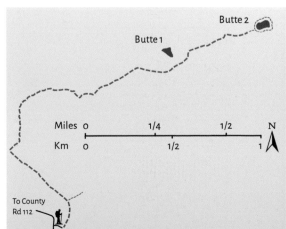

Left: West Pawnee Butte

graces the dry snaking streambed, contrasting with whitish cliffs above. It's difficult to stop taking pictures.

Soon you rise into prairie, but West Butte looks no closer than it did at the start. Is it an optical illusion? Land falls away northward as you ford another dry stream and traverse grassland. This prairie is anchored by buffalo grass and blue grama, whose roots form tough sod that holds well against the wind. It took settlers several generations and a Dust Bowl to realize this stuff should never be plowed. On closer examination, the diversity of vegetation is impressive. Over 400 native species grow here.

The trail dips to arrive beneath the domineering form of West Butte. What is this? A bit of Mars? A hunk of comet? A corroded alien spaceship? Whatever it is, it looks otherworldly, especially in slanting sunlight. And inaccessible! Ringed at the top by 30- to 50-foot cliffs, there appears to be no way to stand on top.

The buttes are very much of this world. Remnants of ancient High Plains that didn't erode into the South Platte, they are protected by caps of sandstone and conglomerate that formed 3 to 20 million years ago. Below the hard caps is softer sediment of the Brule Formation, described geologically as "white to pale-pink blocky tuffaceous claystone and lenticular arkosic conglomerate." It formed 25 to 40 million years ago, before there were words that big.

A trail slants down and up toward East Butte, beckoning you to visit it as well. On the way you'll pass a sign that reads, "Private Land Ahead, Respect Owner's Rights," but it doesn't tell you not to proceed. The Forest Service owns all of West

Prairie view from east side of East Pawnee Butte

East Pawnee Butte

Butte, but only part of East. In fact, most of Pawnee National Grassland is privately owned.

You will arrive at East Butte within minutes. You can enjoy it from the base or circumnavigate it on a trail of sorts. Falling rock and clay-fall are hazards, so don't linger beneath precipices. On the east side, gorgeous rippled "clay barrens" melt into prairie. On the north, notches cut into the Brule mark where some people have attempted to scale the butte. Tempting ... but even if you made it up, how would you get down? Better to enjoy this close encounter from below and respect the summit as a no-go zone.

On the way back you can skirt to the north side of West Butte and confirm there is no summit access there, either. Or you can trust me.

From Denver. Take I-25 north to Exit 269A, then CO 14 east for another 36 miles. Turn left onto CR 77, drive 15 miles, then turn right onto CR 120. Proceed 5.8 miles, veer left onto CR 87 for 0.8 miles, then turn right on CR 122 and drive 0.7 miles into Grover. Turn right onto CR 390 (Railroad Avenue), continue 5.8 miles, and turn left onto CR 112. Proceed 6.4 miles, turn right on CR 107/CR 112, drive 300 feet, then go left to stay on CR 112. In 2 miles turn left at the sign to Pawnee Buttes. The trailhead and its large parking area are 2 miles farther on the left. *2 hours, 40 mins.*

2 Soapstone Prairie's Towhee Loop

THIS HIKE REALLY DELIVERS: ROLLING HILLS, SPRING WILDFLOWERS, VIEWS OF PEAKS AND prairie, and a chance to see pronghorns and bison. Add a mind-boggling archeological site and perhaps a picnic, and it's a fine day near the Wyoming border.

At a Glance

DIFFICULTY	🚶	DISTANCE/TIME	3.5 miles/1.5 hours
TRAIL CONDITIONS	🚶🚶🚶🚶	TRAILHEAD ELEVATION TOTAL HIKING GAIN	6,600 feet 400 feet
CHILDREN	🚶🚶🚶🚶	FEATURES	Prairie and mountain views, grass and shrubland hills, archaeological site
SCENERY	🚶🚶🚶	BEST SEASON	Spring and fall
PHOTO	🚶🚶🚶	OTHER USERS	Bikes and horses on small portion
SOLITUDE	🚶🚶🚶	NOTES	No dogs, toilets at trailhead
PROPERTY	Soapstone Prairie Natural Area	JURISDICTION	City of Fort Collins Natural Areas

In 2009 the City of Fort Collins gave lowland hiking a boost by opening this large tract of prairie and foothills along the Wyoming border. It's off-limits for three months in winter, however, to give wildlife a break from humans.

Begin the **Towhee Loop** on the east side of the parking lot to hike the loop counterclockwise, which puts sustained mountain views in front of you instead of behind you. The view, which is seen first from the parking lot, is dominated by three graceful Mummy peaks: Hagues, Stormy, and Comanche.

Birdsong and breezes accompany you through the grassland. After a quarter mile, say au revoir to the mountains and branch left into a gully covered in mountain mahogany. Spring brings a wealth of wildflowers: purples, yellows, and blues. Interspersed are prickly pear and yucca. Orange-winged grasshoppers scatter and fly and maybe hit you in the eye. Perhaps you'll see a pronghorn antelope; they've been here since the last ice age.

Curve right, then left, and ascend one gully into the next. At just over a mile, Mahogany Loop joins from the

Towhee Loop, Soapstone Prairie

right. Then the high peak views return and stay with you as you walk the hilltop toward them.

Below you, prairie stretches off to infinity. There are few places along the Front Range with such pristine views of the plains. One of the few human incursions you'll see is the Rawhide Energy Station, clearly visible to the southeast, next to a reservoir. This power plant fired up its coal unit in the 1980s. Natural gas generators were added in the 2000s, and a solar section went online in 2016.

At 2 miles Canyon Trail branches right. The junction is an excellent place to sit and bask in the view. Besides the Mummies, you'll see the Medicine Bow Range farther north. You can turn onto Canyon if you'd like and walk along the state border all the way into Red Mountain Open Space. No shortage of miles here!

Staying on Towhee, it's a mile descent through another pleasant valley, one with pinkish cliffs of the soapstone that gives this open space its name. As you near the parking lot the trail becomes pavement and branches right to **Lindenmeier Overlook**. Take it and brace yourself—not for a stunning view but for a stimulated imagination.

In 1924, A. Lynn Coffin and his dad were searching for arrowheads on this portion of what was then the Lindenmeier Ranch. They found some fluted points in the side of a dry streambed that didn't match the others in their collection. It wasn't until two years later,

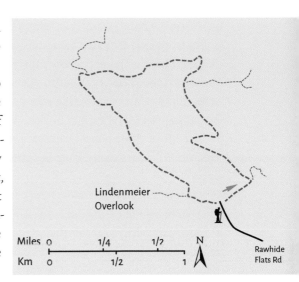

Mummy Range from Soapstone Prairie north trailhead

Prairie view from Towhee Loop, Soapstone Prairie

when similar points were found near Folsom, New Mexico, that their significance began to emerge. The area below the overlook was excavated by the Smithsonian in the 1930s; it is the largest and most complex Folsom Culture site yet found. At the time it shook up prevailing archaeological thinking, which held that humans crossed into North America in about 2000 BC. This site revealed bones of giant bison that were long extinct by then, along with a manmade spearpoint imbedded in one of those bison's vertebrae—proof that humans coexisted with these creatures. Radiocarbon dating has since pegged Lindenmeier artifacts to about 9000 BC.

On the drive back to the entrance, look for modern bison grazing on the right. They were brought from Yellowstone in 2015. Six calves were born here in 2016 through a breeding program that used purged semen and in vitro methods, which ensured the offspring would be free of brucellosis and other diseases afflicting the Yellowstone herd.

From Denver. Take I-25 north about 78 miles to Exit 288, and turn left onto CR 82 (Buckeye Road). Proceed 5.8 miles and turn right onto North CR 15 (Terry Lake Road), a dirt road. Continue 1.1 miles and turn right to stay on North CR 15, now called Rawhide Flats Road. Continue 8 miles to the Soapstone Prairie entrance station and proceed to the large parking lot at North Trailhead. *1 hour, 50 mins.*

3 Coyote Ridge

THIS ALL-AGES, ALL-SEASON WALK OUTSIDE FORT COLLINS TAKES YOU FROM PRAIRIE TO ridgetop for excellent views of waves of earth rising from the plains. From the top, a forgotten valley to the west stirs the imagination.

At a Glance

DIFFICULTY	🚶	**DISTANCE/TIME**	4 miles/2 hours
TRAIL CONDITIONS	🚶🚶🚶	**TRAILHEAD ELEVATION** **TOTAL HIKING GAIN**	5,100 feet 600 feet
CHILDREN	🚶🚶🚶🚶	**FEATURES**	Prairie, hogback ridges, rock escarpment, plains and valley views
SCENERY	🚶🚶	**BEST SEASON**	Fall, winter, spring
PHOTO	🚶🚶🚶	**OTHER USERS**	Bikes, horses
SOLITUDE	🚶🚶	**NOTES**	No dogs, toilets at cabin along trail
PROPERTY	Coyote Ridge Natural Area	**JURISDICTION**	City of Fort Collins Natural Areas

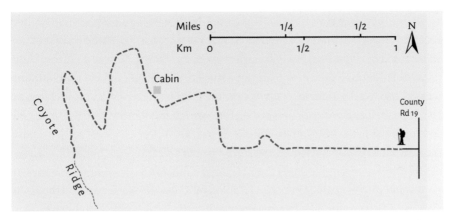

On this hike, you get to "ride" three waves of earth as they build in height to arrive at a ridgetop with striking views of the transition zone from Great Plains to Rockies. About four miles round-trip, this walk delivers a lot for the footsteps and is a great excursion for kids who like to play king of the mountain. Just bring sunscreen and keep an eye out for snakes if you do some rock scrambling at the top.

From your vehicle, walk straight over the prairie toward the hills on **Coyote Ridge Trail**. After 0.5 miles, you'll curve up into the hills to gain the low first ridge. Drop into the next fold of earth and continue to a cabin used for classes and events. All are welcome to enjoy its shady deck and enjoy the quarter-mile **Hidden Clues activity trail** in back.

Start of Coyote Ridge Trail

Ahead is a slot in the hogback ridge, a natural gateway guarded by two slanted rocky hills. The terrain is flowing and evocative here, like waves frozen in motion; these could be gigantic, rolling breakers good for surfing. To get an idea of how it looked millions of years ago, picture the eastern faces of these ridges rising way up into the sky to form a gigantic earthen dome, created when subterranean forces pushed ancient rock upward. Later, erosion washed away the softer stone to expose the hard-rock spines of these hogbacks.

Pass through the opening in the hills and veer left to hike beneath a line of crags. There are brambles here, but the dominant shrub is mountain mahogany, popular winter chewing for the local mule deer. In spring, look for the little yellow flowers of Bell's twinpod, a plant native only to Boulder and Larimer counties.

The wide rocky trail makes two sweeping switchbacks to gain the top of the third wave: Coyote Ridge. Miles of ridgetop cliffs stretch in two directions to create a gorgeous effect; they also provide secluded nesting sites for raptors and bats. To the east, the trailhead and the highway appear farther away than they really are. To the south, you'll see the city of Loveland with its monumental white silo, formerly used to store molasses. More than half a million gallons of the sticky stuff spilled there in 1990, covering two city blocks.

West lies a storybook valley beneath higher hills. A creek cuts through the basin amid a scattering of lonely farmhouses, a scene that looks like an American West landscape painting. Native Americans hunted deer in this valley and collected wild plums and chokecherries before settlers arrived in the late 1800s and

Scrambling to the high point of Coyote Ridge

Coyote Ridge

put it under heavy cultivation. Ranchers farmed dryland grain, pastured horses, planted cherry and apple orchards, and ran turkeys here. Though the valley looks nearly abandoned now, a rail spur once ran from Fort Collins to busy sandstone quarries on the opposite ridge. The railbed is still visible if you go down into the valley.

At the ridge crest, you might sense a promontory a little higher and to the north. And you'd be right. A side path leads to a small escarpment and some unsanctioned, but popular, scrambling routes.

The ridgetop is a fine turnaround point but hardly the trail's end. You can continue south for a quarter mile and then descend into the valley, where the trail enters Rimrock Open Space. From there, paths branch both north and south to connect with Horsetooth Mountain and Devil's Backbone Open Spaces, respectively. No shortage of miles here! But for younger ones, and others, conquering Coyote Ridge is a fine and satisfying milestone for the day.

From Denver. Take I-25 north to Exit 257, then turn left onto US 34 west (Eisenhower Boulevard). After 7 miles turn right onto Wilson Avenue/Taft Hill Road (CR 19) and drive north 5.3 miles. Coyote Ridge Trailhead and its parking lot are on the left. *1 hour, 10 mins.*

4 Horsetooth Rock

THIS POPULAR HIKE OUTSIDE FORT COLLINS SCALES A LOCAL LANDMARK THAT HAS AN interesting creation myth and delivers 360-degree views of plains and peaks.

At a Glance

DIFFICULTY	♟♟♟	DISTANCE/TIME	5 miles/2 hours
TRAIL CONDITIONS	♟♟♟	TRAILHEAD ELEVATION	5,800 feet
		TOTAL HIKING GAIN	1,500 feet
CHILDREN	♟♟	FEATURES	Unique stone peak, rock scramble to summit, panoramic views
SCENERY	♟♟♟	BEST SEASON	All year
PHOTO	♟♟♟	OTHER USERS	Bikes and horses on portion, dogs on leash
SOLITUDE	♟	NOTES	Entrance fee, toilets at trailhead
PROPERTY	Horsetooth Mountain Open Space	JURISDICTION	Larimer County Department of Natural Resources

Climbing Horsetooth Rock is a rite of passage for many Fort Collins residents and university students. The hill's unique summit is a great place to experience a sunrise, and it's conspicuous enough to be part of the logo for the City of Fort Collins. It looks like two giant horse incisors flanked by molars. The route described here goes to the top of the northern molars—a fun scramble that doesn't require technical expertise.

Begin in grassland on **Horsetooth Rock Trail**, which you will follow all the way to the summit. Keep left as Horsetooth Falls Trail branches right and enjoy beau-

Horsetooth Rock Trail

tiful views of red rock hogbacks to the east. When you reach a service road, turn right and continue 0.2 miles until Horsetooth Rock Trail branches left up some stairs. You'll climb through a grassy gully next to some bulbous rock formations to reach a shoulder, where the plains come into view. Ahead the way is evident: along a rocky ridge populated by scraggly aspens.

Continue up some stairs and wind through rocks to a place where the trail briefly joins a bike path. At this junction you'll see a memorial for John Blake, a CSU doctoral student who died in a fall on Horsetooth Rock in 1987. His family installed the plaque, which serves as a reminder that, although climbing the rock is not particularly dangerous, you must be careful.

Keep right as the trails separate. The unmistakable form of Horsetooth Rock immediately appears. A short loop path branches left for additional views to some western snowy peaks including Meeker and Longs.

With such a unique appearance, it's not surprising that creation legends surround Horsetooth Rock. While horses have been in North America for only about 500 years, human beings have been around much longer, and the older legends have

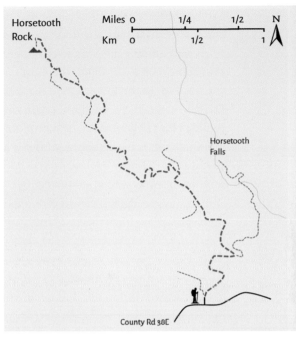

Horsetooth Rock

nothing to do with horses. One tale declares the rock to be the lacerated heart of a giant. This giant was the guardian of the animals living in the "Valley of Contentment" below, which is now filled by Horsetooth Reservoir, but those animals were coveted by hungry human plains dwellers. One night while the giant slept, and his throbbing heart rose above his body, a warrior struck with his tomahawk and made two slashes across the giant's heart, turning the giant to stone.

As you continue climbing, you'll need to mount some carved steps and scramble over some rocks. Just follow the most obvious route and use your hands where you need to. Beyond the rocks, a dirt path crosses beneath the horse's incisors. The trail steepens to reach a notch between the northern summit rocks, where you may find children playing, pretending they are dental floss. Enjoy the high mountain views from here, or scramble left to reach the top of a molar. This last pitch can be dizzying, and requires some hand- and footwork, but your exposure is limited. The reward is unimpeded 360-degree views.

As always, watch for afternoon thunderstorms. In the creation legend, thunder represents the spirit of the murdered giant, and lightning his anger. For you, they herald danger. If a storm approaches, get off the rock immediately.

If you are not knackered as you return to the trailhead, you can take a nice 2.4-mile round-trip on **Horsetooth Falls Trail**. The trail leads down then up to the place where a stream spills through rocks into a picturesque pool. Depending on the season and weather conditions, it can be a trickle or a torrent, but it's a nice hike either way.

From Denver. Take I-25 north to Exit 257, then turn left onto US 34 west (Eisenhower Boulevard). Drive 10.5 miles, turn right onto North CR 27 (Buckhorn Road), then proceed 5.2 miles to Masonville. Turn right onto West CR 38E and continue 3.4 miles. The entrance to Horsetooth Mountain Open Space and its large parking lot are on the left. *1 hour, 20 mins.*

Approach to Horsetooth Rock summit

5 Arthur's Rock & Westridge

A BRISK CLIMB GAINS A ROCKY PRIZE, AND A STROLL IN WOODED HILLS BRINGS HIGH mountain views on this delightful all-season hike outside Fort Collins.

At a Glance

DIFFICULTY	👤👤👤	DISTANCE/TIME	7 miles/3 hours
TRAIL CONDITIONS	👤👤👤👤	TRAILHEAD ELEVATION TOTAL HIKING GAIN	5,600 feet 1,300 feet
CHILDREN	👤👤👤	FEATURES	Rock summit, woods, plains, mountain views
SCENERY	👤👤👤	BEST SEASON	All year
PHOTO	👤👤👤	OTHER USERS	Bikes and horses on portion; dogs on leash
SOLITUDE	👤👤	NOTES	Entrance fee, toilets at trailhead
PROPERTY	Lory State Park	JURISDICTION	Colorado Parks & Wildlife

The trail to Arthur's Rock begins in a stony gulch amid brambles, your destination visible above. It is named not for Arthur the King, who pulled a sword from a rock, but rather Arthur Howard, son of one of the early settlers in the area. Most of the Howards' land is now this state park, which is named not Howard Park but Lory Park, in honor of an early president of Colorado Agricultural College (now CSU).

Ascend the left side of the gulch, keeping left at a fork to stay on **Arthur's Rock Trail**. From here the trail slants gently through a meadow toward the rock. Some say this hunk of pegmatite resembles a person's silhouette. If so, the person has a very large chin and is gazing upward.

As you enter a shady grove, the trail becomes very quiet. Cross a gully and the vegetation shifts from dense stands of fir to more solitary ponderosa pines, then shifts again to grassland as the trail climbs toward Arthur's lower crags. A bouldering trail branches left; keep right and continue the traverse toward the cliffs. A spur at one of the switchbacks leads to a scenic overlook but offers nothing you won't see from the top. Soon the main trail traverses directly below the rock face. You can feel its power and overhanging gravity.

More switchbacks bring a junction with a branch trail to the summit, which is just a short distance up a steep gully. Poised on the summit ridge are some large boulders that look ripe for trundling—by a giant with a crowbar, that is. Walk between them to gain the tip-top, at 1.8 miles.

Below stretches Horsetooth Reservoir, the city of Fort Collins, and its northwest suburbs Bellvue and Laporte. If some of these names sound French, that's because they are. Trappers, many of French descent, began frequenting this area in the

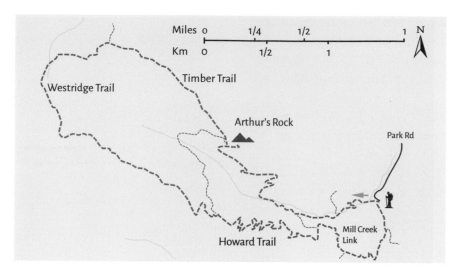

early 1800s. They gave the main river its modern name: Cache la Poudre; that's the river you crossed on the way in. After the gold rush hit in 1858, some French-Canadian families settled Colona, now Laporte, with the idea of creating a "port" on a stagecoach route connecting the Oregon Trail to Denver and the goldfields. A few years later the U.S. Army built a military post called Camp Collins nearby to protect the stage route from Indian attack. The camp got washed out in a flood, and its 1864 replacement was called Fort Collins—although no real fort was ever built there.

The views have everything you could ask for except high snowy peaks. They're here but hidden by the terrain. To see them, take an easy 3-mile walk into the

Arthur's Rock

rolling hills behind the Rock. Continue a short distance on the main trail, then branch right onto **Timber Trail**. After 0.8 miles through pleasant woods, turn left on **Westridge Trail**. Follow this old jeep road as it winds the wooded ridge that concealed the splendid peaks. As the trail tops out, near 7,000 feet, you'll get sustained views of Meeker and Longs to the southwest.

After a lovely half mile on the ridgetop, the trail drops to join **Howard Trail**, which rejoins **Arthur's Rock Trail** in the gulch. Or you can branch right and get to your vehicle via the **Mill Creek Link**, where you'll be treated to views of red hogbacks and rolling grassland. In the field at the bottom is what looks like an assembly of hobbits' cabins. What is it really? A horse jumping course!

Gully to summit of Arthur's Rock

Summit boulders, Arthur's Rock

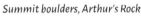

From Denver. Take I-25 north to Exit 269B, then CO 14 west to Fort Collins. Turn right onto Riverside Avenue, which becomes Jefferson Street, and right again onto North College Avenue (US 287). Continue straight on US 287B when US 287 veers north. Pass through Laporte, veer left on Rist Canyon Road, cross the river, then turn left on North CR 23. Proceed 1.4 miles, turn right on Lodgepole Drive (North CR 25G), and continue to the Lory State Park entrance. The trailhead and parking area are 2 miles down the park road. *1 hour, 40 mins.*

6 Greyrock Mountain

THIS PEAK LOOKS LIKE A BIG ICE CREAM SUNDAE, BUT YOU'LL HAVE TO WORK TO EARN THE treat. A favored hiking destination for more than a hundred years, it is a popular backcountry challenge with some bouldering near the top.

At a Glance

DIFFICULTY	🚶🚶🚶🚶	DISTANCE/TIME	8 miles/3.5 hours
TRAIL CONDITIONS	🚶🚶🚶	TRAILHEAD ELEVATION TOTAL HIKING GAIN	5,600 feet 2,000 feet
CHILDREN	🚶🚶🚶	FEATURES	Mountain ascent, views, meadow
SCENERY	🚶🚶🚶	BEST SEASON	Fall, winter, spring
PHOTO	🚶🚶🚶	OTHER USERS	Dogs on leash
SOLITUDE	🚶🚶	NOTES	Toilets at trailhead
PROPERTY	Roosevelt National Forest	JURISDICTION	U.S. Forest Service

Recreational hikers have been climbing this scenic mountain for many years. The first Greyrock trail was constructed in the 1910s under the direction of a visionary forest ranger. The one in use today, **Greyrock Trail** (FS 946), was mostly built in the 1930s, by members of the Civilian Conservation Corps. This popular New Deal program employed young, unmarried men in projects to improve the nation's forest and recreation resources. Enrollees worked six-month stints for up to two years in return for food, clothing, shelter, and $30 a month (about $550 these days). The catch was that most of these young men's earnings had to be sent home to their parents.

Greyrock Mountain

Soon after you cross the footbridge over the Cache la Poudre River, the highway sounds fade away. After hiking 0.7 miles through a gully, you'll turn right at a junction where two valleys meet. Ascend the right-hand valley, much of which was burned in the 2012 High Park fire. The burned area is obvious but not oppressive; some trees survived and there are many other signs of life. In spring you'll find white-violet harebells, blue lanceleaf chiming bells, and purple pasque-flowers. Watch out for poison ivy along the stream banks; this post-fire invader has three shiny green leaflets which turn red in fall.

Eventually the trail curves right into a side gully, then crisscrosses as it climbs. Soon views of the Poudre Valley open up to the south. As you wrap around a shoulder, Greyrock Mountain juts into the air ahead of you: a seemingly inaccessible molten mound. It's hard to believe a hikers' trail goes to the top of it.

Greyrock is a visible extrusion of the Log Cabin Batholith, an emplacement of magma that rose through fractures in overlying gneiss and schist about 1.4 billion years ago. Though undeniably gray, it is classified as Silver Plume granite, which is a slightly pink igneous rock found all over this region of the Rockies.

At 2.3 miles you'll arrive below Greyrock's face, at a junction in a meadow with a park bench. Turn right and traverse steeply, close to the imposing wall. The route markers here can be confusing; wooden posts and metal plates are more reliable than stacked-rock cairns. After climbing right, the route curves left to reach a surprising stretch of sand flats and trees. Continue through them and over some rocks, past a picturesque pothole pool, to the obvious summit.

From the top, the extent of the 2012 wildfire looks extraordinary. In fact, what you see is only part of the damage, which was caused by two adjacent blazes that burned a month

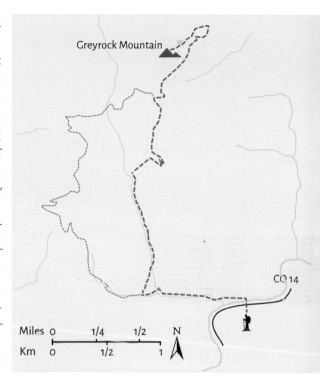

Poudre Wilderness Volunteers install a sign on Greyrock Mountain

Descending from the summit of Greyrock Mountain

apart. The main fire ignited when lightning struck a tree across the valley. Response was rapid, coordinated, and diligent, but more than 87,000 acres burned over several weeks, making it the second-largest wildfire, by area, in Colorado's recorded history.

When you return to the junction below the face, you have a choice: descend by the same route, or extend the hike 1.5 miles by making a loop through the beautiful meadow to the west along the 2.7-mile **Greyrock Meadow Trail** (FS 947). The latter choice is a nice walk, but a tidy amount of exercise since all the elevation lost to reach the meadow is regained—and then some—to get over a ridge before descending a grassy hillside on rocky switchbacks.

Back at the Poudre River, look for a bench on the bank before the bridge. It's an excellent spot to sit and enjoy the flowing water for a spell before getting in the car.

From Denver. Take I-25 north to Exit 269B, then CO 14 west and US 287 north through Fort Collins. Turn left to continue on CO 14 (Poudre Canyon Road) and proceed 8.5 miles to the Greyrock parking lot, on the left. The trail begins on the other side of the road; be careful crossing it. Additional parking is available along the highway. *1 hour, 40 mins.*

7 Mount Margaret

THIS MIGHT BE THE GENTLEST TRAIL YOU'LL EVER TAKE TO CLIMB A MOUNTAIN. AS YOU WIND through tranquil meadows and aspen groves to a low summit east of Red Feather Lakes, you might remember the familiar song of a celebrated "Indian princess."

At a Glance

DIFFICULTY	👤👤	DISTANCE/TIME	8 miles/3 hours
TRAIL CONDITIONS	👤👤👤👤	TRAILHEAD ELEVATION	8,100 feet
		TOTAL HIKING GAIN	negligible
CHILDREN	👤👤👤👤	FEATURES	Forest, meadows, aspens, rock formations
SCENERY	👤👤👤	BEST SEASON	Spring and fall
PHOTO	👤👤👤	OTHER USERS	Bikes, horses, dogs
SOLITUDE	👤👤👤	NOTES	No toilets at trailhead
PROPERTY	Roosevelt National Forest	JURISDICTION	U.S. Forest Service

The rocky hilltop at the end of **Mount Margaret Trail** (FS 167) is actually 150 feet lower than the trailhead, so technically you will "descend to the summit"—a funny idea—but the pleasant, easy trail offers a fun scramble to the top and some nice views in the Red Feather Lakes region.

The trail begins in rolling ponderosa forest where the trees are spaced enough apart to reveal some of the curious rock formations that exist along much of this walk. Aspens soon join the mix and remain profuse, making this trail a brilliant choice in fall. Birdsong is also plentiful along these old logging roads, and you may hear woodpeckers drumming.

At 0.8 miles, you'll reach a willow bottom and cross a stream. Three

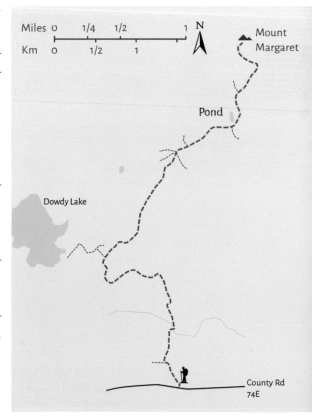

Horse and rider on Mount Margaret Trail

Fall foliage along Mount Margaret Trail

photogenic rock mounds rise behind you. A half mile later, you'll pass through a gated fence; the fence is used to control the cattle that graze here in summer on public land permits. A trail branches left to Dowdy Lake, a short trip worth a jaunt on the return journey. The lake is one of a chain of reservoirs built more than a century ago that were called the Mitchell Lakes—until Princess Redfeather came along, that is.

Tsianina ("*Cha-nee-nah*") Redfeather was a renowned Native American mezzo-soprano and musician. Born on a reservation in Oklahoma, she received sponsorship and moved to Denver at a young age to study music. There she met composer Charles Wakefield Cadman. Cadman's famous piece "From the Land of the Sky-blue Water" became her signature song—and later the

jingle for Hamm's beer. "Princess Redfeather" became a Denver-based celebrity, and when some developers were looking for a new name for the Mitchell Lakes, where they wanted to build a resort in the 1920s, they appropriated her Indian motif and her putative ancestor, a Cherokee leader named Redfeather. According to legend, Chief Redfeather died in a battle against the Pawnees in the region of these lakes.

At 2.5 miles, you'll arrive at a five-way intersection; proceed straight ahead on the main trail. A half mile later, you'll enter a huge meadow with a pond surrounded by a crossbuck fence built to

Abert's squirrel along Mount Margaret Trail

keep out livestock. Keep left as Divide Trail branches right. It seems the woods and flats will go on forever, but soon a valley opens to the right with startling rock peaks across the way. Your destination becomes visible along the ridge to the left, and you realize that after all this downhill progress you really will be climbing a mountain.

Continue to the "End of Trail" sign—but perish the thought. This is the funnest part! From a campfire ring, scramble up the rocks—any way is a good way as long as you remain close to the spine.

The summit is a conglomeration of boulders perched over North Lone Pine Creek Valley, offering views southwest to the Mummy Range. Nestled in the verdant valley to the east is a ranch that looks like a true home on the range. Now called the Maxwell Ranch, it may be the source of this mountain's name. In 1926, a wealthy Denver widow named Margaret Goldsborough bought land there as a wedding present for her daughter. The marriage lasted only a few years, but the name of the mountain endured.

The easy walk back might be tiring for children, but only because of the distance. Save a snack for a rest break along the trail, or take the path down to Dowdy Lake and splash a bit.

From Denver. Take I-25 north to Exit 269B, then CO 14 west and US 287 north through Fort Collins. Continue on US 287 north for about 20 miles to Livermore. Turn left on West CR 74E (Red Feather Lakes Road) and proceed 20 miles to the parking lot for Mount Margaret Trailhead, on the right. *2 hours.*

8 Emmaline Lake

AN EASY VALLEY STROLL MORPHS INTO A STIFF CLIMB THAT ENDS IN A DAZZLING CIRQUE in Comanche Peak Wilderness, where two lakes are tucked up high in remote wildlands.

At a Glance

DIFFICULTY	👤👤👤👤	**DISTANCE/TIME**	12.5 miles/5 hours
TRAIL CONDITIONS	👤👤👤	**TRAILHEAD ELEVATION** **TOTAL HIKING GAIN**	9,000 feet 2,000 feet
CHILDREN	👤👤👤	**FEATURES**	Forest, meadow with mountain views, cirque and lakes
SCENERY	👤👤👤👤	**BEST SEASON**	Summer
PHOTO	👤👤👤👤	**OTHER USERS**	Horses, dogs on leash
SOLITUDE	👤👤👤	**NOTES**	Toilets at nearby Tom Bennett Campground
PROPERTY	Roosevelt National Forest, Comanche Peak Wilderness	**JURISDICTION**	U.S. Forest Service

Don't be put off by the length of this hike. Only the last two outbound miles involve serious uphill going; otherwise, it is a fairly easy stroll. The views are splendid from the start of the hike, where you'll see two cirques dropping from the distant ridge between Fall Mountain and Comanche Peak. You're heading to the cirque on the right.

Follow the jeep road from the parking area, **Forest Road 147**, half a mile to a gate, where it becomes **Emmaline Lake Trail** (FS 945). Continue through a vast grove of small aspens peppered with mountain golden banner and other flowers.

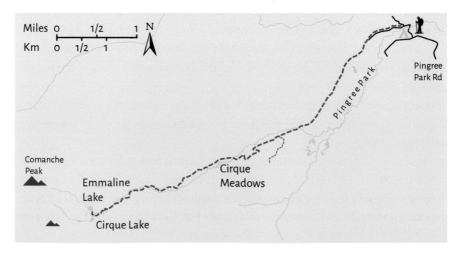

Below, in Pingree Park, you'll see the buildings of CSU's Mountain Campus, where forestry courses have been offered since the 1910s.

Soon young lodgepole pines appear among the aspens—confirmation that this hillside is several decades into fire recovery. The blaze, which raged in the dry summer of 1994, was likely caused by a lightning strike on the northeast ridge. Fueled by dense pines (which had sprouted after another fire all the way back in 1890), the 1994 blaze

Cirque through the trees, Emmaline Lake Trail

burned a 1,275-acre swath through half the campus buildings. This hillside is now an outdoor classroom for the study of forest regrowth.

The murmur of Fall Creek intensifies as you continue down the road. Cross the creek and proceed through mature lodgepoles, keeping right when Mummy Pass Trail branches left. Two hairpin turns signal your arrival at Cirque Meadows, a lovely creek bottom with views to the headwalls. At 3.5 miles it's an attractive destination. But you're more than halfway to the lakes, and have gained half the elevation, so why not carry on?

A right turn takes you through woods at the edge of the meadows and into Comanche Peak Wilderness. Seasonal streams tumble across the trail as it steepens, and bright yellow asters light up the green spaces between trees. When the trail eases, you can sense the headwalls through the woods, but you're not there yet. It's up again and over a hump to cross into a restricted area; beyond is for day visitors only, no camping.

You still have an adventurous mile of uphill hiking to go. Cairns mark the way, but it's easy to miss one and get off track. If this happens, retrace your steps and rejoin the route, which proceeds through an interesting network of waterways, grottoes, marshes, and boulders. Keep at it until you break into the cirque. Here Cirque Lake glitters below you, and there are good seats on the rocks for gaping at the cliffs above.

Emmaline Lake is a few minutes farther, tucked beneath Comanche Peak. Early rancher Frank Koenig kindly named this lake for his mother, and named many other nearby features when he became one of the original rangers of Rocky Mountain National Park. By then the folks at the U.S. Geological Survey had already named the valley "Pingree." Today, many wish they had chosen another name.

Asters along Emmaline Lake Trail

Emmaline Lake

George Pingree came here in 1867 to cut trees for railroad ties, which he floated down the Poudre and sold to Union Pacific. When the railroad moved on, so did Pingree. Three years earlier, Pingree participated in the massacre of Native American women, children, and older men at Sand Creek, in southeast Colorado. He collected 13 scalps that day and was proud of it; in fact, he was reportedly indignant about being jailed for 10 days.

Indignation cuts both ways. In 2015, shortly after the 150th anniversary of Sand Creek, CSU changed the name of its longtime mountain facility from Pingree Park Campus to Mountain Campus.

From Denver. Take I-25 north to Exit 269B, then CO 14 west and US 287 north through Fort Collins. After 10 miles, turn left onto CO 14 west, Poudre Canyon Road. Drive west 26 miles, then turn left to continue 15.5 miles to Pingree Park on CR 63E, a decent-quality dirt road. Turn right, drive past Tom Bennett Campground, and arrive at the small parking lot for Emmaline Lake Trailhead; additional parking is available farther along the road. *2 hours, 50 mins.*

9 Big South

THIS WALK TAKES YOU THROUGH DEEP MOODY FOREST AND ALONGSIDE POWERFULLY
rushing water in an upstream section of Colorado's only Wild and Scenic River.
Rock gorges, waterfalls, and remote wooded hillsides make for a beautiful outing.

At a Glance

DIFFICULTY	👥👥	**DISTANCE/TIME**	7.5 miles/3.5 hours
TRAIL CONDITIONS	👥👥👥	**TRAILHEAD ELEVATION** **TOTAL HIKING GAIN**	8,500 feet 700 feet
CHILDREN	👥👥👥	**FEATURES**	River, waterfalls and gorges, forest
SCENERY	👥👥👥	**BEST SEASON**	Spring and fall
PHOTO	👥👥👥	**OTHER USERS**	Horses, dogs on leash
SOLITUDE	👥👥👥	**NOTES**	No toilets at trailhead
PROPERTY	Roosevelt National Forest, Comanche Peak Wilderness	**JURISDICTION**	U.S. Forest Service

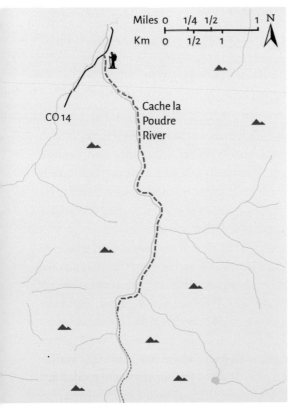

Miles 0 1/4 1/2 1   N
Km 0 1/2 1

CO 14

Cache la
Poudre
River

Get ready for some deep-
woods walking along a wild
section of the Cache la Poudre
River. Here the river flows from
south to north, draining the
western slopes of the Mummy
Range before making a big bend
toward the plains. Hence the
trail's name: **Big South** (FS 944).

Begin in aromatic pine forest
where the river can be heard but
not seen. On the opposite side of
the valley, steep hillsides drop to
the source of the noise. Within
half a mile you'll enter Comanche Peak Wilderness and arrive
in a dramatic gorge.

It's wild indeed, in both a
physical and official sense. From
this point on to its headwaters,
the Poudre is classified as "Wild"

Big South Trail

under the Wild and Scenic Rivers Act of 1968; downstream portions are classified as "Scenic." It's the only river in Colorado to receive these designations (Oregon, in contrast, has 55), which prohibit the river from being dammed or otherwise have its free flow altered. The protection extends a quarter mile on each side of the river, and while it does not confer the same level of protection as a "Wilderness Area" designation, the fact that the river is embedded in Comanche Peak Wilderness gives it a belt-and-suspenders level of security.

As the valley broadens, the trail follows the river from above, then traverses a hillside, reenters the forest, and ambles back to stream level. This sequence repeats again and again: a river bottom, a hillside traverse, lush woods, stream. It is a peaceful, mesmerizing pattern, and the miles roll by. The trail is well maintained by volunteers, but the forest is dense and you are bound to encounter some uncleared treefall.

At 1.5 miles you'll pass through an aspen grove, then, half a mile farther on, you'll reach another gorge. Cross a rockslide on an excellently crafted trail and enjoy good views of waterfalls below. Continue through mixed forest, then cross a bridge; from here the trail veers uphill from the river and its sound becomes faint. You'll descend to rejoin the river, then leave again to climb the next mound.

After passing a seasonal pond, the trail descends via switchbacks to another gorge. This is a good turnaround point, at 3.75 miles—or you can continue; the next stretch is lovely with many good streamside picnic spots. In fact, you could continue onward in the Comanche Peak Wilderness *for days*, but this wild and scenic spot, about midway between two road access points to the river, is about as deep into the Poudre's backwoods as you can get.

This river is likely the one that explorer Stephen Long called "Pateros Creek" when he encountered it out on the plains in 1820. This name may have originated when a Frenchman was found wandering near the river it in a pitiful condition (*pitoyable* being French for "piteous"). The river's current French name, Cache la Poudre,

Cache la Poudre River, viewed through forest on the Big South Trail

also comes from legend. In either the 1820s or 1830s, a company of French trappers was caught in a snowstorm while camping along the river. Forced to lighten their wagon loads, they reportedly dug a pit and cached some of their goods, including a store of gunpowder (*poudre*). After filling the pit, they burned some brush on top to make it look like an old campsite. Had I been in that group, I would have stayed very far away from the fire burning on top of the buried gunpowder!

From Denver. Take I-25 north to Exit 269B, then CO 14 west and US 287 north through Fort Collins. Turn left onto the continuation of CO 14 (Poudre Canyon Road) and proceed another 49 miles up Poudre Canyon to Big South Trailhead and its small parking area, on the left. *2 hours, 30 mins.*

10 Trap Park

AFTER AN INITIAL UPHILL STRETCH, THIS TRAIL IS A WALK IN THE PARK. VIEWS OF GRACEFUL high ridges abound, and in nearer view is a riverine willow habitat favored by moose.

At a Glance

DIFFICULTY	🚶🚶	**DISTANCE/TIME**	7 miles/3 hours
TRAIL CONDITIONS	🚶🚶🚶	**TRAILHEAD ELEVATION** / **TOTAL HIKING GAIN**	10,000 feet / 700 feet
CHILDREN	🚶🚶🚶🚶	**FEATURES**	Gentle trail, meadow and willow basin, mountain views, moose
SCENERY	🚶🚶🚶	**BEST SEASON**	Early summer
PHOTO	🚶🚶🚶	**OTHER USERS**	Bikes on portion, horses, dogs on leash
SOLITUDE	🚶🚶🚶	**NOTES**	Toilets at Long Draw parking lot, 3 miles before trailhead on Poudre Canyon Road
PROPERTY	Roosevelt National Forest, Neota Wilderness	**JURISDICTION**	U.S. Forest Service

Trap Park Trail (FS 995) begins as an old range road, rising in forest to a washed-out hairpin turn above Trap Lake. You might think this name is a legacy of beaver-trapping days, but in truth it refers to the snares set by early settlers to control pesky bears.

You'll traverse on the old road into a narrow valley, where Trap Creek tumbles below. This uphill section doesn't last long, and in about a mile the trail mellows in a basin. Iron Mountain makes its first appearance as a smooth, twin-humped hill in the distance. Nearer on the left are the handsome crags of Flat Top Mountain. Ahead is an expanse of meadow and willow which makes a nice neighborhood for moose. They are likely there even if you don't see them; these largest members of the deer family obscure themselves quite well in the riverine bushes they feed on.

Moose usually keep their distance and pretend to ignore you. If one approaches, it is probably not a friendly matter. Back away slowly and don't throw anything. Moose can be problematic for hikers because they have few natural enemies, show little fear of humans, and hate dogs, which they regard as wolves and have been known to kick. Moose cows are protective of their newborns in spring, and both males and females can be aggressive during fall mating season, when you might hear the low-pitched grunts of bulls and the higher, longer wails of cows. At other times of the year moose can seem entirely benign, curiously approaching cars and houses, even walking onto front porches and staring into windows.

The road becomes a two-track trail in the grass and crosses the creek. Now you get a sense of the park's vastness: it stretches for two miles, to the base of Iron Mountain. As the trail continues above-right of the creek, the mountains approach as if in a slow-motion zoom. After a bit the path rises a little higher into the fringe of shady pines. Higher still on both sides is the boundary of Neota Wilderness. At 10,000 acres, Neota is small for a wilderness area, filling in a space between other reserves. In addition to having no roads, which is a requirement of all federal wilderness areas, Neota also has almost no trails.

As you near the end of the park, the path veers to its center, crosses the stream twice, and fades away in

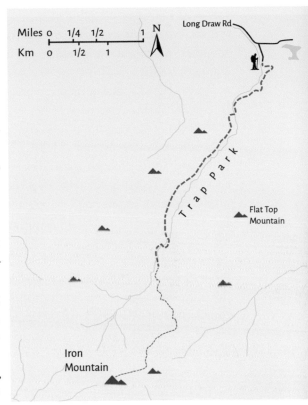

Trap Park Trail

forest. At 3 miles this is a fine picnic spot and a good place to turn around. Or you can explore the woods by continuing on a faint path along the right side of the creek, where you might find moose beds matted down in the grass. A metal sign on a tree lets you know you've entered the wilderness area. The social trail continues left of a small meadow, where there are nice views of the shoulder of Iron Mountain. At a stream crossing, it diverges into several freelance routes.

To kick the day's adventure up a notch, consider hiking up Iron Mountain! It's a straightforward ascent and adds 3 miles (round-trip) and 1,500 feet of elevation to the hike. To do it, follow social trails or make your own way up-left of the stream to where the rocky tundra takes over. From there it's easy to pick a way to the obvious summit, where you'll get great views across Rocky Mountain National Park and a special vista of Mount Richthofen and the formidable Nokhu Crags of the Never Summer Range.

From Denver. Take I-25 north to Exit 269B, then CO 14 west and US 287 north through Fort Collins. Turn left to continue on CO 14 west and proceed another 53 miles up Poudre Valley. Turn left on Long Draw Road (Forest Road 156), drive 2.9 miles, and turn right. The Trap Lake Trailhead and parking lot are 0.1 miles ahead. *2 hours, 50 mins.*

Iron Mountain from Trap Park

11 Twin Crater Lakes

THIS LOVELY LONG WOODSY WALK GOES DEEP INTO RAWAH WILDERNESS NEAR THE Wyoming border, where a sequence of stream valleys leads to a pair of remote alpine lakes set beneath a stony cirque.

At a Glance

DIFFICULTY	🥾🥾🥾🥾🥾	**DISTANCE/TIME**	13 miles/6 hours
TRAIL CONDITIONS	🥾🥾	**TRAILHEAD ELEVATION** / **TOTAL HIKING GAIN**	8,600 feet / 2,600 feet
CHILDREN	🥾	**FEATURES**	Aspens, forested river valley, meadow, high lakes and cirque
SCENERY	🥾🥾🥾🥾	**BEST SEASON**	Summer
PHOTO	🥾🥾🥾🥾	**OTHER USERS**	Horses, dogs on leash
SOLITUDE	🥾🥾🥾	**NOTES**	Laramie River Road closed December to early June, toilets at trailhead
PROPERTY	Rawah Wilderness	**JURISDICTION**	U.S. Forest Service

Lace up your boots well for some rigorous—and rewarding—wilderness walking. It takes some effort to reach the heart of the majestic Medicine Bow Range, but intrepid day-trippers will find it worthwhile. After scoping out the region, you might feel compelled to return with overnight gear and spend days wandering this lonely northern swath of Front Range.

Begin **West Branch Trail** (FS 960) by walking a short distance south alongside Laramie River Road, then curve right to cross a bridge over a confluence of canals. These canals divert summer meltwater east through a tunnel. Continue on a service road beside one of the canals, and then branch left to cross it and head into conifer forest. Aspens mix in and become the predominant species as the trail enters Rawah Wilderness and continues up the valley. Morning mists rise as the trail gains steadily on white stones, making occasional switchbacks to stay above the river. The grade isn't

West Branch Trail to Twin Crater Lakes

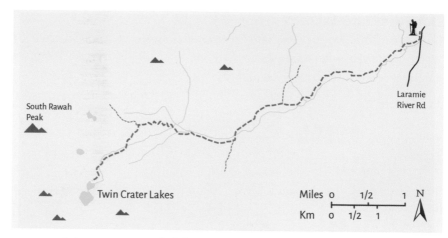

South Rawah
Peak

Laramie
River Rd

Twin Crater Lakes

Miles 0   1/2   1   N
Km   0   1/2   1

steep, and there's an extended downhill stretch that's easy to forget about until the walk back.

Below is the West Branch of the Laramie, on its way to join the North Platte in Wyoming. The river—along with a city, county, fort, and mountain—is named for the French-Canadian trapper and trader Jacques La Ramie. Born in Quebec, La Ramie set out in 1815 for the headwaters of the North Platte, where he helped run an annual rendezvous of independent trappers. In autumn of 1820 he went trapping along what became his namesake river, and didn't show up for the spring rendezvous. It's intriguing to imagine that he spent his last days right here, along this stream, but it's more likely that he met his doom on the Wyoming prairie, where a search party found a partly built cottonwood cabin and a broken beaver trap.

At 2.75 miles keep straight as Camp Lake Trail branches right. Less than a mile

Approach to Twin Crater Lakes

farther, you'll cross the stream and arrive at another fork; turn right here onto **Rawah Trail** (FS 961) to continue along the stream's south bank. You're now about halfway to the lakes. An easy mile takes you through lush forest and subalpine flowers, where you'll cross tributary streams so tiny they're hard to detect. Then, after crossing two substantial streams in quick succession, it is time to climb. Steady switchbacks lead to a hilltop in the woods, where some Medicine Bow peaks finally come into view. At a third fork, turn left onto **North Fork Trail** (FS 962).

You'll ascend a forested ridge, break out of the trees, and level off to wide-angle views of resplendent high cliffs. The beauty only intensifies as the trail crosses a brook in a broad meadow ringed by the mountain theater. After meandering through more meadows and spotty trees, the trail steepens for a final pitch to arrive at the lakes.

It's fun to kick off your boots and go for a victory wade in shining Twin One. You can also visit its partner, though it's hardly a twin. A sliver of the much larger second lake shimmers beneath the cirque-cliffs ahead.

You're now in the heart of Rawah Wilderness, one of five Colorado tracts set aside by Congress in the original Wilderness Act of 1964. Looking around, it's easy to approve of the name. "Rawah" comes from the Ute word *ura'wa*, meaning "crest of a mountain ridge" or "wild place."

From Denver. Take I-25 north to Exit 269B, then CO 14 west and US 287 north through Fort Collins. Turn left to continue west on CO 14 and proceed 57 miles up Poudre Valley. Turn right onto CR 103 (Laramie River Road), a dirt road, and continue for 6.8 miles to the parking lot for West Branch Trailhead, on the left. *3 hours.*

Twin Crater Lakes

12 Blue Lake of Poudre Valley

THIS GENTLE TRAIL INTO THE RAWAH WILDERNESS FEATURES FOREST AND MEADOW-clearings full of summer wildflowers. End rewards include a beautiful high lake and views to graceful snow-clad slopes in the Medicine Bow Range.

At a Glance

DIFFICULTY	👤👤👤	DISTANCE/TIME	10 miles/4.5 hours	
TRAIL CONDITIONS	👤👤👤	TRAILHEAD ELEVATION	9,500 feet	
		TOTAL HIKING GAIN	1,500 feet	
CHILDREN	👤👤👤	FEATURES	Easy grade, forest, wildflowers, streams, alpine meadows, lake	
SCENERY	👤👤👤	BEST SEASON	Summer	
PHOTO	👤👤👤	OTHER USERS	Bikes on lower portion, horses in some seasons, dogs on leash	
SOLITUDE	👤👤👤	NOTES	Toilets at nearby Long Draw Winter Trailhead	
PROPERTY	Roosevelt National Forest, Rawah Wilderness	JURISDICTION	U.S. Forest Service	

Blue Lake Trail (FS 959) begins in moist forest with a creek rushing by on the left. Descend to cross it and continue downhill through arrow-straight lodgepoles. As the trail wraps the hillside, it widens into the bed of a bygone logging road.

Logging was particularly intense here in the late 1860s, when the first trans-continental railroad reached Cheyenne and continued west. These pines made excellent railroad ties and could be floated down the Poudre River to LaPorte for onward transport by ox train to Wyoming. For several years, a "tie hack"—i.e., any man with a saw and a broadax—could make $3 to $5 per day doing this work.

The road stays easy as it curves through the woods. Soon Chambers Lake appears below you on the right, named for a trapper who was scalped here by Indians in the late 1850s, or so the story goes. Later his son promoted local timber to the Union Pacific Railroad, and both the lake and the logging camps took the Chambers name. The lake size has since been increased by damming.

Blue Lake Trail

The footpath branches left from the old road and crosses a bridge over Fall Creek to enter Rawah Wilderness. Continue through a riverine forest, where flowers decorate the greenery between the tree trunks: lavender asters and columbines, orange Indian paintbrush, blue-purple mountain larkspurs, many yellows, all garnished with graceful white yarrow. Sometimes the forest gives way to meadow, and numerous seasonal streams burble across to keep everything green and damp.

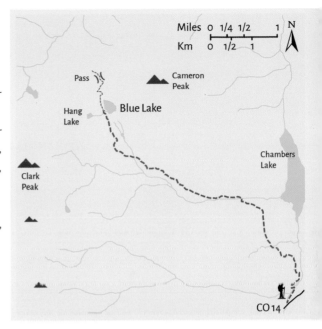

Across the valley, you'll see many standing dead lodgepoles, which indicate that pine beetles have infested the forest. When these ghostly trees fall, the remaining healthy ones will inhabit a much thinner, rejuvenating forest.

Snow-patched higher hillsides appear intermittently as you ascend through the woodland. The trail remains gentle as it alternates between dry, rocky stretches and wet forest and meadow. It's a pleasant walk the whole way, with no pressing need to know how far you've gone or have still to go. In time, the green valley opens up and—perhaps sooner than you expected—

Parry's primroses near Blue Lake

Blue Lake appears downhill to the east. The trail has been so peaceful, you almost want to keep walking right up the green flanks of Clark Peak to the west. At 12,951 feet its unseen summit is the highest point in the lovely Medicine Bow Range.

Meadows slope to the serene stone-ringed lake, and forest carpets the opposite hillside. To reach the lake, drop alongside a tumbling stream through a field of nodding yellow glacier lilies. After relaxing a bit on the shore, you can amble

Blue Lake

over rounded stones to the north end. Here at another inlet stream you'll find a host of water-loving wildflowers, including the less common, bright violet (and rank-smelling!) Parry's primrose.

These beautiful mountains form the northern limit of Colorado's Front Range, which extends into southern Wyoming. Their name comes with a story, as most things do in these parts. As told to early white settlers, Native American groups gathered every summer to make bows in a nearby valley full of mountain mahogany. While there, they performed ceremonies to invoke supernatural powers and cure diseases. This was relayed to the settlers as "making medicine" while "making bow." Near-consensus is that the two terms merged into the name settlers gave to these mountains and their northern river: Medicine Bow.

If you want to hang out longer in this pristine wilderness, head for Hang Lake, higher up the side of Clark Peak.

From Denver. Take I-25 north to Exit 269B, then CO 14 west and US 287 north through Fort Collins. Turn left to continue on CO 14 (Poudre Canyon Road) and drive west 53 miles to the parking lot for Blue Lake Trailhead, on the right; additional parking is available at the nearby Long Draw Winter Trailhead. *2 hours, 40 mins.*

13 Diamond Peaks

THESE TUNDRA KNOBS HIGH ABOVE CAMERON PASS ARE EASY TO REACH, AND THEY MAKE delightful catbird seats from which to look out over the Never Summer and Medicine Bow Ranges.

At a Glance

DIFFICULTY	🚶🚶🚶	**DISTANCE/TIME**	6 miles/2.5 hours
TRAIL CONDITIONS	🚶🚶	**TRAILHEAD ELEVATION** **TOTAL HIKING GAIN**	10,000 feet 1,900 feet
CHILDREN	🚶🚶🚶	**FEATURES**	Forest, alpine meadows, tundra, high mountain views
SCENERY	🚶🚶🚶🚶	**BEST SEASON**	Summer
PHOTO	🚶🚶🚶🚶	**OTHER USERS**	Bikes, horses, dogs
SOLITUDE	🚶🚶🚶🚶	**NOTES**	Toilets at trailhead, thunderstorm exposure above tree line
PROPERTY	Roosevelt National Forest, State Forest State Park	**JURISDICTION**	U.S. Forest Service, Colorado Parks & Wildlife

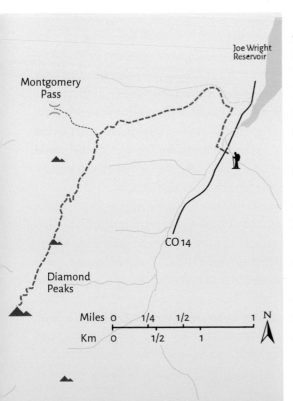

Montgomery Pass Trail (FS 986) begins across the highway from the parking lot, ascending into woods and leveling off parallel to the road. As it approaches a stream, the trail curves uphill along the bank, then leaves the stream and steepens. Soon the grade eases on a forested shoulder where it's nothing but smooth, easy walking among lodgepoles and firs, some of which have blue diamond markers on their trunks. Before you know it, 1.4 miles have passed and a trail junction appears. The right branch leads half a mile to Montgomery Pass. This jaunt drops to a pretty clearing in the

Montgomery Pass Trail to Diamond Peaks

Coyote in Diamond Peaks Bowls

forest before ascending through vast meadows to the broad, formerly cattle-grazed pass.

For a bit more of an adventure, turn left instead onto a trail marked as "Bowls"—meaning backcountry ski bowls. This path is steep at first, but mellows as you arrive at a saddle at timberline with a lovely park basin beyond. A strange crater sits in red dirt in the saddle, for no reason I could discern. Aliens? Above to the right are the bowls: the graceful slopes of Diamond Peaks.

Across the park, the distant castle formation of Nokhu Crags in the Never Summer Range grabs the eyes, along with range-topping, slate-gray Mount Richthofen, behind it. The Japanese-sounding name of Nokhu actually comes from the Arapaho phrase *neaha-no-xhu*, meaning "eagle's nest." Richthofen was named for an adventurous German baron-scientist, who coined the term "Silk Road" and discovered goldfields in California.

The park is a great destination, but a higher saddle on the verdant ridge of Diamond Peaks is even better. There's no established trail, but it's easy to see where to go, and the stony tundra provides a fine walking surface. On reaching the saddle, conquering the next Diamond peak becomes irresistible. A faint trail takes you to its crest in minutes, and the views are great: Never Summers to the south and east, Clark Peak and other Medicine Bows to the north, and forested slopes of State Forest State Park (in which you are now standing) to the northwest. The state park was formerly the Colorado State Forest, and its west-slope hillsides were heavily logged in the 1900s. The largest lumber camp in Colorado was located downhill west of Montgomery Pass; for a time it used German prisoners of war as laborers.

From here the next, and highest, Diamond peak practically begs to be climbed. This delectable smooth green pyramid is only 0.75 miles farther and 270 feet higher. First, drop 150 feet to

Nokhu Crags and Mount Richthofen, from Diamond Peaks Bowls

the saddle, then zigzag uphill through grass on the faintest of trails. The reward is a blasting view of Richthofen and its neighbors, including Seven Utes Mountain, which looks tailor-made for a ski resort. Also on view is a rare southward look all across Rocky Mountain National Park.

Seven Utes was in fact considered for ski resort development—in the 1960s, when Denver was vying to host the 1976 Winter Olympics. Investors ponied up millions of dollars. The games ended up in Austria, and progress on the Seven Utes development slowed under decades of impact studies. In 1993, a California investor tried to build a Vail-scale resort here, but public opposition was vociferous, and the investor gave up.

And so this remote and gorgeous high place remains tranquil and resort-free. As you turn around and make your way back down into the yawning green Bowls, perhaps you can picture returning in winter and doing it on skis—this time with an avalanche beacon in your pocket!

From Denver. Take I-25 north to Exit 269B, then CO 14 west and US 287 north through Fort Collins. Turn left to continue on CO 14 (Poudre Canyon Road) and proceed west another 56.5 miles to the parking lot for Zimmerman Lake Trailhead, on the left. *2 hours, 45 mins.*

14 American Lakes

SOME CALL THEM THE AMERICAN LAKES, OTHERS THE MICHIGAN LAKES; ALL WOULD AGREE they are beautiful. Children, novice hikers, and seasoned mountaineers alike will delight in this gorgeous walk high in the Never Summer Range.

At a Glance

DIFFICULTY	🚶🚶🚶	DISTANCE/TIME	7.5 miles/3.5 hours	
TRAIL CONDITIONS	🚶🚶🚶🚶	TRAILHEAD ELEVATION	9,800 feet	
		TOTAL HIKING GAIN	1,400 feet	
CHILDREN	🚶🚶🚶🚶	FEATURES	Subalpine and alpine meadows, wildflowers, high lakes, majestic peaks	
SCENERY	🚶🚶🚶🚶🚶	BEST SEASON	Summer	
PHOTO	🚶🚶🚶🚶🚶	OTHER USERS	Bikes, horses, dogs on leash	
SOLITUDE	🚶🚶	NOTES	Entrance fee, no toilets at trailhead, thunderstorm exposure above tree line	
PROPERTY	State Forest State Park, Routt National Forest	JURISDICTION	Colorado Parks & Wildlife, U.S. Forest Service	

American Lakes Trail begins modestly on an old logging road in State Forest State Park, formerly the Colorado State Forest, which originated from a 1930s federal land swap and had a mandate to "extend the practice of forestry." In those days, that meant ramping up the logging. Timbering peaked in the 1950s as protests grew over the visibly denuded mountainsides. The last of the lumber camps closed in the early 1970s, shortly after this park was established.

High slopes peek through trees as the road curves in the valley. At 0.5 miles, the spiky Nokhu Crags appear briefly on the right, a titillating preview of scenery to come. At 1.2 miles you'll cross Upper Michigan Ditch, a canal sending western-slope snowmelt east to Fort Collins. Continue toward the multicolored walls of Thunder and Lulu Mountains, through a meadow so stuffed with wildflowers

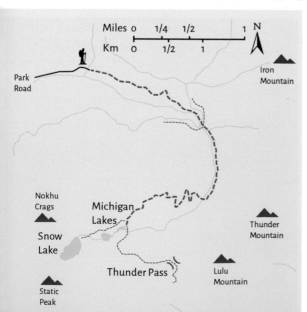

in July it will blow you away. Lulu was named after an 1880s silver mining town on its other side, which was itself named for a mining bigwig's daughter.

At just over 2 miles, you'll cross the stream and make easy switchbacks uphill on a narrower path. The views include rust-colored cliffs and lobes of Iron Mountain to the northeast. As the trail wraps into the upper valley, gray peaks steal the show to the southwest: Mount Richthofen, highest in the Never Summer Range; its box-castle lower partner Static Peak; and, delaying their second appearance for dramatic effect, the spires of Nokhu Crags. Across to the south is the graceful green swoop of Thunder Pass.

The Never Summers are younger than most of the Rockies, formed by volcanic action and intrusive processes less than 30 million years ago. The name, like many others in this vicinity, is a result of a 1914 hiking trip organized by the Colorado Mountain Club. The group wanted to replace the prosaic names settlers had assigned to local landmarks with names Native Americans used. Club members found two Arapaho elders who agreed to trek through the mountains with

Lulu Mountain view from American Lakes Trail

American Lakes

an ethnographer to record names and stories. The U.S. Geological Survey sanctioned dozens of those names but some ambiguity had crept in. When the hiking party reached the Never Summer Range, the Arapaho gentlemen offered a name that could mean either "It is never summer" or "Never no summer." The former was adopted, but as you can see, summer does arrive here—and is exquisite.

At 3.75 miles the first of two American Lakes arrives, gem-set beneath the Crags. This is a nice stopping point where smaller hikers can rest, take in the scenery, and perhaps brave dipping their feet. For those wanting more, the alpine playground beckons. You can go left to lovely Thunder Pass (0.5 miles) or branch right to Snow Lake, which is set higher in a fabulous cirque (0.9 miles). I recommend doing both, and perhaps doing the lake first.

For **Snow Lake**, follow the up-and-down path along the north shore of the two American Lakes. A steep cairn-marked route through scrub and boulders will take you above timberline to the cirque below Static Peak, whose snowfields are reflected in the gray, lake-filled bowl. That route is a lot of fun. For **Thunder Pass**, either return to the lake outlet or shortcut through moorland to join the trail. It's a pleasant undulating stroll to the pass, which sits on the boundary of Rocky Mountain National Park. It's a great place to have lunch or keep walking. A post-marked route heads west up the ridge, offering more rambling in this beautiful high place.

From Denver. Take I-25 north to Exit 269B, then CO 14 west and US 287 north through Fort Collins. Turn left to continue on CO 14 (Poudre Canyon Road) and drive west another 62 miles over Cameron Pass. Turn left to enter State Forest State Park at the Crags fee station, then continue 1.8 miles to the parking lot for American Lakes Trailhead. *2 hours, 50 mins.*

View of Nokhu Crags from Thunder Pass

Loveland &
Longmont

Plains rise to meet a jagged wall

Loveland and Longmont are the gateway cities to Rocky Mountain National Park and the Indian Peaks. The Front Range doesn't get any "fronter" than here, where a wall of thirteeners and fourteeners rises right out of the prairie. Little introduction is needed for the national park, which alone has 300 miles of hiking trails; the best way to get to know this astonishing place is to lace up your boots and go walking. Nine hikes within the park are featured in this chapter, and they will take you into the heart of it—from Black Lake and Chasm Lake to Wild Basin and the Ute Trail.

The term "Indian Peaks" is less well known to most people, even those who live beneath them and enjoy their intense beauty every day. Lying just south of the national park, the Indian Peaks comprise a 16-mile stretch of jagged summits, seven of which are over 13,000 feet. Many people thought the Indian Peaks should have been included in Rocky Mountain National Park when it was created in 1915, and over several decades the Park Service tried to annex them but failed. In 1978, the Indian Peaks finally became protected as a Wilderness Area. This chapter samples their northern reaches; other walks in the Indians are described in the Boulder chapter.

Other adventures here include driving up Big Thompson Canyon for a spring-training ascent of Crosier Mountain, inhaling the butterscotch scent of ponderosa pines on a sunny winter day in the foothills on Bitterbrush and Nighthawk Trails, and making a long, lonely trek to the tundra highlands of Signal Mountain in summer. And kids of all ages will enjoy a thrilling peak-bagging experience on little Lily Mountain.

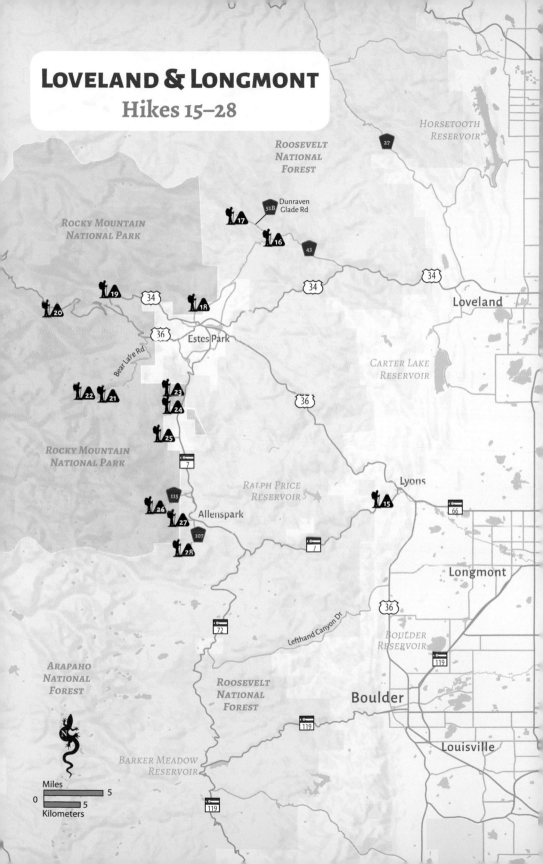

Ouzel Falls in Wild Basin, Hike 26

15 Bitterbrush & Nighthawk

THIS GENTLE ASCENT THROUGH THE TRANSITION ZONE FROM THE EDGE OF THE GREAT
Plains into the foothills of the Rockies delivers a lot: tilted sandstone buttes,
sweeping views, aromatic grass, and woodlands.

At a Glance

DIFFICULTY	🚶🚶🚶	**DISTANCE/TIME**	9.5 miles/4.5 hours
TRAIL CONDITIONS	🚶🚶🚶	**TRAILHEAD ELEVATION** / **TOTAL HIKING GAIN**	5,500 feet / 1,200 feet
CHILDREN	🚶🚶	**FEATURES**	Sandstone buttes, rolling wooded hills, grassy basins, views of prairie
SCENERY	🚶🚶🚶	**BEST SEASON**	All year
PHOTO	🚶🚶🚶	**OTHER USERS**	Bikes on portion, horses
SOLITUDE	🚶🚶	**NOTES**	No dogs, toilets at trailhead, frequent closures in winter and spring due to muddy trail
PROPERTY	Hall Ranch Open Space	**JURISDICTION**	Boulder County Parks & Open Space

The **Bitterbrush Trail** begins with a walk toward two dramatic red buttes:
Indian Lookout Mountain and Hat Rock. The tilted sedimentary layers of these
hills have a story to tell.

The dark basal rock, a granite and gneiss layer called the Fountain Formation,
was deposited about 280 million years ago during the erosion of the Ancestral
Rockies, which rose about 30 miles west of here. Near the top of the buttes is an
eye-catching salmon-pink band of rock called Lyons sandstone. Valued for its
appearance, hardness, and tendency to break into smooth slabs, Lyons sandstone
has been quarried up and down the Front Range for over a century. Some of the

Indian Lookout Peak and Hat Rock from Bitterbrush Trail

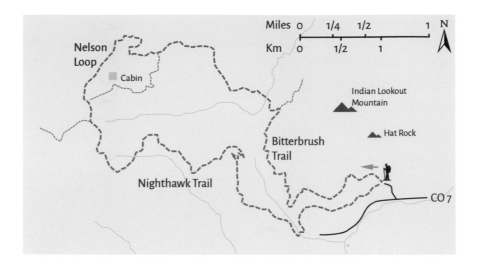

best stone is right here. This Lyons layer hardened from sand dunes that were here when the prairie you see before you was a hot, dry desert bordering an inland sea. Most astonishing is how the layers of the buttes tilt upward like a drawbridge, a result of a major uplift that began about 60 million years ago and created the current Rocky Mountains.

As you make an easy ascent through tall, fragrant prairie grasses, don't be surprised if a bird flits along next to you, landing atop the mullein stalks to ogle you. Soon the terrain changes; there are more boulders and stubby trees. After 2 miles the trail tops out in a big basin called **Antelope Park**, where the twin tops of Mount Meeker and Longs Peak peer over the hills to the west. As you descend into the basin, you'll pass the junction with Antelope Trail, which heads downhill

to the right. You may hear the squeaky barks of prairie dogs and see the busy creatures standing up and running about; look up and you might see an eagle or hawk circling above, looking for a meal. At 6,200 feet, this basin is home to one of the highest prairie dog towns in the county.

Beyond Antelope Park the trail enters some woods, then crosses more grassland with nice views of Meeker and Longs before reaching the junction with **Nelson Loop**, where you turn right. Congratulations, you've done three quarters of today's elevation gain! Although the

Bitterbrush Trail

last uphill climb may cause some huffing, you'll be amply rewarded with great views of Hat Rock and the plains. Keep an eye out for mule deer hopping about in the woods here.

At 4.8 miles, branch right onto **Nighthawk Trail** for a return trip that is off-limits to mountain bikes (alternatively, you can finish the Nelson Loop and double back the way you came on Bitterbrush). Within 10 minutes, you'll pass the junction with Button Rock Trail, which branches downhill to the right.

Stay on Nighthawk Trail as it descends gently through wide-open meadows, sometimes skirting their periphery in thick stands of pines. This pleasant downhill meander is mesmerizing, a kind of walking meditation—but not so much in mud, which can close the trail during snowmelts (in that case, return via Bitterbrush). Farther down, Nighthawk steepens to follow the contours of the hills and ridges, where there are enjoyable views of the South St. Vrain Valley to the south. Save some juice in your legs for the bottom, where the trail grazes Highway 7 and then heads upward again, over a hump and back to the parking lot.

From Denver. Take I-25 north to Exit 243, then turn left onto CO 66 west. After 14.3 miles, bear right onto US 36 and continue 1.5 miles to Lyons. Turn left onto CO 7 and continue 1.4 miles to the large parking lot for Hall Ranch Trailhead, on the right. *1 hour, 10 mins.*

Mount Meeker and Longs Peak from Bitterbrush Trail

16 Crosier Mountain

THIS SPLENDID HIKE WEST OF LOVELAND OFFERS SECLUDED FORESTS AND A GREAT SPRING workout, not to mention a commanding view of peaks in nearby Rocky Mountain National Park.

At a Glance

DIFFICULTY	👤👤👤👤	**DISTANCE/TIME**	7.5 miles/3.5 hours
TRAIL CONDITIONS	👤👤👤	**TRAILHEAD ELEVATION** **TOTAL HIKING GAIN**	7,000 feet 2,300 feet
CHILDREN	👤👤	**FEATURES**	Varied forest, steep ascent, panoramic mountain views, wildflowers
SCENERY	👤👤👤	**BEST SEASON**	Spring and fall
PHOTO	👤👤👤	**OTHER USERS**	Bikes, horses, dogs
SOLITUDE	👤👤👤👤	**NOTES**	No toilets at trailhead
PROPERTY	Roosevelt National Forest	**JURISDICTION**	U.S. Forest Service

From the nondescript trailhead, head up into the woods on the lightly used **Crosier Mountain Rainbow Trail** (FS 981). As you skirt the fence of a neighboring property, you'll enter a zone of ponderosa pines, the first of several tree species growing in fairly distinct bands on the mountainside. The ponderosas bring an immediate sense of solitude, and sometimes bluebirds.

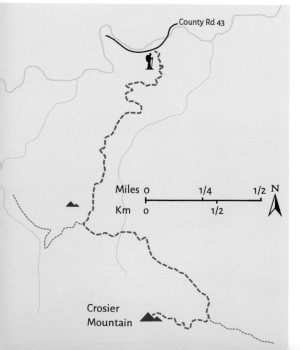

The valley of the North Fork Big Thompson drops away quickly below as you climb switchbacks. Though it appears tranquil, this valley sees major flooding every few decades. In 2013, heavy rains over four days wiped out almost all the storefronts in the nearby hamlet of Glen Haven. An even more damaging flood occurred in 1976. As you walk, enjoy all the glitter underfoot. The silvery sparkle comes from an abundance of mica, a silicate material that cleaves into thin sheets. Any handful of trail dirt yields multitudes of shiny flakes.

Lodgepole pine forest on Crosier Mountain

Mountain views begin at 0.8 miles, first westward through the trees to Mummy Mountain. Soon the path opens into a meadow with views of the valley eastward. The trail continues upward straddling two gullies, where the trees alternate between bands of dense fir and widely spaced ponderosas. Aspens appear as the left-hand gully becomes shallower, and soon they take over with their white trunks gleaming. Eventually the aspens give way to a beautiful large meadow that has abundant wildflowers in summer.

At 2 miles, you'll arrive at a junction on a saddle. Turn left onto **Crosier Mountain Glen Haven Trail** (FS 931) and continue through the ponderosas. If you pause, you can smell the pines' famously vanilla-scented bark, and an Abert's squirrel might stare at you from its perch on a high branch. After the trail dips through gullies and ascends past some lobed rocks, the trees change again: now you're passing through narrow-trunked, densely growing lodgepole pines.

Just when you think you've missed the turnoff and are heading down the mountain on the wrong trail, the path turns upward to meet a junction. Go right to Crosier Mountain's summit. As the path steepens—it gains its final 500 feet over just half a mile—a rocky lower peak appears. It looks much farther away than it should be, but set a steady pace and soon it will be alongside, then below you. You may be huffing and puffing at this point. For distraction you can watch your feet, which continue to move over brightly sparkling ground.

Some surprising views reward you on the ridgetop. Rising to the south are the Twin Sisters and the majestic peaks of Meeker and Longs, with the town of Estes Park nestled below. A few dozen steps more bring Crosier's summit and a

Mount Meeker and Longs Peak, from near the summit of Crosier Mountain

Crosier Mountain summit

180-degree panorama of Rocky Mountain National Park's section of the Continental Divide. Here you can play a naming game of peaks stretching to the Mummy Range.

Crosier Mountain was probably named after a person, exactly who seems lost to time, but it could just as well have been for an object. A "crosier" is a type of staff carried by some high-ranking Christian clergy, with a shepherd's-style hook on the end. Crosier's summit ridge, when viewed from above, does have something of a hooked shape.

Take a moment to congratulate yourself before turning around: you've bagged 2,300 vertical feet and some amazing views! This is a great hike to accomplish in the spring, both for enjoyment and for whipping your mountain legs into shape. From here you can look forward to summer and scope out many more mountain adventures.

From Denver. Take I-25 north to Exit 257, then turn left onto US 34 west (Eisenhower Boulevard). Drive another 21 miles to Drake. Bear right on CR 43 toward Glen Haven and proceed 5.5 miles. The trailhead and small parking lot are on the left, but they are easy to miss, so look sharp. *1 hour, 30 mins.*

17 Signal Mountain

THIS RIGOROUS TREK TO A LONELY TUNDRA SUMMIT JUST OUTSIDE ROCKY MOUNTAIN National Park is a real "hiker's hike," as much about exercise as scenery. But the solitary Scottish Highlands feel at the top is satisfying in every way.

At a Glance

DIFFICULTY	🚶🚶🚶🚶🚶	**DISTANCE/TIME**	10.5 miles/5 hours
TRAIL CONDITIONS	🚶🚶	**TRAILHEAD ELEVATION**	8,000 feet
		TOTAL HIKING GAIN	3,000 feet
CHILDREN	🚶	**FEATURES**	Forested ridge ascent, tundra meadow, granite rock formations, views
SCENERY	🚶🚶🚶	**BEST SEASON**	Summer
PHOTO	🚶🚶🚶	**OTHER USERS**	Horses, dogs on leash
SOLITUDE	🚶🚶🚶🚶	**NOTES**	Toilets at nearby Dunraven Trailhead, thunderstorm exposure above tree line
PROPERTY	Roosevelt National Forest, Comanche Peak Wilderness	**JURISDICTION**	U.S. Forest Service

The lightly traveled **Bulwark Ridge Trail** (FS 928.1) begins in a tranquil valley with an evocative Highlands name: Dunraven Glade. Your first task is to gain Bulwark Ridge, and the trail doesn't joke around in doing it. Don't despair, the entire hike to the summit of Signal Mountain isn't quite as steep as the beginning, and this stiff early climb brings views within minutes: southwest to Longs Peak and Twin Sisters and west to Mount Dunraven and the Mummy Peaks. Rarely are views this good this soon. Enjoy them while they last because they disappear behind trees for much of the trek along Bulwark Ridge.

On the ridgetop the trail levels through cool forest, a pleasant respite amid aspens and wildflowers: golden banner, orange Indian paintbrush, and purple columbine. At 1 mile, turn left onto **Signal Mountain Trail** (FS 928). An easy mile melts beneath your feet as you pass through dense pines, then the trail remembers there is a mountain to climb, and it steep-

Bulwark Ridge Trail to Signal Mountain

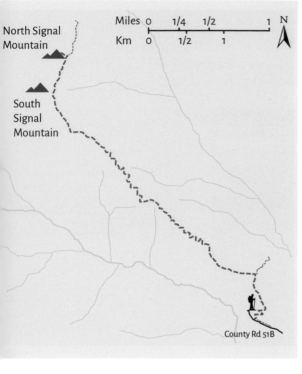

North Signal Mountain

South Signal Mountain

Miles 0 1/4 1/2 1 N
Km 0 1/2 1

County Rd 51B

ens. From here a pattern ensues: ascent, reprieve, ascent, reprieve—all in trees. Each pitch is a little steeper and rockier than the one before it. What a wilderness workout! Eventually you'll reach an extended gentler section on the ridge, with more views than usual through the trees. Then you'll go over a hump and be greeted by South Signal Mountain, to the north: a green summit with interesting granite side protrusions.

Dip through a refreshing downhill stretch, then rise to traverse South Signal's eastern flank, just beneath those granite lobes. You'll pass through the tree line and continue slanting up to arrive in a wide parklike saddle between North and South Signal Mountains. This remote spot has a high Gaelic feel, and there's a big glittery rock to sit on to enjoy views west to the Stormy Peaks.

From the saddle, you get the feeling that many dazzling mountains are hiding behind South Signal. Fortunately, North Signal, 12 feet its senior, is an easy jaunt away. To get there, follow the continuing trail, and after a few minutes cut away

Saddle between South and North Signal Mountain

from it uphill to the left. You can't miss the staked-out summit, which offers a superb view of the Continental Divide as it cuts through Rocky Mountain National Park.

Signal Mountain got its name from early settlers, who purportedly saw smoke signals emanating from this vicinity. Nowadays you may or may not get a cell phone signal from the top. I didn't, and I appreciated that fact. It seems I'm not the only one who relishes seclusion: several

Longs Peak and the Continental Divide, from North Signal Mountain

people who signed the summit logbook wrote that they got a signal and were disappointed!

On returning to Dunraven Trailhead, check the signboard for other trails available to hike another day. One nice option, especially in winter and spring, is to walk the North Fork of the Big Thompson River west into Rocky Mountain National Park.

Dunraven Glade and Dunraven Mountain were named after onetime landowner Windham Thomas Wyndham-Quin, England's 4th Earl of Dunraven and Mount-Earl. On a trip to Estes Park in 1872, he found the big-game hunting to be excellent. He returned year after year and attempted to make Estes his personal estate by persuading Americans to establish homesteads and then buying them out. Dunraven amassed 8,000 prime acres in this manner before angry, litigating locals made life unpleasant for him. He'd stopped coming to Colorado by the mid-1880s but held on to his land here until 1907. Now all that's left of him is the name.

From Denver. Take I-25 north to Exit 257, turn left onto US 34 west (Eisenhower Boulevard), and drive 20.5 miles to Drake. Turn right onto CR 43 and proceed 6.1 miles. Turn right on CR 51B (Dunraven Glade Road) and continue 2.2 miles on a good dirt road. Pass Dunraven Trailhead on the left and continue 0.5 miles on a steeper, bumpier road to Bulwark Ridge Trailhead on the right; there is a small parking area in the grass on the left. Alternatively, park in the large lot at Dunraven Trailhead. *1 hour, 30 mins.*

18 Gem Lake

CRAZY ROCK FORMATIONS ABOUND ON ALL SIDES OF THIS SHORT BUT STEEP CLIMB TO A shimmering pond at the edge of Rocky Mountain National Park, and you don't have to pay an entrance fee to see them.

At a Glance

DIFFICULTY	👤👤	**DISTANCE/TIME**	3.5 miles/2 hours
TRAIL CONDITIONS	👤👤👤👤	**TRAILHEAD ELEVATION** **TOTAL HIKING GAIN**	7,900 feet 1,000 feet
CHILDREN	👤👤👤👤	**FEATURES**	Rock formations, mountain views, rock pond
SCENERY	👤👤👤👤	**BEST SEASON**	Fall, winter, spring
PHOTO	👤👤👤👤	**OTHER USERS**	Rock climbers
SOLITUDE	👤	**NOTES**	No entrance fee, no dogs, toilets at trailhead
PROPERTY	Rocky Mountain National Park	**JURISDICTION**	National Park Service

No one ever stepped out of their car here at the edge of Rocky Mountain National Park and asked, "Why do they call it Lumpy Ridge?" A standard reaction is to stand and gape. So many strange shapes rise above you: towers, balanced rocks, bulbous piles of smooth curved rocks, a triple spire that seems about to topple over. These views aren't fleeting, either; the rocks are impressive all along **Gem Lake Trail**. Aspens, pines, and spruces mix in to create a lovely effect.

The uphill grade is also not fleeting—this short hike gains 1,000 feet. As you climb, Longs Peak and others loom behind you, so there's always an excuse to pause and turn around, and there is always plenty to look at.

Lumpy Ridge is a lump of granite on the order of 1.5 billion years old. Uniform in structure, it was never carved by glacial ice. Rather, it lay pressurized under thousands of feet of sediment, and when the overlaying material eroded, the granite respond-

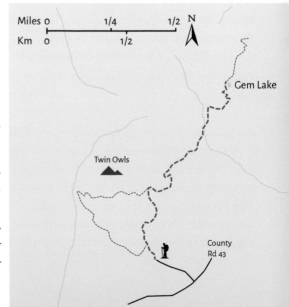

ed by relaxing toward the unconfined side, where it cracked into layers not unlike the rings of an onion. The outer fissures widened farther due to freezing, thawing, and plant action, and some layers fell away or "exfoliated." The exposed rock was then sculpted by wind and other forces into these spectacular landforms.

A mile into the hike, you'll get a brief downhill respite as you head toward another crop of knobby mounds and tilting spire clusters. Next comes a small valley, where narrow switchbacks wind up its throat like a spiral staircase. At a landing, look for a trailside boulder with a porthole through it. This is Paul Bunyan's Boot, and it is clearly in need of some sole repair.

You can feel the lake coming as the trail rises. You'll climb alongside a red stone hill that seems like it's oozing down on you, then arrive at a notch where the rocks look like stacks of pancakes. Gem

Rock formations near Lumpy Ridge Trailhead

Lake sits nestled in an amphitheater of stratified rock. "Lake" might be a stretch. It's more like a pond. Actually, it's a very large puddle, one that fills with precipitation and snowmelt and spills over when it's full. It could fit in somebody's big backyard, but what a backyard that would be! Striated cliffs rise on the opposite side, issuing an irresistible invitation to climb and gaze down at the water. There are decent scrambling routes around back, north of the pond. Or, if rock scrambling isn't your thing, you can stretch out on the coarse-sand beach on the west shore and watch others do it.

Gem Lake makes a superb destination, but you can hike farther if you wish. A sign at the north end of the lake announces "Balancing Rock" 2.1 miles away. The stone mushroom at trail's end is a bit of an anticlimax—especially since you've already seen an example of a mushroom rock near Paul Bunyan's Boot—but it's easy mileage with nice perspectives of Lumpy Ridge and Mummy Mountain.

Returning on the same trail, you can detour near the bottom to add 0.6 miles and a view of an interesting rock wall called Twin Owls. To do this, take a right on the **Black Canyon Trail** connector, traverse downward, and soon they appear. The imposing cliffs offer different images to different imaginations; many see two proud birds with their breasts puffed out. The Owls attract lots of rock climbers, but they are closed to climbing from March through July to allow raptors to nest in peace.

From Denver. Take I-25 north to Exit 243, then turn left onto CO 66 west. After 14.3 miles, bear right onto US 36 and continue 22 miles to Estes Park. Continue straight to join US 34. After 0.5 miles, turn right on East Wonderview Avenue and right again onto MacGregor Avenue. Proceed 1.4 miles (the road becomes Devils Gulch Road, CR 43), then turn left to Lumpy Ridge Trailhead and its large parking lot. *1 hour, 40 mins.*

Gem Lake Trail

Gem Lake

19 Ypsilon Lake

THE LAKE AT THE END OF THIS TRAIL IN ROCKY MOUNTAIN NATIONAL PARK IS PLACID AND lovely, but the star of the show is its namesake mountain, one of the great peaks of the Mummy Range, which watches you along the way.

At a Glance

DIFFICULTY	👤👤👤	DISTANCE/TIME	9 miles/4 hours
TRAIL CONDITIONS	👤👤👤👤	TRAILHEAD ELEVATION / TOTAL HIKING GAIN	8,500 feet / 2,000 feet
CHILDREN	👤👤	FEATURES	Riverine forest, lakes, mountain and cirque views
SCENERY	👤👤👤👤	BEST SEASON	Summer
PHOTO	👤👤👤👤	OTHER USERS	None
SOLITUDE	👤👤👤	NOTES	Entrance fee, no dogs, toilets at trailhead
PROPERTY	Rocky Mountain National Park	JURISDICTION	National Park Service

Among the mountains of the Mummy Range, Ypsilon is a standout. For a closer look at its intense eastern face, begin on the gentle switchbacks of **Lawn Lake Trail**. Soon you'll wrap into a valley where Roaring River flows through a deep gully.

Keep away from the edge that drops to the creek! This steep cut is a result of a flood that occurred in the summer of 1982. Lawn Lake, which feeds the river from the north, was dammed in 1902 for irrigation purposes. Maintenance lapsed, and the dam failed early one morning during peak tourist season. Millions of cubic feet of water rushed down the valley, bringing car-size boulders with it. When the flood reached Horseshoe Park, where you parked your vehicle, it fanned out, broke a downstream dam, and inundated downtown Estes Park.

As the trail levels alongside the stream, the Mummies start to come out. First to show is Fairchild, looking almost flat-topped from this angle. Next is the sheer face of Ypsilon, rising sternly on the left.

At 1.4 miles the trail branches left, crosses the stream, and heads up a long flight of steps. You are now on **Ypsilon Lake Trail**. At the first switchback, you can continue a few dozen yards out onto the ridge for a view of Horseshoe Park and see a swath of boulders and sediment deposited by the flood in a section of park now called the Alluvial Fan.

Next on the trail is an extended forest walk up a ridge: a steady but gentle 2-mile climb that zigzags through lodgepoles and ponderosas. Ground and tree squirrels can be very busy here, though the ones in trees like to pause and scold.

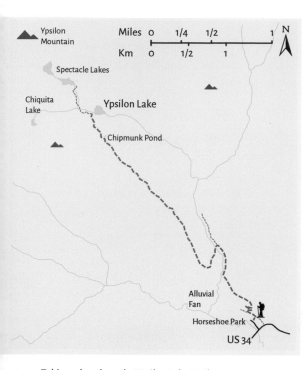

Taking a break on the Ypsilon Lake Trail

You might hear a woodpecker drumming and see its bobbing head. As you surmount a rise, the peaks reappear, with Ypsilon more striking than ever. The trail descends to Chipmunk Pond, where it's good to pause because it offers the hike's best view of Ypsilon, and also reflects it.

Ypsilon has two couloirs running down its headwall that give the mountain its name—sort of. *Ypsilon* is the German word for both the Latin letter Y and the Greek letter Υ (upsilon). As you can see, especially in earlier summer when there is more snow, the upper portions of the couloirs run in parallel and don't really form either letter. Lower down, the left couloir swoops right to—arguably—make a lowercase Y or—definitely—a lowercase U.

The Mummies are a subrange of the Front Range, and separate from the Continental Divide. When viewed from the southeast, especially in winter, some say the shape of a reclining gauze-wrapped cadaver emerges: Mummy Peak is the head, Hagues the tummy, Fairchild the knees, and Ypsilon the feet. People have seen other things in these peaks over the years; before Egypt and mummies became a big part of popular Western culture, the range was sometimes called the White Owls.

From Chipmunk Pond, Ypsilon Lake is less than a half mile downhill. The shore of this large, tree-lined, oblong lake is a relaxing spot

Ypsilon Mountain and Chipmunk Pond

Ypsilon Lake

to kick back, dip toes, and rest a while. For extra adventure, seasoned scramblers can continue up to Spectacle Lakes. The route branches uphill before the inlet stream and climbs 0.8 miles into Ypsilon's cirque. The second half is in a steep boulder ravine marked with cairns; it requires a tricky maneuver across a rock slab that should only be attempted by experienced scramblers. The reward at the lakes is superlative: beautiful close-ups of soaring cliffs and a striated, swooping bowl of stone.

From Denver. Take I-25 north to Exit 243, then turn left onto CO 66 west. After 14.3 miles, bear right onto US 36 and continue 22 miles to Estes Park. Continue straight to join US 34 west and proceed 7 miles, through the Fall River entrance to Rocky Mountain National Park, then turn right onto Old Fall River Road. Lawn Lake Trailhead and its parking lot are immediately on the right. *1 hour, 50 mins.*

20 Ute Trail

THIS HIGH TUNDRA WALK ALONG TOMBSTONE RIDGE IS AS EASY AS IT IS STUNNING, WITH the iconic peaks of Rocky Mountain National Park's Continental Divide staring at you the whole way.

At a Glance

DIFFICULTY	🚶	DISTANCE/TIME	3.5 miles/1.5 hours
TRAIL CONDITIONS	🚶🚶🚶	TRAILHEAD ELEVATION TOTAL HIKING GAIN	11,400 feet 200 feet
CHILDREN	🚶🚶🚶🚶🚶	FEATURES	Easy trail, tundra, high mountain views, wildflowers
SCENERY	🚶🚶🚶🚶🚶	BEST SEASON	Summer
PHOTO	🚶🚶🚶🚶🚶	OTHER USERS	None
SOLITUDE	🚶🚶🚶	NOTES	Entrance fee, no dogs, access road opens late May or early June and closes in fall, no toilets at trailhead, thunderstorm exposure above tree line
PROPERTY	Rocky Mountain National Park	JURISDICTION	National Park Service

This ridge is made for walking! With its high-altitude start and absence of switchbacks, it's a great family choice that delivers a spectacular view of Continental Divide peaks from the moment you get out of the car. Come late on a summer's day, after the likelihood of thunderstorms has abated, and you'll have lovely lighting effects and fewer tourists to contend with.

Ute Trail begins with a short rocky ascent among alpine flowers: yellow avens,

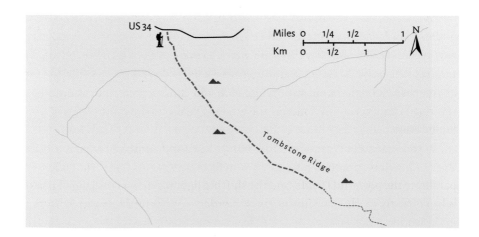

Ute Trailhead

lavender moss campions, and tiny white alpine sandworts. The floral diversity is nearly as remarkable as the view. Prominent across the valley are the dual summits of Stones Peak and the hump of Terra Tomah Mountain; some sharper spires rise in the distance between them.

Native Americans used this ridge as an east-west thoroughfare for hundreds—perhaps thousands—of years, and their paths and cairns were gladly followed by late-coming Anglo trappers and prospectors, who named it Trail Ridge. The section you're hiking is called Tombstone Ridge. Why? Check out the odd stacks of rocks on the crest for your answer.

Follow the ridge as it curves west in the direction of Longs Peak. The trail meanders on a mostly level grade and becomes smoother as you go. It's important to stay in the center of the trail, even when it's rocky, and not trample the fragile tundra alongside it. Leave the scampering to the marmots, who keep you company as you pass through a wide swooping notch and climb a green hill. Behind you, slanting afternoon sun silhouettes the western peaks; to the north, the Mummy Range rises.

As you reach the crest of the hill, Longs Peak and company appear a little closer. Ahead are some new additions: Twin Sisters and Estes Cone. The trail runs parallel to the powerful Divide, and the shifting light playing on the jagged peaks is beautiful to watch. If a name game is in order, a good starting point is Flattop, in the center of the view. Hallett rises just behind it, followed by Otis, The Shark-

Snowdrift Peak and Bighorn Flats, from Ute Trail

stooth, Powell, McHenrys, Chiefs Head, Pagoda, and Longs. Working west (right) from Flattop you'll find Notchtop, Knobtop, Gabletop, and the vast high-elevation Bighorn Flats. Peeking over the flats from a distance are the summit snows of Snowdrift.

Soon the trail begins to curve downhill. At 1.75 miles, it steepens and there is no need to go farther. Before turning around, it's fun to investigate the "tombstones" on the ridgetop. You can scramble to any promontory within minutes and enjoy a good look all around. The Mummies reappear to the north, and in nearer view Trail Ridge Road wraps the ridge's northern slope above Hidden Valley.

This northern slope was home to a ski area until 1991—that's right, a *ski area* in a national park. Begun in the 1930s, Hidden Valley (also known as Ski Estes Park) eventually had lifts that extended on both sides of Trail Ridge Road. The area offered some steep chutes, which you can see, and a substantial 2,000-vertical-foot drop. Over time the Park Service came to view the ski operation as incompatible with the park's mission, yet recognized the social and recreational value it held for area residents. Now that the lifts are gone, sledding is allowed at the former bunny hill, along with ice skating. And yes, you can still ski those upper chutes—but it's quite the winter hike to reach them!

From Denver. Take I-25 north to Exit 243, then turn left onto CO 66 west. After 14.3 miles, bear right onto US 36, and continue 22 miles to Estes Park. Turn left to remain on US 36 and proceed through the Beaver Meadows park entrance for a total of 6.7 miles. Turn left onto US 34 (Trail Ridge Road) and continue 10 miles to Ute Trailhead and its small parking area, on the left. *2 hours.*

21 Black Lake

SOARING GRANITE CLIFFS AND SPIRES, MIRROR LAKES, AND PLUNGING WATERFALLS—THIS is the epitome of alpine gorgeousness in Rocky Mountain National Park.

At a Glance

DIFFICULTY	🚶🚶🚶🚶	DISTANCE/TIME	10 miles/4.5 hours
TRAIL CONDITIONS	🚶🚶🚶	TRAILHEAD ELEVATION / TOTAL HIKING GAIN	9,200 feet / 1,500 feet
CHILDREN	🚶🚶🚶🚶	FEATURES	Cliffs, peaks, waterfalls, reflective lakes
SCENERY	🚶🚶🚶🚶🚶	BEST SEASON	Summer
PHOTO	🚶🚶🚶🚶🚶	OTHER USERS	Horses on portion
SOLITUDE	🚶	NOTES	Entrance fee, no dogs, toilets at trailhead
PROPERTY	Rocky Mountain National Park	JURISDICTION	National Park Service

Three peaks rise west above the trailhead: Thatchtop, Otis, and Hallett. To the southeast is a fourth: venerable Longs Peak, whose deep western gorge is the setting for your destination: Black Lake. You will follow **Glacier Gorge Trail** the whole way.

Begin by descending to cross a creek. Keep straight when a trail branches left to Sprague Lake, and turn left soon thereafter at a second junction toward Alberta Falls. The well-groomed trail curves up through woods to arrive at the popular falls in less than a mile. Hundreds of people might be visiting here by mid-morning; hiker numbers drop off on the more rugged onward trail, which is still very popular (as evidenced by the boldness of the chipmunks).

Climb alongside Glacier Creek, then switchback beneath the cliffs of Glacier Knobs. Keep right when a trail branches left to Boulder Brook, and enter a broad valley with views of higher mountains. You'll level off and curve through trees to arrive at the last major trail junction, where you'll turn left toward Mills and Black Lakes.

Cross a stream and ascend stone stairs; cross another and climb wooden ones. From here the grade mellows as the route crosses large slabs of stone. Look up and you'll see Longs Peak and its jagged southeast ridge, called Keyboard of the Winds, extending to the pyramid of Pagoda Mountain. Within minutes you'll arrive at Mills Lake, which perfectly reflects this scene.

The lake was named for conservationist and nature writer Enos Mills, who was instrumental in the founding of Rocky Mountain National Park. Born in Kansas

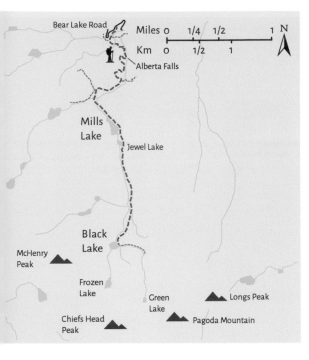

Bear Lake Road
Miles 0 · 1/4 · 1/2 · 1 · N
Km 0 · 1/2 · 1
Alberta Falls
Mills Lake
Jewel Lake
Black Lake
McHenry Peak
Frozen Lake
Green Lake
Longs Peak
Chiefs Head Peak
Pagoda Mountain

in 1870, Enos was a sickly child who wasn't expected to live long. Ill and getting weaker, he left home at age 14 for Colorado. He worked as a housekeeper in an Estes Park lodge, and in 1885 went up Longs Peak for the first time. It was a turning point. Of the many amazing things Mills became, one was a very healthy outdoorsman. Perhaps the mountains cured him, but his great-granddaughter Eryn Mills told me that around this time Enos also discovered he was allergic to wheat.

At 2.7 miles Mills Lake makes a fine turnaround point, especially for young hikers, but keep going for closer encounters with the breathtaking peaks ahead. Continuing left around the lake, you'll arrive at a smaller, grass-ringed lake called Jewel. This is a good place to catch your breath before crossing some narrow boardwalks in the marshes beyond, and then climbing higher alongside cascades and through rocky shrubland. Ahead you'll see the dizzyingly sheer cliffs of Chiefs Head Peak. You'll

Mills Lake

The Spearhead and Chiefs Head Peak, above Black Lake

know you're getting close to Black Lake when you reach Ribbon Falls, a picturesque waterfall sliding down a smooth rock. From here it's a steep climb past some more falls to arrive at the lake.

The dark-hued lake is set in a cirque so dazzling that looking upward might give you chills. Shore access is a little tricky through trees and shrubs; just find a way to sit lakeside and gape. Way above to the southwest, angel-hair waterfalls plunge from cliffs below McHenrys Peak. The point of The Spearhead soars due south, and though it's only a minor projection of Chiefs Head, it looks like something out of Patagonia. Then of course there's Longs Peak, the western side you rarely see; it is just as crazy wild as the often-viewed northeastern side.

Before turning back, consider going left around Black Lake and climbing social trails to two higher lakes. Green Lake is on the eastern side of The Spearhead; Frozen Lake lies to its west.

From Denver. Take I-25 north to Exit 243, then turn left onto CO 66 west. After 14.3 miles, bear right onto US 36 and continue 22 miles to Estes Park. Turn left to remain on US 36 and proceed 3.8 miles, through the Beaver Meadows park entrance. Turn left onto Bear Lake Road and continue 8.3 miles to the parking lot for Glacier Gorge Trailhead, on the left. Additional parking is available at nearby Bear Lake Trailhead. Both lots fill up on summer mornings, after which you will need to use the Park & Ride lot next to Glacier Basin Trailhead and take a park shuttle bus. *2 hours.*

22 Flattop Mountain

THIS IS ONE OF THOSE HIKES WHERE WHAT'S UNDER YOUR FEET IS A BIT OF AN AFTERTHOUGHT. It's all about the mind-blowing views all around you in this glorious park in the heart of the Continental Divide.

At a Glance

DIFFICULTY	🚶🚶🚶🚶	DISTANCE/TIME	9 miles/4.5 hours
TRAIL CONDITIONS	🚶🚶🚶🚶	TRAILHEAD ELEVATION	9,500 feet
		TOTAL HIKING GAIN	2,800 feet
CHILDREN	🚶🚶🚶	FEATURES	Elevation gain, high mountain views, cliffs and gorges in close-up, tundra and wildflowers
SCENERY	🚶🚶🚶🚶🚶	BEST SEASON	Summer
PHOTO	🚶🚶🚶🚶🚶	OTHER USERS	Horses
SOLITUDE	🚶🚶	NOTES	Entrance fee, no dogs, toilets at trailhead, thunderstorm exposure above tree line
PROPERTY	Rocky Mountain National Park	JURISDICTION	National Park Service

Bear Lake is ground zero in Rocky Mountain National Park, and it is right at the trailhead, so be prepared for hordes of other visitors. Only a small fraction of them climb Flattop, however. Though rigorous, this hike is doable by young and old, people carrying babies—anyone in moderately good shape. In truth, it's unfortunate more folks don't accept the challenge and experience the glories beyond the rather unexceptional lake.

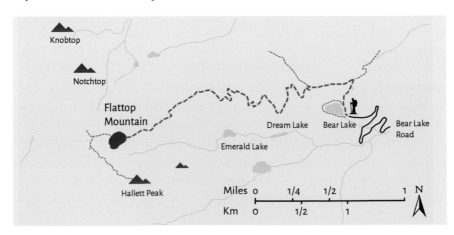

Longs Peak and Keyboard of the Winds, from Flattop Mountain Trail

The soaring, sheer granite cliffs you see across the lake are a sub-ridge of Hallett Peak, whose main summit is hidden. It's another view straight out of Patagonia, and a taste of things to come.

Turn right to hike along the lakeshore, and in minutes branch right onto **Flattop Mountain Trail**. After 0.5 miles, turn left at another fork. As you traverse up through fir and spruce forest you'll see cube-topped Longs Peak staring at you from across the valley, along with its jagged western ridge called Keyboard of the Winds. The trail eases as it changes from one side of a forested ridge to the other. Turn left at the next junction to stay on Flattop.

Now you begin climbing in earnest, making switchbacks along the edge of Tyndall Gorge, which plummets to your left down to sparkling Dream Lake. Trees become stubbier, northward views open up, and a terrific feeling of "getting somewhere" pervades the trail.

Soon you emerge from the stunted pines into a talus field and make a long left-hand traverse toward Hallett. Two ridges away, the steep snowy faces of The Sharkstooth defy gravity. Along the next section of short zigzags, graceful columbines pop out of the rocks, and Emerald Lake appears in the dizzying gorge far below. A sign says, "Do Not Descend"—probably an unnecessary instruction!

From here you'll make a long traverse north, then curve west across tundra. Wildflowers abound here, and the cliffy ridges of Notchtop, Little Matterhorn, and The Gable array themselves ahead. With a half mile to go, the gently rounded summit of Flattop appears above you, holding its snowfield into July; the trail steepens as it zigzags and then makes a beeline for it. You'll meet the snowfield

Hallett Peak, from notch just prior to Flattop Mountain summit

Hallett Peak across Tyndall Gorge, from Flattop Mountain Trail

in a notch with a hitching post. From here it's an easy 10 minutes to the mountaintop, which is actually a vast, stony flats.

Just past the highest point you'll find a junction with a north-south trail, which you can take toward the top of nearby Hallett Peak. It now looks far less formidable than it did from below, and it's only about an hour away. Or you can just enjoy the panorama from here, smack dab on the Continental Divide in what feels like Grand Central Rockies.

Rocky Mountain National Park became the country's tenth national park in 1915 (there are now 60). The original plan was to call it Estes Park, but organizers chose a more generic name in hopes of joining it with other Front Range regions such as Pikes Peak, Mount Evans, and the Indian Peaks. It would take more than 60 years for Mount Evans and Indian Peaks to become designated as Wilderness Areas.

The origin of the name "Rocky Mountains" is not as straightforward as you might think. It resulted from a French translation of the Algonquian word *as-sinii*, meaning "stone," which might have referred to the mountains or might have referred to the western Sioux, whom the Algonquians called "stone enemy" for their practice of boiling meat using hot stones. In either case, by the mid-1700s the French had applied the word to the western mountains, calling them *Les Montagnes de Roche*.

From Denver. Take I-25 north to Exit 243, then turn left on CO 66 west. After 14.3 miles, bear right onto US 36 and continue 22 miles to Estes Park. Turn left to remain on US 36 and drive 3.8 miles, through the Beaver Meadows park entrance. Turn left onto Bear Lake Road and continue 9.4 miles to the large parking lot for Bear Lake Trailhead. The lot fills up on summer mornings, after which you will need to use the Park & Ride lot next to Glacier Basin Trailhead and take a park shuttle bus. *2 hours.*

23 Lily Mountain

THIS SHORT STEEP TRAIL JUST OUTSIDE ROCKY MOUNTAIN NATIONAL PARK PACKS A thrilling punch, with spectacular views to Longs Peak and the Continental Divide. It's great for kids and is accessible in the spring.

At a Glance

DIFFICULTY	👤👤	**DISTANCE/TIME**	4 miles/2 hours
TRAIL CONDITIONS	👤👤👤	**TRAILHEAD ELEVATION** **TOTAL HIKING GAIN**	8,400 feet 1,000 feet
CHILDREN	👤👤👤👤	**FEATURES**	Short, steep climb, great views
SCENERY	👤👤👤👤	**BEST SEASON**	Spring and fall
PHOTO	👤👤👤👤	**OTHER USERS**	Dogs
SOLITUDE	👤👤	**NOTES**	Toilets at nearby Lily Lake Trailhead
PROPERTY	Roosevelt National Forest	**JURISDICTION**	U.S. Forest Service

It's only two miles to the top of this forested peak, which offers close-up views of the Continental Divide running through Rocky Mountain National Park. But Lily Mountain is no pushover, since nearly all 1,000 feet are gained in the second mile.

Lily Mountain Trail (FS 933) starts out as an undulating hillside traverse on a sandy path through ponderosas and rock outcrops, with good views across to Twin Sisters Peaks. CO 7, Colorado's oldest scenic byway, drops away to the right and traffic noise subsides. After a half mile the trail crosses a gash in the hillside, a visible reminder of torrential rains that hit this area in 2013.

After another quarter mile, you are 50 feet *lower* than when you started; now you begin the climb. The trail slants upward to a viewing rock overlooking Estes Park. Here the switchbacks begin in earnest—and don't let up until the summit. It's mostly great trail with many wood-reinforced steps. You'll be climbing the north flank of the mountain, rising through mixed forest, shoulder clearings, and dense stands of lodgepole pines. Set a steady pace and know that the rockier the switchbacks become, the closer the prize.

The last pitch is fun, as you scramble up

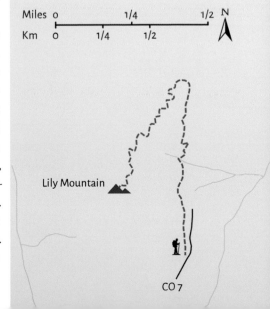

Viewpoint along the Lily Mountain trail

Mount Meeker and Longs Peak from Lily Mountain

rocks using your hands. This hill does a great job of concealing its views until the very end. When you arrive on the granite cap—*boom!*—there they are: Meeker and Longs, looking very much like two distinct mountains and not the "Twin Peaks" they are sometimes called. In fact, Mount Meeker displays its own dual summit quite nicely. A natural exclamation is, "OK, now *those* are mountains!" A heart-thumping view of the Continental Divide continues northward all the way through the national park. It's an ample reward that kids can appreciate. Just be sure to stay away from the dizzying west edge. It's a sheer drop!

What is dubbed "Longs Peak" from Denver is clearly mostly Meeker. Only 350 feet shorter, Meeker is just as much fun to climb, yet almost no one does it. The Twin Peaks are named for two quite different men. Stephen

Long was the country's most active explorer in the 1820s, leading expeditions that scouted more than 26,000 miles from Canada to Texas. Nathan Meeker, on the other hand, was a journalist and novelist, an ardently religious man who tried to establish a utopian colony at Greeley in 1870. When that didn't work out, he got himself appointed as an Indian agent in charge of convincing Utes to convert from nomadic shamanists to settled Christians. While Meeker was pressuring Utes to kill their horses and plant crops, the Utes killed Meeker.

Lily Mountain was named after the natural lake at its base, which was enlarged by a dam

Scrambling down from Lily Mountain

in 1915. The Arapaho called the lake *hebes-okoy*, meaning "beaver lodge." A 1947 survey of local beaver populations documented two beavers and one burrow at Lily Lake, but no lodge. Coincidentally, both Lily Lake and Lily Mountain have a view of a formation on Longs Peak that some say resembles the profile of a beaver. Can you see it? The upper west slope is the back; the sharp drop before the summit is the head.

Lily Lake is a fine place to relax after hiking; it offers an easy 0.75-mile circuit hike, just a half mile south on CO 7. There you might find a paedomorphic tiger salamander; "paedomorphic" means that the adults display juvenile characteristics—not always a bad thing! In the case of the salamanders, they retain a frill of gills.

From Denver. Take I-25 north to Exit 243, then turn left onto CO 66 west. After 14.3 miles, bear right onto US 36, and continue 22 miles to Estes Park. Turn left onto CO 7 (South St. Vrain Avenue). Continue 5.6 miles to the Lily Mountain Trailhead. There are small parking areas on both sides of the highway. *1 hour, 40 mins.*

24 Estes Cone

THIS MEDIUM-SIZED PEAK IS GOOD TRAINING FOR YOUR "MOUNTAIN LEGS." FROM THE TOP, you can look into Rocky Mountain National Park and scout out future visits. On the way down, a side trip to an old mine makes a worthwhile adventure.

At a Glance

DIFFICULTY	🚶🚶🚶	**DISTANCE/TIME**	7.5 miles/3.5 hours
TRAIL CONDITIONS	🚶🚶🚶	**TRAILHEAD ELEVATION** **TOTAL HIKING GAIN**	8,900 feet 2,100 feet
CHILDREN	🚶🚶🚶	**FEATURES**	Lakeside start, forested hillsides, steep final scramble to summit, views
SCENERY	🚶🚶🚶🚶	**BEST SEASON**	Early summer
PHOTO	🚶🚶🚶🚶	**OTHER USERS**	Horses
SOLITUDE	🚶🚶🚶	**NOTES**	No entrance fee, no dogs, toilets at trailhead
PROPERTY	Rocky Mountain National Park	**JURISDICTION**	National Park Service

The trail begins at Lily Lake, where you'll find throngs of tourists in sandals by midday but have the place to yourself at dawn. Your destination is the pretty Estes Cone formation to the west. It appears volcanic, but is really a product of erosion. A second, shorter version rises across the lake.

From the parking lot, head left along the lake trail, then branch left within minutes onto **Storm Pass Trail**. Proceed through treefall before entering a deep forest of lodgepole pines. After dropping 100 feet, you'll arrive at a junction. Continue straight across an excellent bridge and traverse up the hillside on an artisan-

quality stonework trail. Yellow asters light up the spaces between tree trunks, and you'll cross several babbling seasonal streams. The granite lobes to the northeast are Lily Mountain. After a switchback, a long forested traverse wraps around the side of the Cone. Across the valley to the east rise the rocky tops of Twin Sisters Peaks.

As the trail curves over a shoulder, you get expansive views of the severe north cliffs of Mount Meeker and Longs Peak. Soon you reach Storm Pass, a peaceful

Mountain cottontail along the Storm Pass Trail to Estes Cone

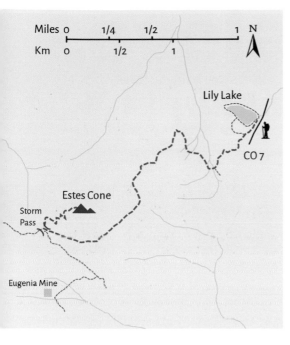

crossroads in the woods that hardly deserves its harrowing name. Turn right here onto **Estes Cone Trail**, and prepare to gain 800 feet in less than a mile.

The rooty, rugged trail makes a few honest switchbacks before giving up the pretense and curving steeply uphill through lichen-covered boulders. The best strategy is to set a slow and steady pace, as if climbing a long flight of stairs. Cairns dot the way and plenty of trees offer shade. The final approach is all boulders; look up when you reach the top and you'll face the Continental Divide, which has saved itself for this fabulous end-reveal. Also popping out are views to the lakeside starting point and the town of Estes Park. Reaching the tip-top of the Cone requires some scrambling along the jagged summit ridge, a fun finale which adds 25 vertical feet but no additional views.

Joel Estes was the first Anglo settler in this area, but he didn't stay long. A Missouri farmer, he moved here with his wife Patsy and the youngest six of their 13 children in 1860. For several years they raised cattle, hunted game, and hosted

Mount Meeker, Longs Peak, and Estes Cone from Lily Lake

Mummy Range from Estes Cone

the occasional visitor. One was William Byers, editor of the *Rocky Mountain News*, who promoted the tourist potential of "Estes Park." The Estes family sold their land and left in the later 1860s, but their name lives on.

Back at Storm Pass, you can take an interesting side trip by continuing straight on **Eugenia Mine Trail**. After walking 1.25 miles downhill through forest and across meadows, you'll arrive at the Eugenia Mine site, a lovely streamside setting ideal for a picnic. There you'll find remnants of a cabin, a tailings pile, and a rusted vertical boiler probably used to power shaft ventilators or water-removal pumps. Eugenia was first staked in 1897, at the end of a short-lived rush to the Longs Peak District. Like all mines this far north, it never produced commercial-grade ore. Had mines here been productive, Rocky Mountain National Park probably wouldn't have been established in its current form. In 1905, two speculators reclaimed the Eugenia site and did some serious digging. By the time they quit in 1911, a fruitless tunnel went 1,500 feet into the mountain (the entrance has since been sealed).

On your way back through the forest on the flanks of Estes Cone, don't be surprised if a mountain cottontail scampers across the trail, then sits and twitches its ears at you.

From Denver. Take I-25 north to Exit 243, then turn left onto CO 66 west. After 14.3 miles, bear right onto US 36, and continue 22 miles to Estes Park. Turn left onto CO 7 (South St. Vrain Avenue), and continue 7 miles to Lily Lake Trailhead. There is no fee for entry to the national park from this trailhead. There are parking lots on both sides of the highway. *1 hour, 30 mins.*

25 Chasm Lake

THIS POCKET OF LONGS PEAK IS A CIRQUE IN THE EXTREME: A GLACIER-CUT BASIN WITH A beautiful alpine lake beneath truly dizzying cliffs. And the hike to get there is one of the best in Rocky Mountain National Park.

At a Glance

DIFFICULTY	🚶🚶🚶🚶	DISTANCE/TIME	8.5 miles/4 hours
TRAIL CONDITIONS	🚶🚶🚶	TRAILHEAD ELEVATION TOTAL HIKING GAIN	9,400 feet 2,500 feet
CHILDREN	🚶🚶🚶	FEATURES	Forest, alpine terrain and lakes, close-up views of high mountain cliffs
SCENERY	🚶🚶🚶🚶🚶	BEST SEASON	Summer
PHOTO	🚶🚶🚶🚶🚶	OTHER USERS	Horses
SOLITUDE	🚶🚶	NOTES	No dogs, toilets at trailhead and along trail, thunderstorm exposure above tree line
PROPERTY	Rocky Mountain National Park	JURISDICTION	National Park Service

The Front Range has many impressive cirques gouged in northeast slopes, where the thickest ancient glaciers formed, flowed, and pried rock into startling cliffs. Longs Peak has such a cirque, and it's on steroids.

To reach this incredible place, begin with a steady ascent on **Longs Peak Trail**. Twin Sisters rises opposite, looking more like quadruplets from this angle. At 0.5 miles, branch left to ascend the wooded hillside where the massif takes shape

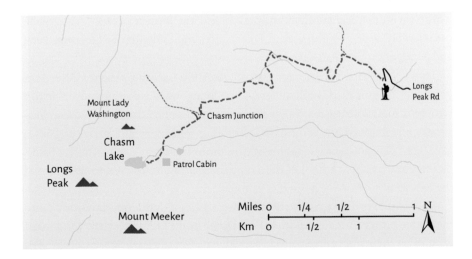

Chasm Junction saddle, with Longs Peak behind

above: Mount Meeker on the left, Longs in the middle, and Mount Lady Washington on the right. If the summer has been moist, squirrels might scurry by carrying mushrooms nearly as big as themselves, and yellow asters will congregate in the spaces between trees.

After crossing two streams you'll break out into meadows and stretches of stunted krummholz trees whose gnarled, snowblasted features look like bonsai. Rising higher, the trail enters a basin of knee-high black birch and willows. The path branches left and climbs to a saddle with heart-thumping views of the cliffs and ramparts of Meeker and Longs.

The saddle, which has a privy and some hitching posts, is called Chasm Junction. Here Longs Peak Trail branches right toward the summit; you'll bear left instead onto **Chasm Lake Trail**, a gentler path that takes you another mile into the soaring amphitheater. Below is Peacock Pool, fed by a pair of waterfalls coursing down smooth granite. You'll descend to cross above the picture-perfect falls and enter a small meadow where there's another privy and, downhill out of view, the Chasm Meadows Patrol Cabin. Built in 2008 to replace the original 1931 structure, it is a base for medical missions and search-and-rescue operations. On any given summer day, well over a thousand hikers and climbers might be on Longs Peak, and accidents sometimes do happen.

Above the meadow are fingerlings of waterfalls backed by the massive, gem-cut cliff of Longs called the Diamond. The Ships Prow formation rises in nearer view on the left, looking like a supersized, listing *Titanic*. Cairns mark the way up a rock gully that involves some easy scrambling, and soon you'll arrive at Chasm Lake. It's a vertigo-inducing moment. The shimmering pool sits 2,312 feet below the mountain's apex, with half the drop falling straight down the sheer face of the Diamond.

Rock climbers didn't seriously consider tackling the Diamond until well into the 20th century. After Yosemite's Half Dome and El Capitan were conquered, experts set their sights on Colorado's great wall, but the Park Service prohibited climbing it. Pressure grew to rescind the ban, and in 1960 two climbers from California, Dave Rearick and Bob Kamps, came to Colorado to support a local team seeking clearance. By the time permission was granted, that team had fallen apart, so Dave and Bob filled out the paperwork themselves. After recruiting a support crew of four locals who gamely agreed to help two Californians bag Colorado's big prize, they completed the ascent over three days. Rearick went on to become a Coloradan and a math professor at CU.

Chasm Lake

Dave and Bob's route is now called D1 or the Casual Route, although its 5.10a rating means it is "extremely severe." Scores of other routes now crisscross the Diamond with names like Black Death, Curving Vine, and Pervertical Sanctuary. As you admire them from the shores of sparkling Chasm Lake, you might be glad you have two boots planted firmly on the ground.

From Denver. Take I-25 north to Exit 243, then turn left onto CO 66 west. After 14.3 miles, bear right onto US 36 and continue 1.5 miles to Lyons. Turn left onto CO 7, drive 24.5 miles, and turn left onto Longs Peak Road. Proceed 1.1 miles to the large parking lot at Longs Peak Trailhead. *1 hour, 40 mins.*

Peacock Pool and waterfalls, from Chasm Lake Trail

26 Wild Basin

THIS WONDERFUL TREK IN ROCKY MOUNTAIN NATIONAL PARK TAKES YOU ON A BEST-OF-the Rockies adventure through creekside forests, past waterfalls, across high meadows, alongside twinkling lakes, and up close to dazzling summits.

At a Glance

DIFFICULTY	🧍🧍🧍🧍	DISTANCE/TIME	15.5 miles/7 hours
TRAIL CONDITIONS	🧍🧍🧍🧍	TRAILHEAD ELEVATION	8,500 feet
		TOTAL HIKING GAIN	3,100 feet
CHILDREN	🧍🧍🧍🧍	FEATURES	Riverine forest, waterfalls, high lakes, peaks
SCENERY	🧍🧍🧍🧍	BEST SEASON	Summer
PHOTO	🧍🧍🧍🧍	OTHER USERS	Horses on portion
SOLITUDE	🧍🧍🧍	NOTES	Entrance fee, no dogs, toilets at trailhead
PROPERTY	Rocky Mountain National Park	JURISDICTION	National Park Service

This hike is simply spectacular, wild and wonderful in many ways. The trail is long but mostly gentle; the basin is gorgeous. There are waterfalls and woods and creeks and mountains, and you reach one of the most beautiful places in the Rockies. Just lace up your boots and do as much or as little as you'd like.

Most hikers begin at Wild Basin Trailhead, but I usually walk in from Allenspark Trailhead (see Finch Lake, Hike 27). That way I always get a parking spot, and I enter Rocky Mountain National Park for free. This alternative adds a few miles, however, and turns an already long day into an epic one.

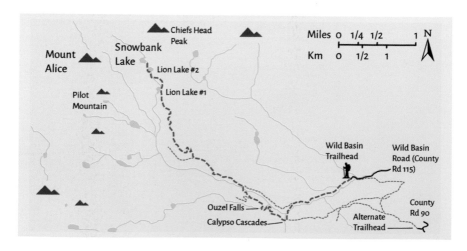

Wild Basin Trail starts out easy along North St. Vrain Creek, wide and smooth in conifers and aspens. At 0.3 miles veer left to visit Copeland Falls, a great destination for teeny-tiny hikers. The path steepens slightly as it continues along more cataracts. At 1.5 miles keep straight when a branch goes right to Pine Ridge. This branch rejoins the trail later on and can be used as a shortcut on the return trip. For now, follow the main trail as it crosses the creek on a lovely bridge and rises to Calypso Cascades, a sequence of waterfalls in the woods. As you continue curving along the hillside, Mount Meeker and Longs Peak appear above-right.

After a couple of switchbacks, you'll arrive at a bridge below Ouzel Falls. To best see the falls, branch left before the bridge and hike uphill for 100 yards. The falls and creek here are named for an aquatic songbird that inhabits clear, fast-flowing water and dives for its food along rocky bottoms. Sometimes the ouzel's sweet song ends as it goes under and resumes without missing a beat on resurfacing.

Keep straight as Bluebird Lake Trail branches left. In minutes, the Pine Ridge branch rejoins from the right; turn left here, toward Thunder Lake. Gorgeous, rolling high ridges appear as the trail ascends the valley. At 5 miles, turn right onto **Lion Lake Trail**. This narrower and more rugged trail is steep in places. As you climb, the sharp point of Mount Alice teases through the trees. A higher outcrop gives views of the severe sides of three of Wild Basin's valleys.

At last the trail eases toward Lion Lake No. 1. Just before you arrive, a view of Chiefs Head Peak's powerful lower headwall appears in the trail gap, which might make you gasp and reach for your camera. At the lakeshore, dazzling Mount Alice reveals her full self. She's had this name since 1905, and no one is sure who she was.

Ouzel Falls

Lower headwall of Chiefs Head on approach to Lion Lake No. 1

There's more to see, and it's not far ahead or difficult to reach. Proceed right around the lake, basking in high-mountain beauty. Curve up-left, following a faint trail through vegetation and cairns across rocks to a well-marked passage up a stone gully. A final traverse through krummholz takes you to Lion Lake No. 2.

One more portage to go. You can see the pocket of Snowbank Lake just a quarter mile ahead. Go left around Lion Lake No. 2, climb uphill alongside the inlet stream, and in minutes the lake pops into view. My favorite lounging spot is a quarter mile right, along the shore of its northern lobe. There's a soft grassy spot there, a perfect place to remove boots, recline, and gaze at the lakeside snowbank and on up to Alice. It's easy to linger in the afternoon and not allow enough time for the long hike back, so be sure to pack a flashlight!

From Denver. Take I-25 north to Exit 243, then turn left onto CO 66 west. After 14.3 miles, bear right onto US 36 and continue 1.5 miles to Lyons. Turn left onto CO 7, continue 21 miles, and turn left onto Wild Basin Road (CR 84/115). Proceed 2.5 miles, through the national park entrance, to Wild Basin Trailhead and its large parking lot. An alternative trailhead, near Allenspark, is described above. *1 hour, 40 mins.*

Snowbank Lake and Mount Alice

27 Finch Lake

DON'T LET THE UNASSUMING TRAILHEAD FOOL YOU. IT IS A GATEWAY TO THE ONE AND only Wild Basin, an area of spectacular scenery in Rocky Mountain National Park, and you won't have to pay to get in.

At a Glance

DIFFICULTY	🚶🚶🚶	DISTANCE/TIME	8 miles/3.5 hours
TRAIL CONDITIONS	🚶🚶🚶🚶	TRAILHEAD ELEVATION / TOTAL HIKING GAIN	8,800 feet / 1,500 feet
CHILDREN	🚶🚶🚶	FEATURES	Gentle-grade trail, views of rugged peaks, forest, lake
SCENERY	🚶🚶🚶🚶	BEST SEASON	Early summer
PHOTO	🚶🚶🚶🚶	OTHER USERS	Horses
SOLITUDE	🚶🚶🚶	NOTES	No entrance fee, no dogs, no toilets at trailhead
PROPERTY	Rocky Mountain National Park	JURISDICTION	National Park Service

This side-door entrance to Rocky Mountain National Park is a great find and gets you free admission to the wild southern end of the park. From the trailhead, cross into the park on **Allenspark Trail** and ascend a set of wood-reinforced steps. The path continues through thick mixed conifer forest, where patches of snow often linger into early June. It doesn't take long for Mount Meeker to peek through the trees, and you might find a moose peeking at you, too. If this happens, give the animal plenty of space until it decides to move on.

Keep straight at 0.8 miles when a trail branches right. At 1.75 miles you'll arrive at a four-way junction. Turn left onto **Finch Lake Trail** and get ready for the best

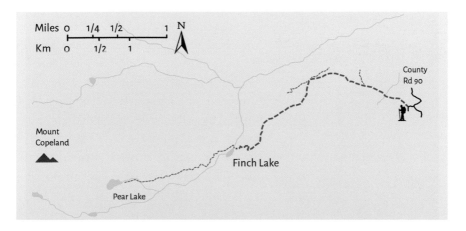

views of the hike. Within a third of a mile the hillside clears to reveal the dazzling rim of peaks surrounding Wild Basin: Longs Peak and the jagged points west of it, the startling pyramid profile of Mount Alice, Pilot Mountain, Tanima Peak, and others. Fingers of glaciers once flowed from the cirques of these peaks and joined in Wild Basin to form a single large glacier system that ebbed and flowed over millions of years. These glaciers left behind U-shaped valleys which are well displayed from this vantage point.

Continue on a gentle uphill grade for another mile before beginning the descent to the lake. Gradually at first, the trail drops into dense firs and then makes two switchbacks before reaching the subalpine shore. It's a tranquil spot ringed with sentinel firs and spruce, a nice spot for a picnic, and it offers mirror-image views of two mountains above. The jagged and more distant peak on the left is Ogalalla, named for a Sioux tribe. The imposing mound on the right is Mount Copeland, purportedly named for a homesteader.

Before 1911 Mount Copeland was called Mount Clarence King, in honor of the surveyor and geologist who was the first director of the United States Geological Survey. King resigned in 1881 to pursue a career in mining consulting, and went on to do something exceedingly curious. In the late 1880s in New York City, when he was nearly 50, he entered into a common law marriage with a black woman named Ada. To avoid the stigma of miscegenation, he pretended to be a light-skinned black railroad porter named James Todd. He kept up this charade for the

Wild Basin from Finch Lake Trail

Ogalalla Peak and Copeland Mountain, from Finch Lake　　　　　　*Moose standing on Finch Lake Trail*

remainder of his life: black railroad porter when home with Ada, with whom he had five children, and esteemed white geologist while on the road. King informed Ada of his true identity shortly before he died in 1901, and she spent several decades trying unsuccessfully to claim his estate.

Here's the zinger: Ada's maiden name was Copeland. So decide for yourself who this mountain was really named after in 1911, 10 years after King died. USGS surveyors needed a new name since King already had peaks named after him in Utah and California (and now there's one in Antarctica). Perhaps the home-steader's name provided a convenient excuse to honor someone else, back when it was a lot tougher to name things after black people.

You don't have to stop at Finch Lake. If you continue 2 more miles on what is now **Pear Lake Trail**, and gain 700 vertical feet, you'll arrive at an adorable alpine loch named for its shape. There you will have even closer views of Ogalalla Peak and (Ada) Copeland Mountain.

From Denver. Take I-25 north to Exit 243, then turn left onto CO 66 west. After 14.3 miles, bear right onto US 36 and continue 1.5 miles to Lyons. Turn left onto CO 7, drive 18.7 miles, and turn left into Allenspark. Take the first right onto CR 90 (South Skinner Road), proceed 1.3 miles, and turn right onto Meadow Mountain Drive. Allenspark Trailhead and its small parking area are 500 feet ahead on the right; additional parking along the road. *1 hour, 30 mins.*

28 Meadow Mountain

THE NAME SUGGESTS A GRASSY WALK, BUT THOUGH YOU'LL PASS THROUGH SOME WOODS and meadows, this steep hike outside Allenspark is all about reaching a rocky top—where the views are superb.

At a Glance

DIFFICULTY	🚶🚶🚶🚶	DISTANCE/TIME	6.5 miles/3.5 hours
TRAIL CONDITIONS	🚶🚶	TRAILHEAD ELEVATION	9,000 feet
		TOTAL HIKING GAIN	2,300 feet
CHILDREN	🚶🚶	FEATURES	Forest, rocky trail, alpine tundra, high mountain views
SCENERY	🚶🚶🚶🚶🚶	BEST SEASON	Summer
PHOTO	🚶🚶🚶🚶🚶	OTHER USERS	Horses, dogs on leash
SOLITUDE	🚶🚶🚶🚶	NOTES	Bumpy access road, 4WD suggested but not required; no toilets at trailhead, thunderstorm exposure above tree line
PROPERTY	Roosevelt National Forest, Indian Peaks Wilderness	JURISDICTION	U.S. Forest Service

The beginning of this rooty, rocky trail gets good aspen color in September, and when conifers mix in, it is a hive of squirrel activity. A branch of Rock Creek murmurs to the left as this section of **St. Vrain Mountain Trail** (FS 915) proceeds up and into its valley. At 0.6 miles, the trail enters Indian Peaks Wilderness and draws alongside the stream. It zigzags to stay above the creek and becomes even rockier, so watch your feet. After several switchbacks, you'll leave the stream and traverse a hillside with great views of thickly forested valleys.

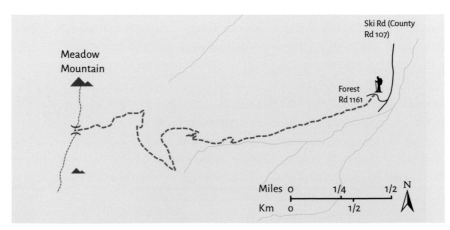

You can't see it now, but the valley confluence below was once the home of the Rock Creek Ski Area. The only reminder is Ski Road, the road you arrived on. The mountain village of Allenspark hosted ski jumping competitions as far back as the 1920s, and in 1947 two rope tows were installed at the nearby valley crux. In 1952, a T-bar was planned to the top of Ironclad Ridge to the east, but interest faltered and the ski area closed. The drive from Denver had always been a bugger, and by then more accessible ski areas elsewhere were attracting all the customers.

Turn and traverse left, where the pines space out in meadow and give the trail a growing sense of arrival. After the next switchback the plains pop into view. Above is the knob of Meadow Mountain, covered in talus, looking more like a Gravel Mountain than a grassy hill. More switchbacks signal the approach to a pass, and anticipation grows. You might find yourself humming "The Bear Went Over the Mountain" as meadows expand, trees shrink, and the tundra saddle comes into view.

What does the bear see? The other side of the mountain, of course—and a fantastic view of Wild Basin and its rugged ring of summits. Copeland Mountain's pyramid peak is complemented by its more jagged cousin, Ogalalla, behind it on the left. Continuing in view northward are Ouzel Peak and more distant Isolation Peak, then a partial view of nearer Tanima. At 3.2 miles the pass makes a great destination, but for the full panorama, go right and follow metal stakes up the side of Meadow Mountain. The summit is just 0.4 miles farther and 450 feet higher, so why not go for it?

On your way up, views expand south to graceful St. Vrain Mountain and southeast to Boulder's foothill peaks and the sunlit plains. Halfway up, the metal stakes vanish and talus takes over com-

Trail to Meadow Mountain

Meadow Mountain saddle, with St. Vrain Mountain beyond

pletely. (The only explanation for Meadow Mountain's name is that some office-bound USGS officer studied a contour map and conjectured a cone of green.) The ascent is not difficult, but it keeps you stepping on rocks to reach the broad summit, where you'll find a stone-built wind shelter and a solar-powered weather station.

Here the fabulous view is made complete: Mount Alice swooping to Chiefs Head Peak and Pagoda Mountain; the jagged Keyboard of the Winds climbing to the crowns of Longs and Meeker; then a long view continuing to Estes Cone, the Mummy Range, and Twin Sisters. It's fun to greet them all.

The setting is wild, tranquil, and remote. On the way back down, especially later in the day, you might not see another human being. But the forest and the creek make for good company, and the squirrels are happy to pause in their foraging to yell at you.

From Denver. Take I-25 north to Exit 243, then turn left onto CO 66 west. After 14.3 miles, bear right onto US 36, and continue 1.5 miles to Lyons. Turn left onto CO 7 and drive 18.7 miles, to Allenspark. Turn left on CO 7 BUS East, and left again to stay on it. Take the next right onto Ski Road (CR 107), a bumpy dirt road, and continue 1.6 miles. Turn right on Forest Road 1161, another dirt road, and proceed 0.5 miles to the small parking lot for St. Vrain Mountain Trailhead. Alternatively, you can park along Ski Road in a small area on the left 1.3 miles past Allenspark, and walk the rest of the way. *1 hour, 40 mins.*

Looking down from Meadow Mountain

Boulder

Outdoor fitness mecca and trail nexus

Boulder has championed the preservation of open space since 1898, when its citizens voted to purchase land for public use on the slopes of the Flatirons, the famous stone spears rising above town. Fast-forward 120 years and you'd be hard pressed to find a place more outdoorsy or hiker-friendly than this college town 40 minutes outside Denver. That first purchase has expanded into a massive "city" park and spawned dozens of other wonderful open spaces, many on former mountain ranchland.

Many foothills trails are walkable all year, delivering lovely forests and dramatic rock formations. In addition to the Flatirons, a must-hike destination, you can take in dizzying Eldorado Canyon from Rattlesnake Gulch, or marvel at Devil's Thumb while heaving yourself up South Boulder Peak. If it's the chilly dead of winter, or you'd like an easy family outing, Walden Ponds offers a short level trail and birdlife encounters, or you can find a forgotten mesa-top reservoir on Eagle Trail.

Drive up Boulder Creek's canyon and you'll reach the laid-back town of Nederland and a host of dazzling high-summer walks. A good way to hook a youngster—or anyone—on hiking is to go to Blue Lake beneath Mount Toll, where there's a waterfall and some bouldering, or to Pawnee Pass, where Navajo Peak's stone pyramid stares you in the face. For a close-up of a near-vertical snowfield, hike up South Arapaho Peak; it's hard to decide which is better, the views or the wildflower-stuffed meadows. And do yourself a favor and hike to Heart Lake, then climb the green tundra hillside above it to Rogers Pass. Utter gorgeousness!

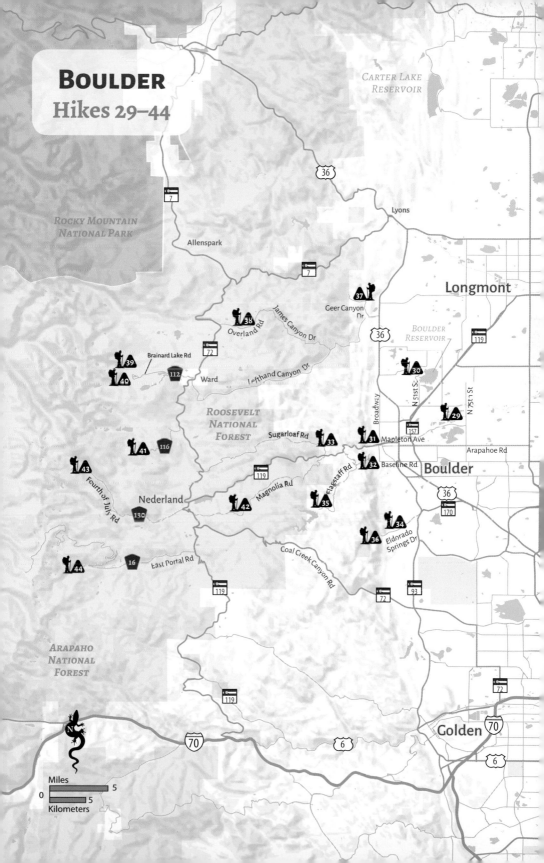

BOULDER
Hikes 29–44

ROCKY MOUNTAIN
NATIONAL PARK

CARTER LAKE
RESERVOIR

Allenspark

Lyons

Longmont

7

7

37

Geer Canyon
Dr.

36

BOULDER
RESERVOIR

119

38
Overland Rd

James Canyon Dr

72

112

Lefthand Canyon Dr

Ward

30

N 51st St

N 75th St

29

157

ROOSEVELT
NATIONAL
FOREST

39

40

Brainard Lake Rd

Sugarloaf Rd

33

31

Mapleton Ave

Broadway

Arapahoe Rd

Boulder

41

116

119

Magnolia Rd

Flagstaff Rd

32

Baseline Rd

35

36

43

Fourth of July Rd

Nederland

130

42

34

Eldorado
Springs Dr

36

170

44

16

East Portal Rd

Coal Creek Canyon Rd

119

72

93

ARAPAHO
NATIONAL
FOREST

119

72

N

Golden

70

6

70

6

Miles
0   5
Kilometers
5

29 Walden Ponds

THIS SHORT TRANQUIL WALK IN BOULDER'S BACKYARD TAKES YOU THROUGH A WETLAND habitat reclaimed from a gravel-mining operation. The reinvention of the landscape has created a pleasant open space for hikers, bird-watchers, fishermen, and kids to enjoy.

At a Glance

DIFFICULTY	🚶	**DISTANCE/TIME**	2.5 miles/1 hour
TRAIL CONDITIONS	🚶🚶🚶🚶	**TRAILHEAD ELEVATION** / **TOTAL HIKING GAIN**	5,100 feet / negligible
CHILDREN	🚶🚶🚶🚶🚶	**FEATURES**	Wetlands, bird life, mountain views
SCENERY	🚶🚶🚶	**BEST SEASON**	All year
PHOTO	🚶🚶🚶🚶	**OTHER USERS**	Bikes, horses, dogs on leash
SOLITUDE	🚶🚶	**NOTES**	Toilets at trailhead
PROPERTY	Walden Ponds Wildlife Habitat, Sawhill Ponds Wildlife Preserve	**JURISDICTION**	Boulder County Parks & Open Space (Walden), City of Boulder Open Space & Mountain Parks (Sawhill)

Who would have thought an old gravel quarry could become a wetland wildlife refuge? After county road builders stripped the floodplain down to bedrock here in the 1960s, the pits they left behind filled with groundwater and a new ecosystem began to emerge. Nature got a hand in 1974 when extensive reclamation work began. Now, more than four decades later, the Walden Ponds and adjacent Sawhill

Ponds preserves are quiet areas full of plants and animals where you can set yourself footloose for a few hours. Scores of species of year-round, seasonal, and migratory birds find their way here; you might also see a beaver, a red fox, or a painted turtle. This short hike is great for children, and anglers of all ages can enjoy catch-and-release bass fishing along the way.

The hike begins with great views of the towering, snow-topped Indian

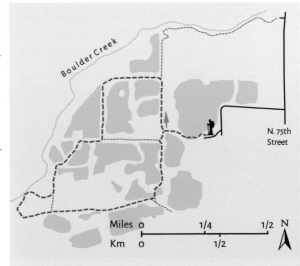

Left: Boulder Creek, near Walden Ponds

Boulder's Flatirons from Walden Ponds

Peaks. The ponds are set back enough from the Front Range to get a good view of the higher mountains. Walk west through the cattails along the boardwalk at the south end of the marsh; here a series of interpretive displays gives the lowdown on the preserve's history and wildlife. At the end of the boardwalk, join the main trail and continue west, with Duck Pond on your left, veering right and then left to make a counterclockwise trip around **Bass Pond** and **Ricky Weiser Wetland**. The trail is easy to follow but can be soggy after rain or snowmelt. There are many good places to stop and fish, and it is fun to count the different types of waterfowl.

At the southwest edge of **Ricky Weiser Pond**, little ones might be ready to turn left and follow a trail leading back to the car. Hardier hikers can turn right and continue southwest around the **Sawhill Ponds**. The landscape is a little wilder here, and it's possible to forget there are cities or roads or old gravel pits nearby. After half a mile, look for a trail branching right into a stand of cottonwoods. Enjoy these hardy pioneer trees, always among the first to colonize a disturbed landscape, as you follow this path to a rushing cataract of Boulder Creek. From here, loop counterclockwise to rejoin the main trail and head east along the southern edge of Sawhill Ponds. Be sure to branch left (north) at the triangular junction amidst the ponds to get back to your vehicle; if you keep going straight you'll arrive at a different parking lot.

You can extend the hike another mile by retracing your steps north along the earthen dike between **Cottonwood Marsh** and **Bass Pond**. The industrial facility ahead on the right is Boulder's wastewater treatment plant, but don't worry, it's not stinky or noisy. Man-made and literally antiseptic, it makes an interesting juxtaposition with the swampy wetlands to your left. Continuing north along the gravel path called **Heatherwood Walden Link**, the trail soon veers northeast to follow Boulder Creek. A tranquil streamside walk leads to 75th Street and another car park. You can return to the Cottonwood Marsh lot by retracing your steps or by walking south along 75th Street and turning right onto the road you arrived on. The latter route brings you past **Wally Toevs Pond**, where you will be greeted by flocks of waterfowl year round. The Canada geese sitting and flapping on the water can create quite the honking ruckus.

Walden Ponds boardwalk at Cottonwood Marsh

Back in the car, consider driving into downtown Boulder for a saunter down the Pearl Street pedestrian mall, where coffee, snacks, and street performers abound.

From Denver. Take I-25 north to Exit 217A, then US 36 west to Boulder. Turn right onto Arapahoe Road (CO 7) and drive east for 5 miles. Turn left on 75th Street and travel 2 miles to the entrance to Walden Ponds Wildlife Habitat on the left. Park in the second lot, at Cottonwood Marsh. *50 mins.*

Walden Ponds trail to Bass Pond

30 Eagle Trail to Mesa Reservoir

KIDS PAST THE "CARRY ME!" STAGE WILL FEEL PROUD TO COMPLETE THIS 5-MILE WALK through a wide swath of prairie to an abandoned hilltop reservoir. Adults get a pleasant, easy hike with space to connect with the land, the past, and each other.

At a Glance

DIFFICULTY	🚶	DISTANCE/TIME	5 miles/2 hours
TRAIL CONDITIONS	🚶🚶🚶🚶🚶	TRAILHEAD ELEVATION / TOTAL HIKING GAIN	5,300 feet / 200 feet
CHILDREN	🚶🚶🚶🚶	FEATURES	Prairie, mesa, abandoned reservoir, raptors, coyotes
SCENERY	🚶🚶	BEST SEASON	All year
PHOTO	🚶🚶	OTHER USERS	Bikes, horses, dogs
SOLITUDE	🚶🚶	NOTES	No toilets at trailhead
PROPERTY	Boulder Valley Ranch	JURISDICTION	City of Boulder Open Space & Mountain Parks

Begin by walking wide, level **Eagle Trail** toward the foothills. The grassland appears tough but is rather fragile. In May and June you will find the bright yellow blossoms of Bell's twinpod, a low-growing plant of the mustard family that is rare in most places but native and plentiful in these Front Range shale soils. Shafts of white yucca blossoms abound in spring as well. In winter, the yuccas' frosted balls of spikes populate the stark landscape like a minefield.

After half a mile, turn left at the junction with Sage Trail, staying on Eagle. Ahead, cattle graze the working ranch in the center of the open space. The trail heads downhill to a pond and curves clockwise to skirt the ranch perimeter. Trees

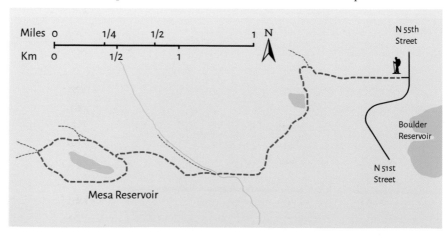

Eagle Trail

Coyote viewed from Eagle Trail

line the way on the approach to Farmers Ditch, an irrigation canal built in 1862.

Eagle Trail is aptly named. Especially in winter, it's a great place to watch golden eagles and hawks hunt for their meals. Don't be surprised if a coyote rises from the grass, trots away, then turns and stares at you from a distance. Keep staring back and don't worry—she's after prairie dogs, not you.

At 1.5 miles, branch left and ascend the side of a low mesa. Considering its location so close to town, the top feels wonderfully remote. No real civilization can be seen to the south, and to the west are more foothills. To the north all you see is rolling ranchland, some distant houses, and the bald cone of Haystack, an extinct mini-volcano out on the prairie.

As you pass through a gate it gets even better, for here is the strange reincarnation of **Mesa Reservoir**, which lost its water connection many years back. This oblong, mesa-top body is gorgeous and spooky in its abandonment. Cottonwoods have sprung up inside the sloping shoreline, and reeds and grasses fill the shallow waters of the bed, where ducks and other waterfowl paddle. The place feels eerie and forgotten. Of course it has a story.

Mesa was the last reservoir in a line served by the Silver Lake Ditch, the last irrigation ditch to use water from Boulder Creek. Construction of the ditch began in 1888 when two men who owned high, dry land north of Boulder tapped into the creek about a mile up Boulder Canyon and ran the waterway. Being latecomers, their water rights were junior, which meant their ditch got lots of water during wet years and little or none during dry. In 1907, W. W. Degge bought the irrigation ditch and added the reservoir. He also purchased tracts of land in north Boulder and tried to develop a suburban community called Wellington Gardens, a project that unraveled in rancorous fashion when stockholders accused him of fraud and embezzlement. Degge's scheme did not materialize, but from your perch on the top of the mesa you can see a distant housing development—proof that Boulder was destined to grow and grow. The Silver Lake Ditch is still in operation, owned by a consortium of users who periodically run water to Mesa Reservoir to help maintain it as a wetland habitat.

Turn left to circle the reservoir. At its west end, the trail descends to a junction with Degge Trail before returning to the reservoir. Late on a winter afternoon, a distant coyote might begin to cry, joined in chorus by others. Enjoy the howls as you take a last look at the lost reservoir and begin the return walk.

From Denver. Take I-25 north to Exit 217A, then US 36 west to Boulder. Take the exit for CO 157 N/Foothills Parkway, drive north 4.8 miles, and turn left on Jay Road. Drive 0.2 miles and turn right onto 51st Street. Continue north 2 miles to the parking lot for Eagle Trailhead, on the left. *50 mins.*

Mesa Reservoir

31 Mount Sanitas

A RUGGED ASCENT FROM OLD TOWN BOULDER TAKES YOU TO A TRANQUIL MOUNT WITH good views of the inhabited plains below. It's been a favorite of health-and-wellness enthusiasts for more than a hundred years.

At a Glance

DIFFICULTY	🚶🚶🚶	DISTANCE/TIME	3 miles/2 hours
TRAIL CONDITIONS	🚶🚶🚶	TRAILHEAD ELEVATION	5,500 feet
		TOTAL HIKING GAIN	1,300 feet
CHILDREN	🚶🚶🚶	FEATURES	Steep trail, colorful boulders, sweeping views of foothills and city
SCENERY	🚶🚶🚶	BEST SEASON	All year
PHOTO	🚶🚶🚶🚶	OTHER USERS	Horses, dogs
SOLITUDE	🚶	NOTES	Toilets at nearby Centennial Trailhead
PROPERTY	Centennial/ Sanitas	JURISDICTION	City of Boulder Open Space & Mountain Parks

Mount Sanitas is great year round, except when snow blankets Boulder and its surrounding hillsides. That said, a sunny dry day in January is a fantastic time to put boot to trail here and give your legs and lungs an awesome winter workout.

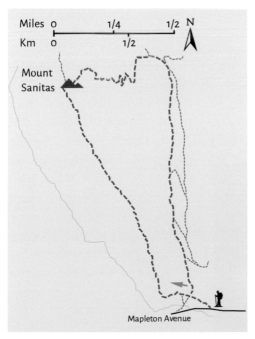

Just before you get to the trailhead, you'll pass the hospital that gives the mountain its name. Originally a "sanitarium" founded by Dr. John Harvey Kellogg, the cereal king, it was built in 1896 as part of a national wellness movement. In addition to fresh air and healthful foods, the sanitarium offered mountain hikes and spring-fed tonic baths as part of the physical regimen of its "outdoor gymnasium." A 1902 brochure proclaimed that a trail had been completed to the top of the mount, which, if you want to pronounce the name correctly, is not the Spanish-inflected "san-EE-tas"

Mount Sanitas Trail

but rather "*SAN-eh-toss*"; Sanitas was also the name of the company that sold Kellogg's corn flakes.

Mount Sanitas Trail begins at the picnic area next to an electrical substation west of the hospital and proceeds up the log-reinforced steps toward some rock cliffs. The steep trail winds through boulders and trees. It is well maintained, but it requires some fancy stepping on the many large rocks that make up the trail bed. Try to stay in the center of the trail as tramping through the adjacent dirt and brush will increase erosion. Views begin after the first 15 minutes, when the trail tops the spine of the ridge and continues up along it. Find a good steady pace and enjoy the workout as the incline continues unabated. It really feels like you are climbing a backbone, complete with knobby vertebrae of reddish rock. Views

Approach to Mount Sanitas Summit

abound to each side: west out to foothills, east down to city and plains.

After 0.75 miles, the grade mellows briefly where some power lines cut across overhead; you're now at the final approach to the summit. The area to the east of the trail is off-limits between February 1 and July 31 for the protection of falcons, golden eagles, and other raptors that nest and roost here. When you reach the apex you will have climbed 1,323 feet in just a little over a mile. Your reward is a catbird seat with unimpeded views from north to south: the hills rolling down to the plains, which curve off to infinity.

Descend eastward to make a return loop along Sanitas's **East Ridge Trail**. This section can be tricky in winter, when the shaded upper

Mount Sanitas Summit

reaches may be icy. You will encounter the most troublesome spots within a few minutes, and can then decide whether to continue on or turn back and descend the mountain the way you came. The trail weaves through a network of ridgetop boulders in the woods and sends you through a slot between two huge rocks that feels like a magic door. From here the trail zigzags down a grassy hill to join the Sanitas Valley Trail. You can follow the valley floor back to your vehicle or use the trail that tops Dakota Ridge, the hogback that runs just east of Sanitas.

Before getting in the car, consider taking a 10-minute stroll to Boulder's charming Pearl Street, where for once you won't have to hunt for parking. This saunter takes you along the aptly named Mapleton Street, a mansion- and maple-lined street that is particularly nice in fall colors.

From Denver. Take I-25 north to Exit 217A, then US 36 west to Boulder. Turn left onto Baseline Road, proceed 1 mile, then turn right onto Broadway. Continue 1.8 miles and turn left onto Mapleton Avenue. Go 0.4 miles, past a hospital on the right, and park either in the spaces to the right or in the lot at Centennial Trailhead, farther along on the left. *45 mins.*

32   The Flatirons

GET FACE TO FACE WITH THE ICONIC CRAGS OF BOULDER ON A POPULAR HIKE THAT TAKES you near the tops of Flatirons One and Two, with an astonishing perspective of the climbers' mecca: Flatiron Three.

At a Glance

DIFFICULTY	🚶🚶🚶	DISTANCE/TIME	4 miles/2 hours	
TRAIL CONDITIONS	🚶🚶🚶	TRAILHEAD ELEVATION TOTAL HIKING GAIN	5,700 feet 1,400 feet	
CHILDREN	🚶🚶🚶	FEATURES	Flatirons, meadows, ponderosa forest, steep mountain trail with cliff views	
SCENERY	🚶🚶🚶🚶	BEST SEASON	All year	
PHOTO	🚶🚶🚶🚶	OTHER USERS	Dogs, horses (lower portion)	
SOLITUDE	🚶🚶	NOTES	Toilets at trailhead, some hand-and-foot scrambling, may be icy in winter	
PROPERTY	Boulder Mountain Park	JURISDICTION	City of Boulder Open Space & Mountain Parks	

Geologically speaking, a flatiron is a steeply slanted layer of erosion-resistant rock set on a softer base. The term was coined right here for the many stone spears rising above Boulder, which resemble clothes irons sitting on their ends. In the days before electricity, such devices were heated by fire and called "flatirons."

Preservation of these strikingly slanted hills began in 1898 when the citizens of Boulder voted to purchase several dozen acres on Green Mountain for a "Chautauqua," one of a network of high-minded adult education and cultural centers that were sweeping the country at that time. Chautauqua Auditorium opened here that year, and over the ensuing decades much of the nearby foothills were

Chautauqua Meadow and the Flatirons

added to the parcel. The auditorium is still very much in use, as are the mountain trails, which are now part of a city park.

To begin, walk a quarter mile up **Chautauqua Trail** on a wide dirt path, straight toward the First Flatiron. Branch right onto **Ski Jump Trail** and continue on, crossing the hillside of what was an off-and-on ski area in the 1950s and 1960s, offering a rope tow powered by a truck engine. A left turn onto the **Bluebell-Baird Trail** takes you into a tranquil ponderosa forest. Within 10 minutes, make a right at a four-way junction onto **Flatirons Loop**, then branch right again onto **1st/2nd Flatirons Trail**. You have only 0.7 miles to go, but get ready to climb.

You'll cross a boulder field, the First Flatiron looming above you, and then reenter the woods. A wooden bridge branches right for rock climbers' access. Don't take it. Instead, go left and make a steady traverse up the wooded hillside. The Third Flatiron will begin to peek at you through the trees. As you climb higher, you will emerge from the woods for a very up-close-

Flatiron 3 from 1st/2nd Flatirons Trail

Trail down from Flatiron 2

and-personal Flatirons moment when the side of the Second Flatiron is within arm's reach and the Third is staring you in the face. More switchbacks take you on a steep but safe trail over rocks and roots that require you to scramble a little, using handholds and toeholds, before you reach a notch just below the Second Flatiron.

The views of the Third Flatiron here are breathtaking. This is a world-famous climbing crag, and you are enjoying a startling view that you can't get from below: the slanted profile of its east face and the vertical drop of its west. The east face is a busy multi-pitch climbing route—when it is open, that is. From February through July, the Third Flatiron is closed to protect raptors during mating and nesting season. Here, peregrine and prairie falcons duke it out for prime cliff-nesting sites, and are sometimes able to coexist.

From the notch the trail descends slightly and then makes a few switchbacks through stubby twisted trees to a higher notch. The mound of rock just above you is the back side of the First Flatiron, a place that looked quite inaccessible from below.

Descend back to **Flatirons Loop** the way you came. Turn right and cross a boulder field, then descend past the Third Flatiron access trail to a junction with **Royal Arch Trail**. You can turn right and hike 0.7 more miles to Royal Arch, a famous rock formation, or save it for another day (the trail can be quite icy in winter). Turning left at the Royal Arch junction, it is 20 minutes back to the parking lot through ponderosas and meadow, via the lovely **Bluebell Mesa Trail**.

From Denver. Take I-25 north to Exit 217A, then US 36 west to Boulder. Turn left onto Baseline Road, proceed 1.7 miles, then turn left into Chautauqua Park, where there is a large parking lot. If the lot is full, you can park on Baseline or on another nearby street. *45 mins.*

33 Canyon Loop

THOUGH JUST MINUTES OUTSIDE BOULDER, THIS TRANQUIL WALK ON GENTLE HILLSIDES through forest and grassland feels like a wilderness respite, and it's snow-free much of the winter.

At a Glance

DIFFICULTY	🚶	**DISTANCE/TIME**	3.5 miles/1.5 hours
TRAIL CONDITIONS	🚶🚶🚶🚶	**TRAILHEAD ELEVATION** / **TOTAL HIKING GAIN**	6,500 feet / 400 feet
CHILDREN	🚶🚶🚶	**FEATURES**	Foothills, grassland, ponderosa forest
SCENERY	🚶🚶	**BEST SEASON**	All year
PHOTO	🚶🚶	**OTHER USERS**	Bikes, horses, trail runners, dogs on leash
SOLITUDE	🚶🚶	**NOTES**	Toilets at trailhead
PROPERTY	Betasso Preserve	**JURISDICTION**	Boulder County Parks & Open Space

Unlike most hill hikes, **Canyon Loop Trail** begins and ends near its high point. Topping out at 6,800 feet, it is doable year round. There are fine views right away across the fields and rolling forested hills. In winter the grasses are a rich shade of tan. Early spring is the best time for wildflowers.

The loop is described here in the clockwise direction, but either way it is downhill for the first half of the hike. Excellent trail quality and gentle grades make the loop popular with mountain bikers and trail runners. If you'd prefer not to encounter bikes, choose a Wednesday or Saturday, when the trail is closed to them.

The grassy cone of Sugarloaf Mountain looms to the left as the trail leaves the parking lot on an easy upslope. Within minutes, you'll enter ponderosa forest and reach the loop's high point. You may get the feeling you are being watched; turn around and you might stare a mule deer in the eyes.

At 0.75 miles the path opens into a clearing with views of the plains through

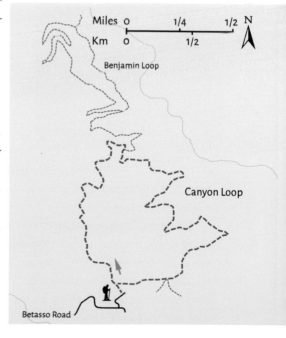

Sugarloaf Mountain from the start of Canyon Loop

Mule Deer on Canyon Loop

a slot in the hills. Ten more minutes brings the junction with the Loop Link Trail. Go right to stay on Canyon Loop. Alternatively, you can go left and add 4 miles to the hike by doing the Benjamin Loop, which passes through similar terrain above Fourmile Canyon. Benjamin Loop is a mecca for trail runners and delightful in its own right, though it offers a less remote vibe since houses are often in view, and sounds of birdsong get mixed with "traffic song."

Continue on Canyon Loop as it alternates between meadow and forest, curving along the hillside and bottoming out in a gully. The gentle return ascent begins at the 2-mile mark, enters another gully, and wraps along a south-facing hillside of grassland and widely spaced trees.

Tree densities are managed here in the Betasso Preserve to reduce the risk of catastrophic fire. Before ranching and fire suppression, natural fires occasionally swept through here, killing shrubs and small trees but leaving established pines standing. Now trees are selectively felled, ferried by helicopter to clearings, and then converted to wood chips, which are trucked out and fed to biomass burners that heat Boulder County Jail and Parks & Open Space buildings.

Continue past an industrial facility operating quietly downhill to the left. This is the Betasso Water Treatment Plant, gravity-feeding the City of Boulder most of its potable water from reservoirs higher up in the hills. Tree density management helps protect that water supply. Free facility tours are available on weekdays if you make arrangements in advance.

Two trails branch left above the treatment facility in a V formation. One is the Betasso Link, heading downhill past the plant. The other leads up to a picnic spot. Keep right of both branches and you'll complete Canyon Loop within minutes.

It's easy to feel the affection Ernie Betasso had for this land when he sold it to Boulder County in 1977. His dad, Steve Betasso, had bought out a homestead here in 1915 and expanded it using profits from mining tungsten and gold in Fourmile Canyon. Steve and his sons used to winter their cattle in these fields and drive them higher in summer months to rangelands below the Indian Peaks. Ernie helped oversee the preserve—the county's first open-space purchase—until his death in 1983, and he'd be pleased to have you enjoy it.

From Denver. Take I-25 north to Exit 217A, then US 36 west to Boulder. Turn left onto Canyon Boulevard (CO 119 west) and continue 6.3 miles. Turn right onto Sugarloaf Road, proceed 1 mile, then turn right on Betasso Road. Continue 0.5 miles to the parking lot for Betasso Preserve Trailhead, on the left. *1 hour.*

Forest of Canyon Loop

34 South Boulder Peak

THIS RIGOROUS HIKE TO THE HIGHEST POINT IN BOULDER MOUNTAIN PARK BRINGS thrilling views from the top and close encounters with freaky Devil's Thumb along the way.

At a Glance

DIFFICULTY	🚶🚶🚶🚶	DISTANCE/TIME	8.5 miles/3.5 hours
TRAIL CONDITIONS	🚶🚶🚶	TRAILHEAD ELEVATION TOTAL HIKING GAIN	5,600 feet 3,000 feet
CHILDREN	🚶	FEATURES	Steep gully ascent, old cabins, expansive views, rock formations
SCENERY	🚶🚶🚶🚶	BEST SEASON	Spring and fall
PHOTO	🚶🚶🚶🚶	OTHER USERS	Dogs, horses on portion
SOLITUDE	🚶🚶	NOTES	Parking fee for vehicles not registered in Boulder County, toilets at trailhead
PROPERTY	Boulder Mountain Park	JURISDICTION	City of Boulder Open Space & Mountain Parks

South Boulder Peak is the highest of Boulder's four summits, but it's obscured from downtown by its neighbor, Bear Peak, so it doesn't get as much glory—or quite as many visitors.

As you cross South Boulder Creek and walk toward the hills, the crooked tower of Devil's Thumb demands notice, jutting up between the two peaks ahead of you. You will get to know this rock intimately, along with South Boulder, the charred-tree peak to its left. Veer left onto **Homestead Trail** and ascend through

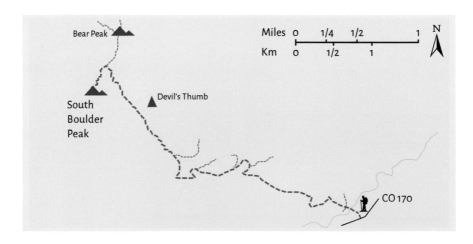

grass, shrubland, and ponderosas. At 1.5 miles turn left on **Mesa Trail**, then left again on **Shadow Canyon South**.

While Devil's Thumb is hiding, a different stone spear rises on your left. Beneath it, you'll see the weathered roof of McGillvray Cabin peeking over the bushes. Abandoned now, it was once a cozy homestead, and the lilacs planted there still bloom every spring. The trail climbs and levels off into the canyon crux, where another cabin perches against a boulder. This is Stockton Cabin, likely a miner's lodge before it was acquired by writer Jessie

Bear Peak from South Boulder Peak

Stockton, who homesteaded here in 1910. Her grandsons remember driving up here in a Ford Model T.

Just past the cabin, the easy freeway trail ends. Turn left onto a narrower trail and get serious about climbing. With 1.5 miles to go and 2,000 feet to gain, there isn't much to say except, "Just do it." It's a steep but decent path with stone steps, boulders, and tree roots, all in thick woods. Devil's Thumb reappears on your right—towering, bizarre, and taunting now, since you must climb 700 feet *above* it to reach your summit. Probably better not to look at it much—a difficult thing

Shadow Canyon Trail

Devil's Thumb from Shadow Canyon Trail

to do! Expert rock climbers love the Thumb, of course; there's a route on its north face called "Cheating Reality."

Hoist your body uphill. The last stretch to the saddle is easier, on switchbacks through a burn area. Gazing back through scorched trees, you'll see Devil's Thumb finally below you, and a pod of Denver skyscrapers sprouting on the plains.

This is the edge of a fire that started on this peak's western slope during a lightning storm in 2012. Stirred by winds, it raced uphill and forced standby evacuation orders for thousands of south Boulder residents. I was picnicking at Chautauqua Park with my kids that day when they told us to get out. Heavy rain the next day brought relief, as did quick action from air tankers that dropped thousands of gallons of Phos-Chek, a fire retardant also known as "red slurry." The Forest Service dumps about half a million gallons of this chemical on Colorado every summer but limits its use within 600 feet of waterways because it can kill fish.

You'll turn left at the saddle and climb through more burn. The last bit is an easy scramble over reddish rocks. In late afternoon, the slanting sun over the Indian Peaks illuminates nearby Bear Peak's rocky ridge to beautiful effect. As you take in the views, many old mountain friends show up to say, "Hello! Glad you came!": Mount Evans, James Peak, all the Indians, Meeker, and Longs. Devil's Thumb can do no mischief now; it is but a minor oddity compared to the majesty around you.

Congratulations! You've reached the crown of Boulder. If you'd like to climb Bear Peak, too, you can. It's easy from the saddle: only a half mile and 400 vertical feet.

From Denver. Take I-25 north to Exit 217A, then US 36 west to McCaslin Boulevard. Turn left and make an immediate right onto CO 170 (Marshall Road). Proceed 3.8 miles, turn left to stay on CO 170 (now called Eldorado Springs Drive), and continue 1.9 miles to the parking lot for South Mesa Trailhead, on the right. Additional parking is available across the street at Doudy Draw Trailhead. *45 mins.*

35 Meyers Homestead

THIS PLEASANT WALK FOLLOWS A WIDE PATH THROUGH AN HISTORIC MOUNTAIN RANCH
outside of Boulder. Beautiful meadows intersperse with stands of pine, fir, and
aspen on the way to an 8,090-foot promontory that is enjoyable all year round.

At a Glance

DIFFICULTY	🚶🚶	**DISTANCE/TIME**	5.5 miles/2.5 hours
TRAIL CONDITIONS	🚶🚶🚶🚶	**TRAILHEAD ELEVATION** **TOTAL HIKING GAIN**	7,300 feet 700 feet
CHILDREN	🚶🚶🚶🚶	**FEATURES**	Meadows, woodlands, bluebirds, view of Indian Peaks
SCENERY	🚶🚶🚶	**BEST SEASON**	Fall, winter, spring
PHOTO	🚶🚶🚶	**OTHER USERS**	Bikes, horses, dogs on leash
SOLITUDE	🚶🚶	**NOTES**	Toilets at trailhead
PROPERTY	Walker Ranch	**JURISDICTION**	Boulder County Parks & Open Space

The wide trail starts out easy: a half-mile walk downhill through grassland
into gently sloped **Meyers Gulch**. The remains of an old ranch building appear
across the way. Andrew Meyers was the first homesteader here, in 1890, but the
structure dates to a later period after his neighbor, James Walker, bought him out.
Continue up the valley through meadows and stands of ponderosa pine on a

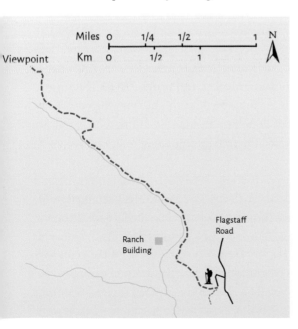

trail never steep enough to require a switchback. As you go
along, aspens join the conifers;
dense Douglas firs populate
the north-facing hillside across
from you. In spring and summer, watch for the bright flash
of mountain bluebirds; many
birdhouses have been placed in
and around the gulch for them.
Wildflowers are plentiful here,
and so are dark, long-eared
Abert's squirrels, which you
can see scrambling around in
the ponderosas. In winter you
have a good chance of seeing
elk and mule deer grazing.

Meyers Homestead Trail

Walker Ranch, through which this trail runs, is listed on the National Register of Historic Places. A pioneer success story, Walker arrived from Missouri in 1865, poor and sick with yellow fever. According to his granddaughter, who lived up here into the 1980s, Walker wanted to see some Indians and breathe Rocky Mountain air before he died. He camped in these high meadows and was cured by the combination of fresh air, herbs, and Arapaho Indian skill. He started a hard-scrabble homestead, married a schoolteacher, and got a big boost when a group of Englishmen leased a rocky hill on his property, hoping to extract gold using a cyanide process. The gold operation was short-lived, but the first lease payment allowed Walker to launch a successful ranching operation using tough Scottish Galloway cattle. By the mid-1900s, Walker Ranch had grown to 6,000 acres.

At 1.5 miles the trail veers uphill to the right and curves left through a dense stand of aspens. These trees look healthy and they are; they like the combination of moist soil, elevation, and plentiful sunshine on this hillside. Here you get a sense that the trail is ending, but it's not done yet. Another half mile, a little steeper now, takes you through a pretty basin before the trail reaches its terminus on the ridgetop among trees.

From a bench at the trail's end, you can enjoy the view of Boulder Canyon and beyond. Across the way stands the cone of Sugarloaf Mountain. Backing it in the distance is the lovely skyline of the Indian Peaks. It's interesting how distances can be deceiving in the mountains. Although they are as pretty as ever from this perspective, the Indian Peaks might feel farther away from you here, atop a foothill, than when you stare at them from the plains. In fact, they are closer.

Head back down the hill and you'll be back in the parking lot in short order. Though this is a fairly high hike, surpassing 8,000 feet in elevation, it can be done

Aspen grove on Meyers Homestead Trail

in midwinter as long as you can make it up to the trailhead on Flagstaff Road—an adventure in itself. The trail might have patches of snow, but the slope is gradual and the trail is easy to follow. On a different day, consider returning to hike the adjacent Walker Ranch Loop, a 7.8-mile up-and-down mountain adventure best done later in spring when its switchbacks in shady woods aren't coated in ice.

From Denver. Take I-25 north to Exit 217A, then US 36 west to Boulder. Turn left onto Baseline Road and drive west 7.5 miles as it becomes Flagstaff Road and heads steeply up and over the foothills. The parking lot for Meyers Gulch Trailhead is on the right. *1 hour.*

Old ranch building along Meyers Homestead Trail

36 Rattlesnake Gulch

A HIKE IN ELDORADO CANYON GIVES YOU CLOSE ENCOUNTERS WITH SOME DRAMATIC climbing walls, an ascent to wide vistas, and a chance to explore the remains of a summer resort hotel.

At a Glance

DIFFICULTY	👥	DISTANCE/TIME	4 miles/2 hours
TRAIL CONDITIONS	👥👥👥	TRAILHEAD ELEVATION / TOTAL HIKING GAIN	6,000 feet / 1,000 feet
CHILDREN	👥👥👥	FEATURES	Canyon cliffs, hotel ruins, views of the Continental Divide
SCENERY	👥👥👥	BEST SEASON	All year
PHOTO	👥👥👥	OTHER USERS	Bikes, dogs on leash
SOLITUDE	👥	NOTES	Entrance fee, toilets at park entrance and at the visitors center
PROPERTY	Eldorado Canyon State Park, City of Boulder Open Space	JURISDICTION	Colorado Parks & Wildlife, City of Boulder Open Space & Mountain Parks

Eldorado Canyon is awesome, and Rattlesnake Gulch Trailhead is located smack in the middle of the awesomeness. Astonishing views begin in the parking area, where 1,000-foot cliffs stare down on you as you get out of the car.

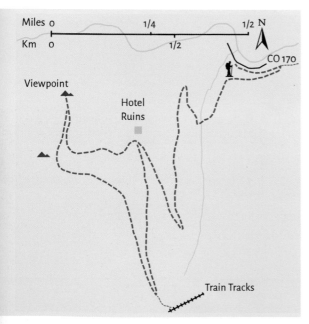

The cliffs have been a rock climbing mecca since the beginning of the sport. Parents be warned: a trip here might inspire your kids to take up the pastime!

The surreal right-tilting walls remain in view as you start down **Fowler Trail**, headed toward a snippet of prairie that appears through a slot in the canyon. After a couple of minutes, branch right and head into **Rattlesnake Gulch** on the namesake trail. Switchbacks deliver more dizzying views, the canyon walls appearing to swoop down and then jut up into a castle-like formation called

El Dorado Canyon from Rattlesnake Gulch

the Bastille, to the east. Above you on the hillside, train tracks cross steep red scree.

At 1.25 miles, you'll reach a hillside plateau that was the site of the luxurious Crags Hotel, where guests arrived by train, wagon road (now this trail), or gravity-powered funicular. The hotel opened in 1908 and lasted five seasons before burning down in mysterious circumstances. Fragments of foundation remain, along with a circular water fountain and the kitchen fireplace.

In fact, this rustic state park was once a major commercial resort area. In full swing by 1906, Eldorado Springs hosted tens of thousands of summer visitors drawn by its artesian water-filled swimming pools and carnival atmosphere. Fine hotels catered to honeymooners such as Dwight and Mamie Eisenhower. Glenn Miller played the dance hall.

The Crags Hotel ruins, Rattlesnake Gulch

From the ruins, continue on Rattlesnake Gulch and turn right when it forks into a loop. Within minutes you'll arrive at an overlook with views of Indian Peaks from South Arapaho to Shoshoni. A few hundred yards farther up the loop trail, an unmarked spur leads to a rocky point with an even better view. It's a sheer drop-off on the other side, so be very careful if you go here.

The loop continues on a pleasant wooded traverse and tops out near the red dirt scar of the train tracks. Here, at a stop called Scenic Siding, guests disembarked to ride burros or walk to The Crags. The railroad still brings travelers every day, but they don't get off. Amtrak's California Zephyr between Chicago and San Francisco passes eastbound in the morning and westbound in the afternoon.

Return to the hotel ruins by continuing the loop along a section that might once have been used by an arsonist. The hotel burned in autumn 1912, after it had closed for the season. Lightning strikes are possible at this time of year but not commonplace.

For an interesting short side trip at the end of the trail, turn right on **Fowler Trail** and walk to the Bastille. A climbers' access path heads down to the road on the west side of this startling hunk of rock. Follow that trail to the bottom, then look up and imagine a cable strung 600 feet overhead, across the canyon to the facing cliff. Imagine a man named Ivy Baldwin walking across it dozens of times over several decades. Baldwin's last tightrope walk here was in 1948, when he was 82 years old. Today, slackliners sometimes perform this feat.

There are other wonderful trails in this park, including the climbers' trail along spectacular West Ridge. This winding rock staircase gains 1,100 feet in less than a mile to reach a secluded notch in Cadillac Crag. No rock climbing is required—but it is great fun to watch the climbers in action.

From Denver. Take I-25 north to Exit 217A, then US 36 west about 14 miles to the McCaslin Boulevard exit and turn left. Make an immediate right onto CO 170 (Marshall Road) and continue 3.8 miles. Turn left to stay on CO 170 (now called Eldorado Springs Drive) and proceed 3.4 miles west to Eldorado Canyon State Park; the last stretch is along a good dirt road. Rattlesnake Gulch Trailhead and its small parking area are half a mile beyond the park entrance on the left. *50 mins.*

Indian Peaks from Rattlesnake Gulch Trail viewpoint

37 Wapiti Trail & Ponderosa Loop

A GENTLE YEAR-ROUND WALK IN THE FOOTHILLS AND PONDEROSA PINES NORTH OF Boulder brings a chance to see mule deer, elk, and other wildlife.

At a Glance

DIFFICULTY		DISTANCE/TIME	8 miles/3.5 hours
TRAIL CONDITIONS		TRAILHEAD ELEVATION	5,900 feet
		TOTAL HIKING GAIN	900 feet
CHILDREN		FEATURES	Ponderosa forest, mule deer, elk, views of hogbacks and red sandstone
SCENERY		BEST SEASON	Fall, winter, spring
PHOTO		OTHER USERS	Bikes, horses
SOLITUDE		NOTES	No dogs, toilets at trailhead, trails can be muddy in winter and spring
PROPERTY	Heil Valley Ranch	JURISDICTION	Boulder County Parks & Open Space

"Wapiti," an English synonym for elk, derives from a Shawnee word that means "white rump." Here your best chance to see such rumps is in winter, when wapitis come down from Indian Peaks Wilderness to munch on grasses and shrubs between the ponderosa pines. Today this protected area helps them complete their annual migration to the eastern plains. Once close to extermination in Boulder County, the elk population is now quite healthy. In 2017, the first-ever legal elk hunting in county open space was allowed, at nearby Rabbit Mountain.

From the parking lot, **Wapiti Trail** traverses a field and heads left up the hillside in swooping, bike-friendly switchbacks. Mountain bikers sharing these trails are by and large courteous, and are required to yield to pedestrians. Continue up

Mule deer along Wapiti Trail

Viewpoint

Wild Turkey Trail

Ponderosa Loop

Lichen Loop

Geer Canyon Drive

Miles 0   1/4   1/2   N

Km 0   1/2   1

through trees interspersed with grasses, shrubs, and mullein spires. In winter, you will likely see groups of mule deer dancing around in the clearings, eyeing you but not running away. At 1.9 miles, you'll arrive at the remains of a stone house set in the trees.

For thousands of years, Native Americans camped among widely spaced trees on these hillsides, where every few decades a natural fire would sweep through, killing the seedlings but leaving mature trees standing. Beginning in the 1880s, ranching and modern fire suppression techniques promoted higher tree densities and elevated the fire risk. When Boulder County purchased this land from the Heil family in the mid-1990s, land managers implemented a program of prescribed burning and selective tree thinning in an effort to return these forests to a state closer to primeval. The result is the parklike landscape you see here.

After 2.7 miles and 800 feet of elevation gain, turn left onto the **Ponderosa Loop**. Climb another hundred feet to reach the highest point of the hike, where you'll be rewarded with the first of many views of the dual summits of Mount Meeker and Longs Peak, to the northwest.

The trail meanders in a very pleasant fashion

View from the South St. Vrain Valley overlook, Ponderosa Loop

along the hilltop to reach some park benches with delightful views of the South St. Vrain Valley, at 4.2 miles. This overlook is just beyond the halfway point and makes a perfect spot to break for a snack and enjoy the scenery. In this majestic display, the Great Plains rise to meet the Rockies in slanted ridges of reddish Lyons sandstone. This distinctive stone was formed about 280 million years ago from sand dunes at the edge of an ancient inland sea. It has been quarried here for over a century and used in construction throughout Boulder County, including in many University of Colorado campus buildings.

From the viewpoint you have a trail choice. Branch right for the most direct return route along the **Ponderosa Loop** back to the junction with **Wapiti Trail**. For a 2-mile longer walk, take the left branch and continue on **Wild Turkey Trail**, another loop; it will return to **Ponderosa Loop** shortly before it rejoins **Wapiti**. Both choices offer very pleasant walking on gentle up-and-down paths through forested terrain. You might see a wild turkey on either trail, especially in winter when they stand out among patches of snow.

If you're not too knackered a half mile before reaching your vehicle, branch left onto the **Lichen Loop**. Turn left again and walk the eastern half of this pretty 1.3-mile trail. This hikers-only path heads up along a forested hillside, then down into meadows with fine afternoon views of the foothills and peaks to the south.

From Denver. Take I-25 north to Exit 217A, then US 36 west to Boulder. Continue about 8 miles, then turn left onto Lefthand Canyon Drive (CR 94). Proceed 0.5 miles, turn right on Geer Canyon Drive, and proceed 1.3 miles to the Heil Valley Ranch Trailhead and parking area. *1 hour.*

38 Ceran St. Vrain & Miller Rock

THIS KID-FRIENDLY HIKE TAKES YOU THROUGH A CREEK VALLEY IN DEEP WOODS BEFORE climbing a sunny hillside to a startling hunk of granite. Views from the top are superb.

At a Glance

DIFFICULTY	🚶🚶	**DISTANCE/TIME**	6 miles/2.5 hours
TRAIL CONDITIONS	🚶🚶🚶	**TRAILHEAD ELEVATION** **TOTAL HIKING GAIN**	8,300 feet 1,000 feet
CHILDREN	🚶🚶🚶🚶	**FEATURES**	Forest, creek, rock scramble to views
SCENERY	🚶🚶🚶🚶	**BEST SEASON**	Spring and fall
PHOTO	🚶🚶🚶🚶	**OTHER USERS**	Bikes, horses, dogs, 4WDs on a small portion
SOLITUDE	🚶🚶	**NOTES**	No toilets at trailhead
PROPERTY	Roosevelt National Forest	**JURISDICTION**	U.S. Forest Service

The first two miles of this pleasant hike make a gentle descent through forest along South St. Vrain Creek. The trail then climbs to Miller Rock, which offers sweeping views of the Continental Divide. Often snow-free by April, this hike is a great warm-up for summer adventures in the nearby Indian Peaks Wilderness and Rocky Mountain National Park.

Begin **Ceran St. Vrain Trail** (FS 801) by crossing the well-made bridge at the trailhead. This fine trail was built in 1979 with the help of the Youth Conservation Corps (YCC), a program by then in its waning days. The YCC was set up in the early '70s on the model of the Civilian Conservation Corps, a fondly remembered Depression-era program.

The trail traverses a steep hillside

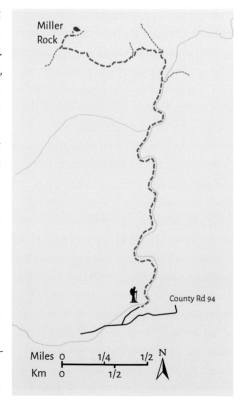

through tall pines, as the creek rushes in the narrow valley below. Cliffs appear across the way, and some aspens sprinkle in among the conifers. After a mile, the valley widens and the path descends to continue in lush forest along the creek. The sound of flowing water mixes with squirrel scolds and birdcalls to create a soothing backwoods soundtrack. After crossing a tributary, you will head onto a ponderosa hillside strewn with boulders.

The trail bottoms out at 2 miles, where it turns left onto a jeep road and heads uphill. Within minutes, you'll branch left onto an **unnumbered trail spur** to climb to Miller Rock. It is a brisk march uphill, but the orange trunks of ponderosas keep you company. As the trail mellows, a bike path joins from the right, and soon some Indian Peaks appear through the trees. At 3 miles, turn right at the intersection with **Forest Road 252A** (a jeep road). You won't wonder where Miller Rock is much longer—it appears on the left within minutes.

From a campfire ring at the rock's base you can shimmy up a chimney to the top. If skilled rock scrambling is not your cup of tea, or if you have small children with you, you should meander around to the north side, where a fun and easier vegetated route leads to the same place. The views from the top are a thrill for all ages: east to the plains, south to James Peak, west to the jagged Indians, and north to Mount Meeker, Longs Peak, and the Mummies.

On the return, enjoy the soulful forest

Bridge at start of Ceran St. Vrain Trail

Ceran St. Vrain Trail

along the creek, headed upstream this time. The last two miles go quickly, and the gentle ascent is barely noticed.

This trail and creek are named after Ceran St. Vrain, an early trader. Born in St. Louis to a well-to-do French military family in 1802, St. Vrain went west and helped establish a booming trading business with the prominent Bent family. They established St. Vrain's Fort where this creek joins the South Platte, out on the prairie below. Sacagawea's son worked out of this fort in the early 1840s, floating bison tongues and hides downriver to St. Louis.

The fort site makes an interesting side trip on the way home. To get there, take CO 66 east to Platteville. Head north on US 85, turn left on CR 40, and drive until the road ends. A monument installed in 1911 marks the lonely spot, which has a beautiful view of the river and creek confluence. Also in view is the Fort St. Vrain Generating Station across the river to the southwest. This power plant is now fired by natural gas, but it began life in the 1970s as Colorado's only nuclear power plant.

From Denver. Take I-25 north to Exit 217A, then US 36 west to Boulder. Continue about 8 miles and turn left onto Lefthand Canyon Drive (CR 94). Proceed 5.3 miles and turn right onto James Canyon Drive (also CR 94). Continue 7.7 miles, passing through Jamestown, and turn right into the parking lot for Ceran St. Vrain Trailhead. *1 hour, 30 mins.*

View from Miller Rock

39 Blue Lake of Indian Peaks

MOUNT TOLL SOARS LIKE A GIANT INCISOR TOOTH ABOVE THIS HIGH LAKE'S WONDROUS setting. Alpine terrain doesn't get much more spectacular, or more accessible, than this.

At a Glance

DIFFICULTY	🥾🥾	**DISTANCE/TIME**	5 miles/2.5 hours
TRAIL CONDITIONS	🥾🥾🥾🥾	**TRAILHEAD ELEVATION** / **TOTAL HIKING GAIN**	10,600 feet / 900 feet
CHILDREN	🥾🥾🥾🥾	**FEATURES**	High ponds and lake, cliffs, high mountain views
SCENERY	🥾🥾🥾🥾🥾	**BEST SEASON**	Summer
PHOTO	🥾🥾🥾🥾🥾	**OTHER USERS**	Dogs on leash
SOLITUDE	🥾🥾	**NOTES**	Parking fee, toilets at trailhead, thunderstorm exposure above tree line
PROPERTY	Brainard Lake Recreation Area, Indian Peaks Wilderness	**JURISDICTION**	U.S. Forest Service

This hike to Blue Lake is terrific, but you have to show up early or come later in the day. Parking places go fast at the trailhead, which is shared with an equally popular trail to Mount Audubon.

The **Mitchell & Blue Lakes Trail** (FS 912) begins in fir forest on a gentle but rocky path. After crossing a stream you'll continue in level woods and soon arrive at Mitchell Lake. A spur leads to its shore, where there are views of a majestic shoulder of Audubon.

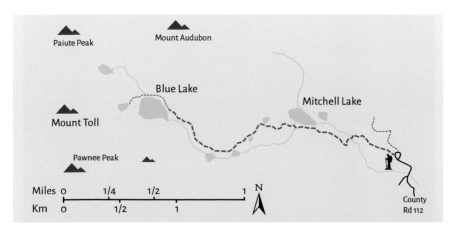

Trail to Blue Lake

After continuing on through woods, you'll climb a hillside with views down to the lake. The grade then mellows in a lovely area of ponds, where the prominent tooth of Mount Toll points over the rise. Don't turn around yet! None of those ponds is Blue Lake, and the scenery just gets better. Soon you'll reach a postcard-perfect basin, where a stream splashes down a rock-and-shrub meadow. Above, Mount Toll presents its dizzying profile as if it were the Matterhorn. It becomes even more transfixing at the 2.5-mile mark, where it stands in stunning juxtaposition with shimmering Blue Lake beneath it.

If you think scenery like this belongs in Rocky Mountain National Park, you're not alone. The glorious Indian Peaks were included in the park when it was originally proposed, but were removed to appease local logging, mining, and grazing interests. The park opened in 1915, but the Indian Peaks didn't get their own protected wilderness status until 1978. The Indian names were suggested by a botany teacher named Ellsworth Bethel in the early 1900s, both to honor the Indian nations and for fear that leaving so many blank spaces on the map would discourage Congress from enacting the park legislation. Of the eleven Indian peak names Bethel suggested, six are used today: Apache, Arikaree, Kiowa, Navajo, Ogalalla, and Pawnee.

There's much to explore here at the lake. Kids will probably find it cold for swimming, but might enjoy getting a closer look at the intriguing cliffs across the water. The trail continues along the northern shore, then slants uphill opposite the sheer face of a shoreline that looks tailor-made for cliff diving. Here a waterfall spills off the rocks and plunges into the lake. Even as late as mid-September, yellow and lavender flowers add color to the intoxicating landscape. After crossing some boulders above the lake's western end, the trail ascends to a higher basin, where it finds a grassy flat and a pond beneath ever-looming Mount Toll.

There is no Indian nation called Toll. The peak is named for Roger Wolcott Toll, the second superintendent of Rocky Mountain National Park. Toll was an avid mountaineer and conservationist, and his book *Mountaineering in the Rocky Mountain National Park* is a granddaddy of modern hiking guides like this one. Toll might have become director of the National Park Service if he hadn't been killed in an auto accident in 1936, while investigating possible locations for a series of international parks along the Mexico border.

Would you like to climb Mount Toll? It's just 1.25 miles farther and 1,000 feet higher. It requires no fancy skills or equipment—just legs and lungs. To do it, ascend the rocky slope past the pond, left of the snowfields and cliffs. You'll arrive in a higher basin where you'll need to hop across boulders. After that, the easiest way to the saddle is up the most vegetated part of the hillside. Once there, a few more minutes will take you to the apex of this little Matterhorn.

From Denver. Take I-25 north to Exit 217A, then US 36 west to Boulder. Continue about 8 miles then turn left onto Lefthand Canyon Drive. Proceed 10.7 miles to CO 72, turn right, and make a near-immediate left onto CR 112 (Brainard Lake Road). Continue 5.6 miles to the large parking lot at Mitchell Lake Trailhead. *1 hour, 30 mins.*

Mount Audubon, from the Blue Lake Trail

Blue Lake and Mount Toll

40 Pawnee Pass

THIS SUMMER HIKE HAS IT ALL: A FORESTED LOWLAND LAKE, A SPARKLING ALPINE LAKE, and a stunning ridge climb to a yawning pass with incredible views—all in the heart of the gorgeous Indian Peaks.

At a Glance

DIFFICULTY	🚶🚶🚶🚶	**DISTANCE/TIME**	9 miles/4.5 hours
TRAIL CONDITIONS	🚶🚶🚶	**TRAILHEAD ELEVATION** **TOTAL HIKING GAIN**	10,500 feet 2,000 feet
CHILDREN	🚶🚶🚶	**FEATURES**	Moose encounters, lakes, high mountain pass, summit scrambles
SCENERY	🚶🚶🚶🚶	**BEST SEASON**	Summer
PHOTO	🚶🚶🚶🚶	**OTHER USERS**	Dogs on leash
SOLITUDE	🚶🚶🚶	**NOTES**	Entrance fee in summer, toilets at trailhead, thunderstorm exposure above tree line
PROPERTY	Brainard Lake Recreation Area, Indian Peaks Wilderness	**JURISDICTION**	U.S. Forest Service

Besides being some of the most beautiful craggy mountains in the world, the Indian Peaks are close to Denver and very popular on summer days. So do yourself a favor: get up early and get to the trailhead before 7 a.m. to ensure a parking spot and a head start. Many of the folks arriving later will keep to the lower elevations, but today you're going up high.

From the trailhead, take the streamside forest trail to Long Lake, an easy,

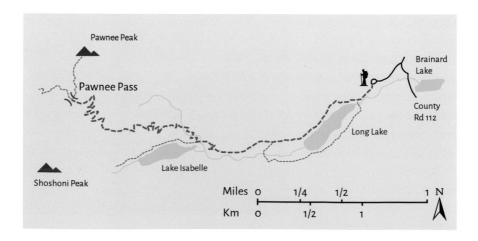

Navajo Peak from Pawnee Pass Trail

quarter-mile saunter. Keep your eye out for moose, which frequent the stream. At the lake, stay right on **Pawnee Pass Trail** (FS 907) to walk along the north shore, then continue through the gentle valley. Note the Jean Lunning Trail branching left, but don't take it now. Instead, continue on. If the weather is fair, you'll get nice views of the sun-drenched Niwot Ridge rising above you to the south.

When the trail steepens through woods, you will be nearing the trail to Lake Isabelle. The picturesque alpine lake is visible down and to your left from the junction at 2.1 miles. From here, a short trail leads to the lakeshore. You can enjoy the side trip either now or on the return trip. Lake Isabelle also makes a fine destination in its own right, particularly for young hikers who show signs of tiring early. There's good fishing here, too. You might want to return another day and explore past the lake; a stunning trail climbs to its feeder glacier and the peaks above.

From the junction, go right to stay on Pawnee Pass Trail and climb through stubby trees and rocks alongside another stream. The trail is safe and easy to follow, a dizzying delight as it winds up through the cliffs. Staring you in the face is the startling stone pyramid of Navajo Peak, a favorite climb for many Indian Peak baggers. Lake Isabelle sparkles below you again before the trail levels out into a large grassy basin. You can linger here before walking a half mile through fields speckled with yellow alpine sunflowers. But you know what's coming. You can see the switchbacks ahead, leading higher up the rocky hillside. Set a steady pace and follow the turns, and soon the trail mellows again for the final approach to the wide saddle of Pawnee Pass, at 4.5 miles.

Pawnee Pass from the side of Pawnee Peak

Moose in stream near Long Lake Trailhead

If, after catching your breath, you're in the mood for more, take the easy ascent north from the pass to the summit of Pawnee Peak, at 12,943 feet. The 400-foot climb is mostly on a narrow trail marked by cairns, with some easy rock scrambling at the top. Here you are rewarded with top-of-the-world views up and down the Continental Divide. For a more challenging scramble, you can ascend through boulders south from the pass to the top of 12,967-foot Shoshoni Peak. This climb gives jaw-dropping views down to the Isabelle Glacier and across to Navajo and Apache Peaks. You can also descend west from Pawnee Pass for 1.5 miles to Pawnee Lake, visible from the pass, but this is a challenging route in a steep boulder field with some sections of trail lost to rockslides.

On the return to the lowlands, you will likely encounter many later-arriving hikers. If you prefer less company, branch right onto **Jean Lunning Trail** and follow it around the south edge of Long Lake. It's a slightly longer route, but also less traveled, and the trail is newer and smoother than its north-shore counterpart. With fewer ups and downs and some lovely boardwalks, it's a foot-friendly way to end the day.

From Denver. Take I-25 north to Exit 217A, then US 36 west to Boulder. Continue about 8 miles and turn left onto Lefthand Canyon Drive. Proceed 10.7 miles to CO 72, turn right, and make a near-immediate left onto CR 112 (Brainard Lake Road). Continue 5.8 miles to the large parking lot for Long Lake Trailhead. *1 hour, 30 mins.*

41 Rainbow Lakes

THIS POPULAR FAMILY TRAIL OUTSIDE NEDERLAND LEADS TO A SERIES OF LAKES GOOD FOR fishing and dipping toes. Above, a graceful peak rises amid terrain that has long been a source of silver ore and artistic inspiration.

At a Glance

DIFFICULTY	👤	**DISTANCE/TIME**	2.5 miles/1.5 hours
TRAIL CONDITIONS	👤👤	**TRAILHEAD ELEVATION**	9,900 feet
		TOTAL HIKING GAIN	300 feet
CHILDREN	👤👤👤👤👤	**FEATURES**	Forest, lakes and ponds, mountain view
SCENERY	👤👤	**BEST SEASON**	Early summer
PHOTO	👤👤👤	**OTHER USERS**	Horses, dogs on leash
SOLITUDE	👤	**NOTES**	Toilets at trailhead
PROPERTY	Indian Peaks Wilderness	**JURISDICTION**	U.S. Forest Service

This short hike is a good training ground for little legs and lungs, and a great place to introduce children not only to mountain walking but also to trout fishing. As for views, lovely Caribou Peak hovers west above the trailhead and is a recurring companion.

Rainbow Lakes Trail (FS 918) begins uphill and soon curves west through pine forest. Keep straight at 0.3 miles when Arapaho Glacier Trail branches right. After some gentle up-and-down walking, you'll climb to the first lake on what becomes a very rocky path. The lake sits in a pretty setting beneath the eastern slope of Caribou, which is particularly attractive in early summer when snowfields cling

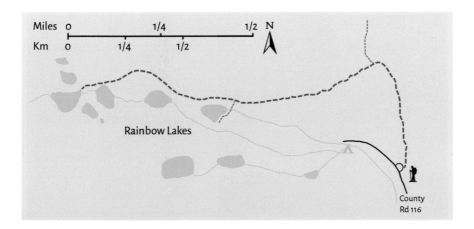

to its bowl. A path heads left along the lakeshore; you can explore it now or on the way back.

Stay right to continue west along the lake through aromatic pines. After more up-and-down walking, you will surmount a rocky hump and arrive at the next lake. The onward shoreline trail has some good spots for picnicking, with more views of the now-closer mountain. Then it's more woods walking on a rocky trail—challenging for the feet, especially little ones—to arrive at a marsh. Skirt the woods to its right to reach another lake, where the trail ends abruptly at its shore. Caribou rises from its opposite end.

Rainbow Lakes Trail

The mountain was named for one of two silver veins discovered southeast of its summit in 1869. Five years earlier, a man named Sam Conger collected some interesting rocks while hunting deer on its slopes. He eventually showed them to some experienced miners, who recognized them as silver ore. Together they located the source outcropping at 10,500 feet. One vein they named Carriboo, probably after a mining district in British Columbia (real caribou, which are North American reindeer, don't live this far south). The second they named Poor Man, though it proved to be the richer vein.

Boom and bust ensued in the mining camp of Caribou, where about 3,000 people lived at one point. After the prime ore was extracted, the mine changed hands and the new owner began milling the ore downhill in a settlement called Middle Boulder. Folks began calling the town "the Netherlands" after a group from Holland purchased the mine in 1873. Later, the town's name was officially changed

Caribou Peak and one of the Rainbow Lakes

to Nederland, a Dutch word for "low land." Set at an oxygen-thin elevation of 8,200 feet, the town was indeed low compared to the ore source.

A platinum boom hit 100 years after the silver boom, though not in the metallurgical sense. In 1971, a record producer bought the Caribou Ranch (you drove through its northeast corner to get here) and converted a barn into a recording studio. Joe Walsh christened it, and by 1974 Elton John had recorded his album *Caribou* there. Over 14 years, more than 150 artists recorded at Caribou, including Joni Mitchell, U2, Stevie Nicks, and Michael Jackson. Some used it repeatedly. Amy Grant was set to cut a fifth album there in 1985 when the control room caught fire. The studio never reopened.

The official trail ends at the third lake, but the basin is good for roaming, and social trails meander among nearly a dozen lakes and ponds that are good for trout fishing. It's a great place for kids to practice map and compass skills. Along the way they might find signs of beaver work, such as lodges and chewed trees.

From Denver. Take I-25 north to Exit 217A, then US 36 west to Boulder. Turn left onto Canyon Boulevard (CO 119) and continue 17 miles west to Nederland. From the roundabout, continue straight onto CO 72 and drive 7 miles. Turn left onto CR 116 and continue on a good dirt road for 5 miles. The parking lot for Rainbow Lakes Trailhead is on the right. *1 hour, 40 mins.*

42 Red Dot/Yellow Dot

THIS HIGH FOOTHILLS HIKE OUTSIDE NEDERLAND DELIVERS PLENTY OF ASPENS ON A MELLOW trail that offers solitude, elusive views of snowy peaks, and interesting stories of fire and ice.

At a Glance

DIFFICULTY	🚶🚶	DISTANCE/TIME	4 miles/2 hours	
TRAIL CONDITIONS	🚶🚶🚶	TRAILHEAD ELEVATION TOTAL HIKING GAIN	8,400 feet 300 feet	
CHILDREN	🚶🚶🚶🚶	FEATURES	Gentle trail, forest, aspens, views of snowy peaks and lowlands	
SCENERY	🚶🚶	BEST SEASON	Spring and fall	
PHOTO	🚶🚶🚶	OTHER USERS	Bikes, horses, dogs	
SOLITUDE	🚶🚶🚶	NOTES	No toilets at trailhead	
PROPERTY	Roosevelt National Forest	JURISDICTION	U.S. Forest Service	

There's a period in spring when the snowpack above 10,000 feet can stall in its retreat. The high mountains look alluring, but continued cold and snowfall keep them white. Lower elevations go into a snow-then-melt cycle that can go on for months. This high foothills walk is great to do while waiting for higher terrain to open up. It's also wonderful in fall, when the aspens light up gold in the sun, and it's easy enough for kids any time of year.

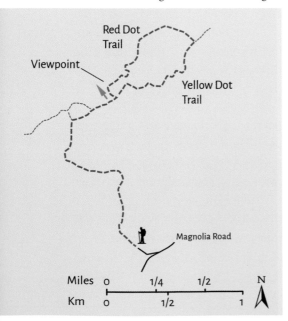

The pines smell great as you begin walking on old **Forest Service Road 357** (now gated for recreational use). Soon, pretty cliffs come into view across the valley. The trail continues alongside dense lodgepole pines to reach a meadow. Look back and you can see cliffs, the back side of the Boulder Mountains, and through Eldorado Canyon to the plains. Ahead, if the aspens are bare, you'll see Mount Meeker and Longs Peak peering between the trunks.

After about a mile, fork right and enter a flat. As the path heads toward

Eldora Ski Resort from Red Dot Trail

cliffs, it becomes a tunnel through aspens—dazzling in fall. In the grove, fork left onto a loop trail. The outbound and inbound portions of this loop are known to mountain bikers as **Red Dot** and **Yellow Dot**, respectively. You may see colored trail markers that were originally the painted tops of tin cans. The homegrown nature of this signage hints at the bootleg origins of these lovely paths, now part of the Dot Trail System.

There are nice views of the Arapahos and other Indian Peaks on this loop. For the best vista, scramble up rocks to the left when the trail begins to ascend from the flats. You'll enjoy a panorama of Eldora Ski Resort and the snowies behind it, all the way north to Longs.

In the valley you'll see evidence of the 2016 Cold Springs fire. Look carefully and you can spot a successfully defended mansion sitting in the middle of the devastation. The fire forced nearly 2,000 evacuations, burned almost 600 acres, torched eight homes, and totally freaked out the normally laid-back (and I mean *very* laid-back) town of Nederland. One woman rode her horse through the flames to escape. The fire started when two guys failed to completely extinguish their campfire. They pled guilty to fourth-degree arson and apologized. The judge sentenced them to two years of work release and ordered them to pay up to $1.25 million in restitution.

The trail traverses through dense pines, then descends by snakelike switch-backs to reach another aspen flat. Skirt right of the flat and you'll soon reach an intersection with an old jeep road, which marks the transition from Red Dot to

Aspen grove, Red Dot Trail

Yellow Dot. Turn right for a brisk uphill walk and then continue along a gentler forested incline. The only sounds you'll likely hear are the wind in the trees and maybe a distant train whistle. Top out on a level hilltop with encore glimpses of snowy peaks before heading down to the loop junction and back to your vehicle.

If you visit in early March there will probably be some snow on the trail, but you can take part in Nederland's "Frozen Dead Guy Days" on the way home. This festival has a long backstory involving a Norwegian guy and his mom who came here with a dead grandpa stored on dry ice, hoping to reanimate him later. Son and mom were deported, but the dead guy remains in a Tuff Shed outside town. Part of the festival proceeds go toward buying more dry ice.

From Denver. Take I-25 north to Exit 217A, then US 36 west to Boulder. Turn left onto Canyon Boulevard (CO 119 west) and continue 17 miles to Nederland. From the roundabout, continue south on CO 119 for 2 miles and turn left onto Magnolia Road (CR 132). Proceed 3.8 miles and turn left to arrive at the Front Range Trailhead and its small parking lot. *1 hour, 30 mins.*

Fall foliage along Red Dot/Yellow Dot Trail

43 South Arapaho Peak

THIS TREK IN THE INDIAN PEAKS IS A QUINTESSENTIAL ROCKY MOUNTAIN SUMMER HIKE: blue skies, jagged peaks, beautiful wildflowers—even a glacier. Intrepid hikers can add a thrilling ridge scramble to neighboring North Arapaho Peak.

At a Glance

DIFFICULTY	🧍🧍🧍🧍🧍	DISTANCE/TIME	9 miles/4 hours
TRAIL CONDITIONS	🧍🧍🧍	TRAILHEAD ELEVATION TOTAL HIKING GAIN	10,100 feet 3,300 feet
CHILDREN	🧍🧍	FEATURES	Forest, wildflowers, tundra, talus, glacier and mountain views
SCENERY	🧍🧍🧍🧍🧍	BEST SEASON	Summer
PHOTO	🧍🧍🧍🧍🧍	OTHER USERS	Horses, dogs on leash
SOLITUDE	🧍🧍	NOTES	Toilets at trailhead, thunderstorm exposure above tree line
PROPERTY	Indian Peaks Wilderness	JURISDICTION	U.S. Forest Service

Golden asters greet you at the beginning of this glorious hike, harbingers of things to come. **Arapaho Pass Trail** (FS 904) takes you across some boardwalks in fir forest, then into a clearing with a view to a flank of your mountain destination. From here the flowers only increase in number and variety: Indian paintbrush, columbine, buttercups, little sun flowers, and many others—about 90 species in all. Across the valley, peaks rise majestically and a creek tumbles from Diamond Lake.

Make some switchbacks in the woods and then stay right, at 1.25 miles, where Diamond Lake Trail (FS 975) goes left. Soon you'll enter a hillside meadow stuffed with wildflowers. Also gawk-worthy are the expanding views of the peak-ringed valley. It gets steeper here, but take heart: you are bagging some vertical gain. After the trail levels off in a basin, you'll reach a junction near a pile of tailings from

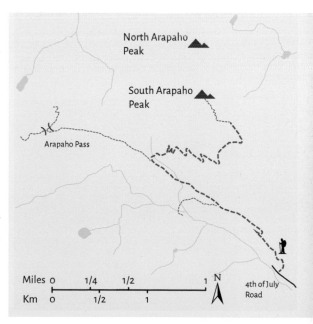

Arapaho Glacier Trail

the old Fourth of July Mine. Turn right here onto **Arapaho Glacier Trail** (FS 905). That's South Arapaho Peak above you.

The mine, staked on Independence Day 1872, was thought to have a major silver lode. A shaft was dug 230 feet deep, and the camp grew to include bunkhouses, stables, and a blacksmith's shop. But the cost of extraction exceeded profits, and inactivity set in by decade's end. Some folks tried to revamp it as a copper mine in the early 1900s. Three million dollars of stock was sold, and the road was upgraded, but almost nothing of value was unearthed.

After you cross a marshy area you'll break out of stubby trees to make your way upward in tundra. As you rise, the mountainscape unfolds to reveal Mounts Evans, Bierstadt, Grays, and Torreys to the south. Below to the east is Eldora Ski

South Arapaho Peak

Resort. You'll reach a meadow shoulder speckled with alpine avens and bluebells, and then traverse to a saddle where the knife-edge of South Arapaho Peak soars above. Don't worry; it's not as hard to climb as it looks.

The view from the saddle is awesome. The mighty face of North Arapaho Peak and its jagged ridge stare at you, and Arapaho Glacier plummets almost vertically to a series of lakes and reservoirs. This glacier, the largest in the Front Range, is owned by the City of Boulder. You can get in big trouble for hiking in the next two valleys, which supplied all of Boulder's stored water needs from the 1920s to the 1950s, and still meet about a third of the city's requirements.

At 4 miles this stunning saddle is a superb destination, but if you have half a mile and 600 vertical feet left in you, head for the spear towering above you. You can do it! Just follow the cairn-marked social trail up through boulders and talus, climbing as you would a long flight of stairs. The route is safe but veers close to the drop-off, sending thrilling chills down the spine.

Reach the summit and bask in glory. What a view! Neighboring North Arapaho Peak and its ridge are breathtaking and will entice some hikers onward. Getting to the highest point in the Indian Peaks is no cakewalk; it's 0.75 miles of skilled scrambling with some stirring moments. It's also one of my favorite ridge crossings. While not overly dangerous, it is best to go with someone who has done it before.

But you don't have to go farther. The summit of South Arapaho is entirely satisfying, and it's a great vantage point for plotting future hikes in this gorgeous mountain neighborhood.

From Denver. Take I-25 north to Exit 217A, then US 36 west to Boulder. Turn left onto Canyon Boulevard (CO 119 west) and continue 17 miles to Nederland. From the roundabout, continue south on CO 119 for 0.6 miles. Turn right onto Eldora Road and proceed 4 miles to where the pavement ends. Continue 0.8 miles on a good dirt road, bear right at a fork, and proceed 4 miles on bumpier Fourth of July Road to the parking lot for Fourth of July Trailhead. Additional parking is available along the road. *1 hour, 40 mins.*

View from Arapaho Glacier Trail

44 Rogers Pass

A VINTAGE RAILROAD TUNNEL MARKS THE START OF A GLORIOUS HIKE ALONG SOUTH Boulder Creek to a high tundra pass. It takes you through an enchanting landscape of streams, lakes, meadows, and crags.

At a Glance

DIFFICULTY	🚶🚶🚶🚶	DISTANCE/TIME	10 miles/5 hours
TRAIL CONDITIONS	🚶🚶🚶🚶	TRAILHEAD ELEVATION	9,200 feet
		TOTAL HIKING GAIN	2,700 feet
CHILDREN	🚶🚶🚶	FEATURES	Historic rail portal, forest and streams, alpine terrain, lakes, views
SCENERY	🚶🚶🚶🚶🚶	BEST SEASON	Summer
PHOTO	🚶🚶🚶🚶🚶	OTHER USERS	Horses, dogs on leash
SOLITUDE	🚶🚶	NOTES	Toilets at trailhead, thunderstorm exposure above tree line
PROPERTY	James Peak Wilderness	JURISDICTION	U.S. Forest Service

You don't have to hike all the way to the pass to enjoy this trail's top-rated scenery, but it's certainly worth the effort. Begin at the east portal of the Moffat railroad tunnel, where you'll see some abandoned bungalows where there was once a busy construction town. In the distant background, a wall of pretty peaks rises.

The tunnel is named for David Moffat, who began his career as a messenger boy in New York City and ended as a railroad bigwig. In 1904, Moffat spearheaded the construction of a temporary rail line from Denver over nearby Rollins Pass, with his eye on California. This route proved too steep and snowy to be profitable, and Moffat was unable to raise money for a tunnel before he died in 1911. The 6.2-mile tunnel you see opened 17 years later, funded by a state-issued bond. President Coolidge connected two ends of the pilot tunnel during a ceremony in 1927 by detonating a blast via telegraph from the White House.

Turn right from the service road onto **South Boulder Creek**

Moffat Tunnel East Portal, Rogers Pass Trail

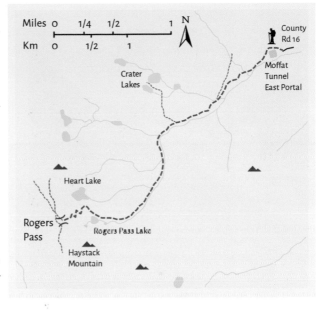

Trail (FS 900) and walk through aspens and wildflowers into James Peak Wilderness. The trail takes you through an enchanting riverine wetland and fir forest, where moss hanging from the branches gives a fairy-tale feel. Harebells and columbines add their colors trailside. Keep straight when Forest Lakes Trail (FS 809) branches right and continue along the creek, making occasional switchbacks, to where Crater Lakes Trail (FS 819) branches right. A steep side mile leads to these lakes, but the most remarkable terrain lies 2.5 miles straight ahead.

Refreshing streams cascade beside you as the trail curves upward and levels off in a stunning peak-ringed basin. A small tree-lined lake appears on your left; a larger unseen lake is on the right. In just a few minutes you'll reach Rogers Pass Lake, nestled at timberline beneath crags and snowfields. At 4 miles it's a gorgeous

Rogers Pass Trail

James Peak from Rogers Pass Trail

and satisfying turnaround point. But if you have another mile and 900 vertical feet left in you, keep going!

Turn right along the lakeshore and climb a green hill to an intermediate ridge. James Peak is now well in view to the south, beyond the pyramid aptly called Haystack Mountain. Ahead is charming Heart Lake, popular with tent campers. To the left, switchbacks spiral toward Rogers Pass.

Head for the hill! It's only six switchbacks, and while you're heaving breaths you can check out Heart Lake's shape, as well as the magnificent jagged ridge leading to James Peak. Look and listen for small tourist aircraft plying the airspace; the scenery here is that renowned.

Finish the switchbacks and traverse toward the pass, which was named for an early Central City mayor who proposed a different railroad tunnel beneath it. A corniced snowfield clings just below the pass into July. In the wide grassy saddle, the trail intersects with the Continental Divide Trail, which continues north to Canada and south to the top of James Peak and onward to Mexico. Views northward include the Arapaho peaks and other Indians; west is Winter Park and the Fraser/Granby valley.

On the way back, you might hear the wail of a train. Moffat's railroad outlasted most other lines in Colorado, and the entire route (save for the portion over Rollins Pass, which was dismantled in the 1930s) is still very much in use as a freight artery of Union Pacific. Passengers also travel each way, each day, on Amtrak's California Zephyr.

From Denver. Take I-25 north to Exit 217A, then US 36 west to Boulder. Turn left onto Canyon Boulevard (CO 119) and continue 17 miles west to Nederland. From the roundabout go south on CO 119 for 4.8 miles to Rollinsville. Turn right on East Portal Road (CR 16) and proceed 8 miles on a good dirt road to the large parking lot at East Portal Trailhead. *1 hour, 40 mins.*

Denver

Metro with a wild backyard

Even in the heart of Denver, you are never far from a wilderness experience. Most of the trails in this chapter are well within an hour's drive from the center of downtown, and can be walked year round. Jefferson County, which covers the western side of the metro area up into the foothills, does a superb job managing its many open spaces. There are also some great state parks in the vicinity, including Roxborough, Staunton, Golden Gate Canyon, and Barr Lake. Put these all together and Denver is a paradise city for anyone with itchy feet.

For the classic Colorado scene—tilted red rocks, emerald hillsides, and deep-blue sky—look no farther than Carpenter Peak or Morrison Slide. For birds try Barr Lake, and for aspens in full autumn blaze, head for Black Bear-Frazer in Golden Gate Canyon in early October.

One of the best things about so many of these Denver hikes is the counterpoint between the city and the wilds at its backdoor. You'll get sweeping views of both peaks and skyscrapers from Green Mountain and Lone Tree Bluffs, for instance, and an interesting perspective on Rocky Mountain water and beer from Mount Galbraith. And while it's easy to forget that Denver is nearby while you're tramping through the forest on Plymouth Mountain, it's a different story at the top, where it all spreads out before you.

The dazzling high-mountain summer walks nearest to Denver are covered in the next two chapters, but herein lies a tease: Chief Mountain, with close-up views of 14,271-foot Mount Evans.

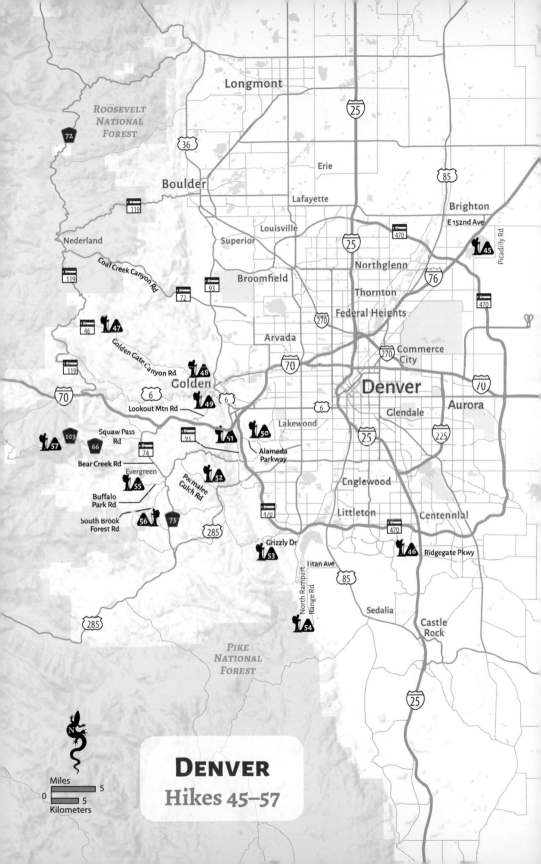

Roosevelt National Forest

72

36

Boulder

119

Nederland

Coal Creek Canyon Rd

119

46 47

Golden Gate Canyon Rd

119

70

48

Golden

6

Lookout Mtn Rd

6

49

Squaw Pass Rd

57 103

66

74

Bear Creek Rd

Evergreen

55

Buffalo Park Rd

South Brook Forest Rd

56 73

285

Longmont

25

Erie

Lafayette

Louisville

Superior

Broomfield

93

72

Arvada

Federal Heights

270

Northglenn

Thornton

Commerce City

270

Denver

Glendale

Lakewood

51

50

Alameda Parkway

52

Pajmalee Gulch Rd

53

Grizzly Dr

Titan Ave

North Rampart Range Rd

285

54

Pike National Forest

85

Brighton

E 152nd Ave

45

Picadilly Rd

76

470

470

70

Aurora

225

25

Englewood

Littleton

Centennial

470

46

Ridgegate Pkwy

Sedalia

Castle Rock

25

N

Miles

0   5

Kilometers

5

DENVER
Hikes 45–57

45 Barr Lake

TAKE A LONG WALK IN THE WETLANDS OF A WORLD-FAMOUS BIRD RESERVE, ONLY 40 minutes from downtown Denver. Bring binoculars!

At a Glance

DIFFICULTY	👥	DISTANCE/TIME	9 miles/3.5 hours
TRAIL CONDITIONS	👥👥👥👥	TRAILHEAD ELEVATION	5,100 feet
		TOTAL HIKING GAIN	negligible
CHILDREN	👥👥👥	FEATURES	Wetlands, bird-watching, eagles
SCENERY	👤	BEST SEASON	All year
PHOTO	👥	OTHER USERS	Bikes, horses, dogs on leash
SOLITUDE	👤	NOTES	Entrance fee, no dogs on southern portion, seasonal waterfowl hunting north of dam, toilets at trailhead
PROPERTY	Barr Lake State Park	JURISDICTION	Colorado Parks & Wildlife

You may want to leave your dog at home on this one. The southern half of Barr Lake is a wildlife refuge where no pets are allowed. Walking the lake clockwise lets you enjoy the refuge first; it also gives the option of going out and back through the reserve instead of walking around the entire lake. If you do bring your dog, you are welcome to walk the northern half of the lake. Children will love a shorter walk within the reserve as there is much to see. They might also enjoy the Eagle Express, a motorized shuttle to wildlife viewing spots that runs on weekend mornings in summer.

Once a buffalo wallow on the prairie, this natural basin was a rest stop for cattle drives before a dam was built in the 1880s and a canal was run from the South Platte River. A larger dam and canal were built a decade later. Trees moved in, grew tall, and a world-class bird habitat was born; in fact, nearly 350 species of birds have been sighted here. The reservoir is famous for its raptors—

Left: Rockies from Lone Tree Bluffs, Hike 46

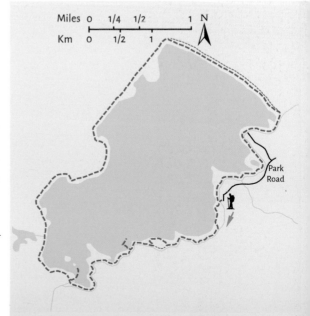

falcons, hawks, eagles, and also owls that migrate through or reside in the cottonwoods and willows. As many as 40 bald eagles winter here, and since 1986 at least one pair has made the park their year-round residence. In winter you might see a red fox on the ice, and deer moving among the trees.

Begin on the **Niedrach Nature Trail**, a series of boardwalks over the water, then rejoin the main trail and continue southwest along the shore. The first of several wildlife viewing stations appears in minutes off to the right. Also recommended is **Fox Meadow Loop**, which branches right at 1 mile to another viewing station. At 1.3 miles, the **Gazebo Boardwalk** extends onto the lake and offers prime raptor viewing (binoculars come in handy here) and a beautiful perspective of the giant shoreline cottonwoods. At 3 miles, another boardwalk called **The Rookery** beckons you again onto the lake.

Commit to walking at least another mile as the trail curves around the southern shore and heads north near the train tracks and highway. Don't let the proximity and white noise of civilization deter you—this is a wild and isolated stretch, and the birds seem to know it. It's easy to become overwhelmed by the sheer number of birds teeming in the woods and wetlands. Fortunately, the trail remains smooth and wide, so you can keep your eyes on the trees. Don't be surprised if blue herons rise and flap out over the water, or if you see white pelicans in summer.

It's hard to imagine this place in the 1930s, when a cleanup expert quoted in the *Denver Post* dubbed it the "biggest sewage lagoon in the United States." Situated downstream from Denver, it was the depository of the city's human and stockyard effluent for decades, but the water quality has improved dramatically, and in 2004,

Birdwatching at Barr Lake

Barr Lake was designated a drinking water resource.

When you reach the backyards of some houses, you are at the boundary of the wildlife refuge. From here you can either complete the circuit of the lake or return through the refuge. Either way it's about 4 miles.

Continuing on, the trail parallels the tracks and crosses the 1.5-mile-long dam. You can walk along the crest of the dam except during winter hunting season, when you must use the path below the dam. In winter, windblown slabs of white ice pile on the dam's inner wall and along the northeast shore to create a remarkable effect.

From Denver. Take I-25 north to Exit 216A, then I-76 east to Exit 22, East Bromley Lane. Turn right off the exit ramp onto East 152nd Avenue, then right again onto Picadilly Road. Drive 4 miles to the entrance to Barr Lake State Park, on the right. Park in the large lot next to the nature center. *40 mins.*

Gazebo Boardwalk at Barr Lake

Southwest Shore, Barr Lake

46 Lone Tree Bluffs

OUT OF SUBURBIA RISE THESE DRY BLUFFS, WHICH ARE HOME TO A LOOP TRAIL THAT OFFERS a vista of the Rockies limited only by the curvature of the Earth. It also offers a water lesson.

At a Glance

DIFFICULTY	🚶	**DISTANCE/TIME**	3 miles/ 1.5 hours
TRAIL CONDITIONS	🚶🚶🚶🚶🚶	**TRAILHEAD ELEVATION** / **TOTAL HIKING GAIN**	6,000 feet / 400 feet
CHILDREN	🚶🚶🚶🚶🚶	**FEATURES**	Grassland bluffs, panoramic views of city and Rockies
SCENERY	🚶🚶🚶	**BEST SEASON**	All year
PHOTO	🚶🚶🚶	**OTHER USERS**	Bikes, horses, dogs on leash
SOLITUDE	🚶	**NOTES**	Toilets at trailhead, very little shade
PROPERTY	Bluffs Regional Park	**JURISDICTION**	Douglas County Parks, Trails & Building Grounds

As you begin walking **Bluffs Regional Park Trail** toward the namesake grassy bluffs, Denver's neoteric suburb of Lone Tree, incorporated in 1995, sprawls behind you. Keep left after 500 feet to walk the loop clockwise and get the best views sooner rather than later. Behind a fence sit two giant cement disks: the tops of underground gravity-fed water tanks which supply houses and lawns below. There are more tanks farther uphill, out of sight. At a half mile, make a sharp right to continue on the loop; the left-hand path dead-ends by the tanks.

Within seconds the Rockies come out—and I mean they *really* come out. Even

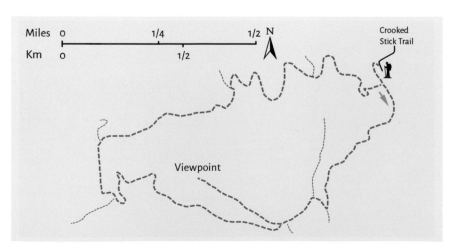

if you see them every day, you probably don't see this much of them. Keep going and soon the whole sweep from Pikes Peak to the Mummy Range is revealed. Also on view in near entirety is the Denver metro area, looking like a forest compared to the treeless bluff on which you are standing and the open prairie in the distance. You can imagine what this scene looked like before settlement: dry, high-altitude plains, devoid of trees except in creek bottoms. A trail branches right to an overlook, but you can skip it so long as you turn right onto the second one, where a viewpoint is visible 0.3 miles away: a park bench silhouetted against the mighty mountain backdrop.

From this bench you'll also look out over the vast spread of master-planned communities collectively known as Highlands Ranch. What you see was mostly dry-land farms and ranchland well into the 1980s, when the company that developed a similar-scale community in California's Orange County got to work here. Other developers piggy-backed. Since the mid-1990s, Douglas County has consistently been

Lone Tree Bluffs Trail

one of the fastest growing counties in the U.S. To put it in perspective, in 1980 the county had 7,789 homes; by January 2017 there were 120,580 homes, with about 3,000 still being added each year.

Back on the main trail, continue the loop as it swoops down a couple of switchbacks to near-backyard level. From here the trail traverses the sides of the bluffs in an up-and-down fashion, wrapping to a low point before making a concerted final push uphill via curves. Along the way, it's fun to try to spot mule deer milling about on the hillsides. They can be sneaky, living inconspicuously among the shrubs year round. Look for their large, mule-like ears and prominent white rumps. In summer, males will be growing antlers covered in a velvety layer which carries blood to stimulate more antler growth.

After gaining 100 feet, the trail tops out with a view of the teeming southeast metro area and the plains. Included in the view is the Rueter-Hess Reservoir, which began filling in 2011 as part of an effort to wean all these homes off well water. When suburban growth exploded in the mid-1990s, the consensus was that the groundwater would last forever. Also, Colorado law allowed anyone owning land in the Denver Basin to draw from its vast aquifer. Two decades and hundreds of ever-deeper wells later (some wells are more than 2,000 feet deep), this con-

Denver from Lone Tree Bluffs

sensus has proven wrong. Consumption has outpaced replenishment, and now surface water and rehabilitated wastewater must be pumped to Rueter-Hess and other reservoirs to satisfy the huge demand.

For a real treat, take this walk in early October, at the height of fall colors. At this time the "urban jungle" looks like a pointillist painting!

From Denver. Take I-25 south to Exit 193. Turn right onto Lincoln Avenue, drive 0.8 miles, then turn left onto RidgeGate Parkway. Continue 0.2 miles and turn right onto Crooked Stick Trail. Proceed 0.4 miles to the Bluffs Regional Park trailhead and its large parking lot, on the right. *30 mins.*

Rocky Mountains view from Lone Tree Bluffs

47 Black Bear Trail & Frazer Meadow

AN ADVENTUROUS RIDGE TRAIL IN THE FRONT RANGE WEST OF GOLDEN OFFERS VIEWS OF snowy peaks, some scrambling on rocky hills, and a gorgeous aspen meadow with a story.

At a Glance

DIFFICULTY	🚶🚶🚶	DISTANCE/TIME	5.5 miles/2.5 hours	
TRAIL CONDITIONS	🚶🚶🚶	TRAILHEAD ELEVATION	8,200 feet	
		TOTAL HIKING GAIN	1,000 feet	
CHILDREN	🚶🚶🚶	FEATURES	Ridge walk with views, aspen meadow, homestead relics	
SCENERY	🚶🚶🚶	BEST SEASON	Spring and fall	
PHOTO	🚶🚶🚶	OTHER USERS	Bikes and horses on small portion, dogs on leash	
SULITUDE	🚶🚶	NOTES	Entrance fee, toilets at nearby visitors center	
PROPERTY	Golden Gate Canyon State Park	JURISDICTION	Colorado Parks & Wildlife	

From the trailhead, **Black Bear Trail** ascends through ponderosa pines and aspens. As you traverse left, pleasing views of the green woodland valley open up

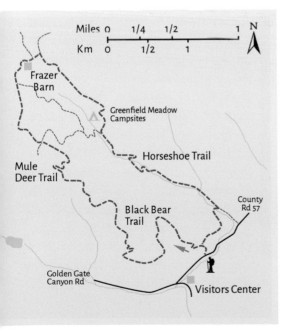

to the southeast. The aspens do turn gold in autumn, but this canyon is actually named for prospector Tom Golden, who platted Gate City at its mouth in the early days of the gold rush. The name "Golden's Gate" became applied to the whole canyon as well as to its toll road, which ran to the mines at Black Hawk, about five miles from here. No gold was ever extracted here in this canyon, but plenty of timber was taken for mine shafts, which required lots of logs for support. The trees you see around you are second growth, less than 150 years old.

Along the Black Bear Trail

Within 1.5 miles the first snowy mounts appear to the west: James Peak and Mount Bancroft. As you climb the ridge on a trail marked with bear-paw signs, Mount Evans joins the view club. The route turns straight upward for a jaunt over some boulders—there's no real trail, but the way is well marked, and it's fun to scramble a bit. The trail keeps to the spiny ridge for a stretch; weaving among the rocks feels like negotiating the back of a stegosaurus. The impressive stone nobs of Tremont Mountain rise to the northwest across the Frazer flats.

Head down through woods to those pretty flats, which are dynamite in fall when the aspens are changing. At a four-way junction, continue straight onto **Mule Deer Trail**, and keep straight when Horseshoe Trail branches right.

After walking through aspens, you'll arrive at a log structure with its roof fallen in. It was built by pioneer John Frazer after he left the goldfields in 1868. If it seems like a big house for one guy, that's because it was his hay barn. Frazer kept two

horses and a few cattle, and cut his hay by hand. He didn't bother to file a homestead claim until 1883, when he borrowed $200 to file as a squatter under the Preemption Act. His associate, Samuel Parker, a black man, signed as witness. This is a great spot for a picnic, and a lovely place to amble about or just sit among the aspens.

Frazer left his beautiful meadow one snowy morning in the 1890s and never returned. On the way to Black Hawk to trade timber for victuals, his wagon load broke free and logs rolled on him. Frazer's land became part of Gap Ranch, which in turn was acquired by the Harmsen family of Jolly Rancher candy fame. By then

Horseshoe Trail

John Frazer's barn in Frazer Meadow

it was the 1950s and the Harmsens, having made their fortune, were looking for a mountain retreat where they could really be jolly ranchers.

A branch trail leads to a spring that is nothing special: just a trickling PVC pipe. Instead, continue a quarter mile and branch right toward the Greenfield Meadow campsites for a gentle downhill walk. The meadow is named for the Greenfield family, who, late to the game of homesteading, arrived from Kansas in the 1920s. Past the campsites, you'll turn left onto **Horseshoe Trail**, which was the Greenfields' wagon road. It will take you down through more aspens back to **Black Bear Trail**, where you'll turn right to return to the car.

Before leaving the park, you can drive up to **Panorama Point**, a popular wedding spot, for a super view of the Continental Divide.

From Denver. Take US 6 west to Golden. At the intersection with CO 58, continue straight on CO 93 north for 1.4 miles. Turn left onto Golden Gate Canyon Road and proceed 12.7 miles to Golden Gate Canyon State Park. Turn right on CR 57 (Crawford Gulch Road). Continue past the visitors center a quarter mile to the parking area for Ralston Roost Trailhead. *50 mins.*

48 Mount Galbraith

THOUGH JUST A BITE-SIZE MOUNTAIN ASCENT, THIS CLOSE-TO-DENVER CLIMB IS NO pushover. The burning in your legs is well rewarded by views down to the plains and up to the snowy peaks.

At a Glance

DIFFICULTY	👥	DISTANCE/TIME	4.5 miles/2 hours
TRAIL CONDITIONS	👥👥	TRAILHEAD ELEVATION TOTAL HIKING GAIN	6,200 feet 1,000 feet
CHILDREN	👥👥	FEATURES	Varied terrain; views of plains, city, hogbacks, and high peaks
SCENERY	👥👥	BEST SEASON	Fall, winter, spring
PHOTO	👥👥	OTHER USERS	Dogs on leash
SOLITUDE	👥	NOTES	Toilets at trailhead
PROPERTY	Mount Galbraith Park	JURISDICTION	Jefferson County Open Space

This hikers-only hill rising from Golden offers a delightful and rigorous hike to a single destination: the summit. You return to your vehicle with a terrific sense of accomplishment.

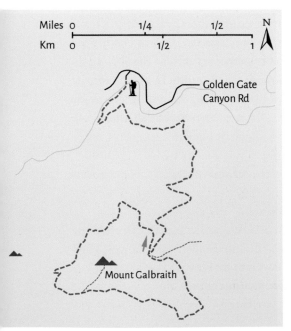

Cross a footbridge and stretch your legs along **Cedar Gulch Trail** for a minute or two before making a switchback and traversing uphill over scrubby ground. Below is the mouth of Golden Gate Canyon, where Golden Gate City once stood. Established in 1859, bustling by 1860, the town was the starting point for one of several competing toll roads that led to gold mines in the hinterland. Remnants of the road can still be seen along the northern park boundary. Little remains of the old town, which was eclipsed by neighboring Golden City when an easier road opened in Clear Creek Canyon, south of Mount Galbraith.

The towns were named for a man,

not the metal: Tom Golden of Georgia, who arrived during the 1858 gold rush. A jack-of-all-tradesman, Golden was instrumental in starting both towns. He left after the Civil War started, leaving only his shiny name behind.

Coors Brewery from Mount Galbraith Loop

As you scramble over a rocky shoulder, the plains come into view. The trail wraps into a gulch, ascends to another shoulder, and repeats, setting a pattern. At 1.2 miles, you'll arrive at a four-way junction with **Nightbird Gulch Trail** and the **Mount Galbraith Loop**. Turn right onto the loop to make a counterclockwise circuit of the summit. You'll start by ascending a grassy hillside. From here, the cliffs of Table Mountain and the distant Denver skyline will seem to watch you climb.

Nearer by spreads the city of Golden and its behemoth Coors Brewery. Even from up here, Coors looks huge. Begun in a converted tannery in 1873 by young Adolph Kuhrs, an orphaned German brewer's apprentice who stowed away on a ship to reach America, the business is still going strong. That's no small feat considering that, in order to survive 17 years of Prohibition, Kuhrs had to diversify into malted milk, near beer, and other products including china dinnerware. In fact, Coors quarried clay for its porcelain operation on 75 acres that were later donated to help create this park.

Past a notch with bushes where birds flit in winter, the trail heads through dense north-facing firs and steepens through rocks before traversing through a burned area to a saddle. The rocky face looming opposite the saddle is not Galbraith; it is its lower, unnamed western neighbor.

Getting to the top of Galbraith requires a little freelancing because the trail does not take you up it, but rather around it. One good way is to cut uphill after the saddle, just as the trail begins to descend into meadow on the south-facing hillside. You'll arrive at the rocky 7,247-foot summit within minutes and enjoy views in many directions, including to snowy humps of high peaks to the west.

Western view from Mount Galbraith's south hillside

This hill is named for Den Galbraith, an early surveyor who was a graduate of Golden's Colorado School of Mines.

Several social trails diverge from the top of Galbraith, but it's best to retrace your steps to continue on the loop trail. A good landmark to orientate your descent is Lookout Mountain, the one with the switchbacking road southeast of you, across Clear Creek Canyon. You might encounter bighorn sheep as you make your way down to the trail.

Hook left through a notch to finish the loop at the four-way junction where it began. Continue on **Cedar Gulch**, and soon the shoulder–gulch–shoulder pattern resumes for a relaxing return to your car.

From Denver. Take US 6 west to Golden. At the intersection with CO 58, continue straight onto CO 93 north for 1.4 miles. Turn left onto Golden Gate Canyon Road. Mount Galbraith Park and its parking lot are 1.5 miles ahead, on the left. *30 mins.*

Cedar Gulch Trail on Mount Galbraith

49 Beaver Brook

ON A PERCH ABOVE THE PLAINS AND CITY, TURN AND ENTER THE WOODS, KNOWING THAT recreational hikers have been enjoying this gentle wilderness trail for a hundred years.

At a Glance

DIFFICULTY	👥👥	**DISTANCE/TIME**	9 miles/4 hours
TRAIL CONDITIONS	👥👥👥	**TRAILHEAD ELEVATION** / **TOTAL HIKING GAIN**	6,900 feet / 400 feet
CHILDREN	👥👥👥	**FEATURES**	Forest, creek gullies, canyon views
SCENERY	👥👥👥	**BEST SEASON**	All year
PHOTO	👥👥👥	**OTHER USERS**	Dogs on leash
SOLITUDE	👥👥👥	**NOTES**	No toilets at trailhead
PROPERTY	Windy Saddle Park, private easements	**JURISDICTION**	Jefferson County Open Space, private landowners

Spring through fall are lovely on this hikers-only ridge outside Golden, but don't let winter deter you. The trail begins at 6,900 feet and varies little in elevation through miles of backcountry. If snowy patches remain in shadier woods, they will be mostly level and usually stomped out. You can assess the trail condition at the beginning and be confident it will remain similar throughout.

Having made the hairpin-turn drive up Lariat Loop Road, your car has done much of the climbing for you. Look for paragliders and hang gliders launching from the top of nearby Mount Zion, just north of the trailhead. From there it's a

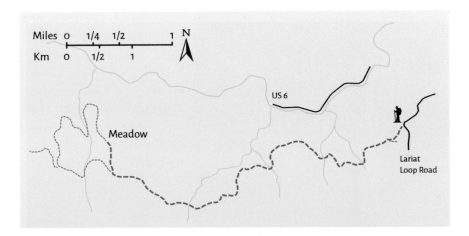

900-foot glide down to a landing spot at the mouth of Clear Creek Canyon. Also look for turkey vultures and other large birds taking advantage of the thermal updrafts. There's a reason this is called Windy Saddle Park.

Turn away from Denver and head into dense woods on **Lookout Mountain Trail**. Within minutes you'll branch right onto **Beaver Brook Trail**. The path is narrow but easy to follow, and it is marked with endearing metal "B/B" signs at regular intervals; distance markers are posted every half mile. After rounding a shoulder and descending into a gully, the trail traverses the steep hillside along some rocky ledges. Be careful and go slowly, especially if there is snow. The ruggedness soon ends and what follows is all smooth trail, alternating between forested gullies and shoulders with clearings.

Through the trees, the bare south-facing slope of Clear Creek Canyon stares back at you. If the faint traffic hum from Highway 6 below annoys you, be patient. After a couple of miles, the road veers north and the trail veers south, and that's the last you'll see or hear it. Things get very quiet as you become immersed in the undulating gully–shoulder–gully pattern of the hillside trek. Distance markers roll by. "How many gullies has it been?" you may ask yourself. "Three? Five?" It's okay to lose track.

If this deep-woods trail feels old, that's because it is. Beaver Brook was one of the first trails built in Colorado for hikers, by hikers. It opened in 1918 when

Beaver Brook Trail

Beaver Brook Trail

walking the backcountry for fun was a novel concept. Back in the day, enthusiasts from Denver would take a trolley to Golden and board the narrow-gauge railway into Clear Creek Canyon. They'd disembark five miles up at Beaver Brook Station, which became something of a tourist depot and was equipped with a dance pavilion. From there they'd hike up the brook and spend the night at Chief Hosa Lodge, which still stands alongside Interstate 70. The intrepid would walk this charming trail all the way back to Golden.

At 4 miles, you'll round a parklike shoulder and get a long view down the canyon toward Golden and its Coors brewery, miniscule from this distance. This is a fine turnaround point, but a better one lies 0.5 miles ahead. In minutes, branch right onto **Gudy Gaskill Trail** and descend into a vast meadow. This is a great place to recline and watch red-tailed hawks circle in the sky.

The return trip is more down than up. Regain the rhythm, let the miles roll by, and you'll find yourself at the car sooner than you might have expected.

On a different day, you might walk Beaver Brook Trail to Genesee Park on I-70 and have someone pick you up there. That trip is 9 miles one way and involves a descent into Beaver Brook's valley, followed by an interesting 1,000-foot ascent alongside the namesake stream on the old tourists' route.

From Denver. Take US 6 west to Golden, exit at 19th Street, and turn left. Proceed 0.3 miles and bear left onto Lookout Mountain Road. Continue uphill 2.8 miles as the road changes name to Lariat Loop Road. Windy Saddle Trailhead and its small parking lot are on the right. *35 mins.*

Meadow on Gudy Gaskill Trail branch from Beaver Brook

50 Green Mountain

LEAVE THE SUBURBS BEHIND ON A PEACEFUL RAMBLE ON A BEAUTIFUL GRASSY HILL IN metro Denver's west end. It's an easy peak to bag, and it has views galore.

At a Glance

DIFFICULTY	🚶🚶	DISTANCE/TIME	5.5 miles/2.5 hours
TRAIL CONDITIONS	🚶🚶🚶🚶	TRAILHEAD ELEVATION / TOTAL HIKING GAIN	6,200 feet / 700 feet
CHILDREN	🚶🚶🚶🚶	FEATURES	Grassland, views of city and mountains
SCENERY	🚶🚶🚶	BEST SEASON	All year
PHOTO	🚶🚶🚶	OTHER USERS	Bikes, horses, dogs on leash
SOLITUDE	🚶🚶	NOTES	Toilets at trailhead, very little shade on trail
PROPERTY	William Frederick Hayden Park	JURISDICTION	City of Lakewood Parks, Forestry & Open Space

This surprising walk climbs from Denver's backyard to a vast countryside that has the feel of rural highlands. As you rise, civilization drops away and a sense of peace pervades the trail. The city is often in view, but only as a silent background.

From the north end of the parking lot, get right down to business—or up to business, rather—by climbing the first switchbacks of **Green Mountain Trail**. It's steep, but rewards come quickly. The suburbs fall away and in minutes you gaze down on them. Farther east, the little clump of skyscrapers that is downtown Denver looks like something you could hold in the palm of your hand.

As the trail mellows out, you'll round a corner and head toward a distant radio tower. The yucca plants here are huge—big balls of spikes sitting in the grass. Stay on Green Mountain Trail as Hayden Trail branches left. After you fork left at the radio tower, the trail widens to a service road and follows the crest of the hill. The city is behind you now,

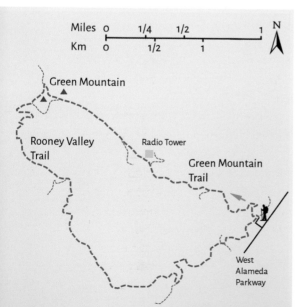

Green Mountain Trail

and Mount Evans stares you in the face. The only sound is the tramp of your feet grinding through the dirt.

Much of this land was acquired from the Haydens, a longtime Lakewood family. Platted in 1889, Lakewood was for decades a popular place for wealthy Denverites to build out-of-town estates. As it grew in the 1900s, it acquired a munitions factory. This hill was used for military exercises by the Colorado National Guard from 1935 through the end of World War II, and its north slope was bombarded with artillery. Most—but not all—of the shells exploded. As recently as 2015, searchers combed the area with high-tech metal detectors looking for buried ordnance.

As you approach the top of the trail, check out the grassland to the right to see how it has recovered from a 2016 wildfire. Two rounded summits appear, seemingly equal in height, and the trail heads into a divot between them. The true tippy-top of Green Mountain is on your left.

Summit bagged, it's time for a detour down the mountain's flanks. The best meander is via **Rooney Valley Trail**, which will take you through delightful gullies, meadows, and shrublands. Two trails lead from the summit, one before and one after the divot. Take either one. They will merge into a single path that looks like it is taking you westward and down to CO 470, miles away from your vehicle, but don't worry. Enjoy views of Red Rocks Amphitheater across the valley before hooking left at a paraglider launching point and descending into canyon lands. Green in spring and summer, these hillsides turn yellow-gold in winter; they are especially beautiful when patches of snow lie among shrubs in the shadier folds.

Downtown Denver from Green Mountain

Buffalo once roamed here; today you might see mule deer grazing and maybe a coyote quickly trotting by.

At a fork in a gully, turn left to stay on Rooney Valley Trail, which wraps southeast in an up-and-down fashion. The trail is named for the Rooney family, who homesteaded here in the 1860s and still run a ranch between Green Mountain and Dakota Ridge. Alexander Rooney came from Iowa for the gold rush and ended up a very successful cattle rancher. The two-story stone house he built in 1865 still stands on Rooney Road, south of Alameda Parkway.

Follow the trail until it joins the **Green Mountain loop** near the bottom of the hill. Here you'll turn left for the final mile: a curvy up-and-down jaunt to the car.

From Denver. Take US 6 west to the Kipling Street cloverleaf, then go south on Kipling Street (CO 391) for 1.1 miles. Turn right onto West Alameda Avenue and continue 2.0 miles as the road curves to the left and becomes West Alameda Parkway. Turn right to enter William Frederick Hayden Park; the parking lot for Hayden–Green Mountain Trailhead is immediately on the right. *25 mins.*

Green Mountain

51 Morrison Slide

A FOOTHILL TREK TO A CLIFF-TOP PROMONTORY GIVES YOU STARTLING VIEWS OF THE FAMOUS Red Rocks, a good view of a dinosaur ridge, a visit to an old cemetery, and an interesting history lesson.

At a Glance

DIFFICULTY	🚶🚶	**DISTANCE/TIME**	4.5 miles/2 hours
TRAIL CONDITIONS	🚶🚶🚶	**TRAILHEAD ELEVATION** TOTAL HIKING GAIN	6,200 feet 600 feet
CHILDREN	🚶🚶🚶🚶	**FEATURES**	Red rock formations, foothills and plains views, historic cemetery
SCENERY	🚶🚶🚶🚶	**BEST SEASON**	All year
PHOTO	🚶🚶🚶🚶	**OTHER USERS**	Bikes, horses, dogs on leash
SOLITUDE	🚶🚶	**NOTES**	Toilets at trailhead
PROPERTY	Matthews/ Winters Park	**JURISDICTION**	Jefferson County Open Space

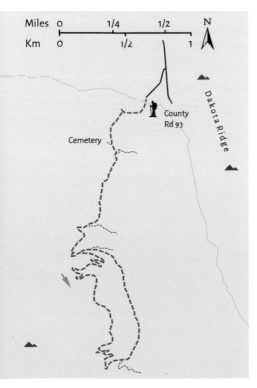

This interesting hike begins in a nondescript spot in the foothills where an important settlement once stood. Named Mount Vernon, it was established in 1859 as a supply town along a wagon road that led to the gold mines of Central City. For a short time, it was a seat of territorial government.

Cross a stream and begin on **Village Walk Trail**. On your right, an old Ute trail, better known now as Interstate 70, hums with traffic headed to Idaho Springs. As you make your way south across sloping fields, the highway buzz fades and Mount Morrison rises to the southwest. To the east, the city of Denver hides quietly behind Dakota Ridge. After a few minutes, you'll pass a small fenced cemetery on

1860 gravestone in Mount Vernon Cemetery

the right—a remnant of old Mount Vernon that we will revisit at the end of the hike.

At 0.5 miles, branch right onto **Red Rocks Trail**. Half a mile later, turn right again onto **Cherry Gulch**. Silence descends as you cross that gulch and wrap around the hillside into another gulch to meet a junction. Turn right onto **Morrison Slide Trail** which, after six stiff switchbacks, traverses through boulders to gain a flat shelf on the hillside.

From this vantage point, south Denver presents itself beyond Dakota Ridge. Bushy green junipers stand along the plateau's edge like sentinels. The trail ambles along the rim of the cliff, which is known as the Morrison Slide, and the first glimpses of red rocks arrive. It's iconic Colorado: blue sky, green hills, and tilted slabs of red sandstone, some forming a natural amphitheater at the world-famous Red Rocks music venue next door.

The Dakota Ridge opposite is also world-famous. For over 100 years, its quarries have yielded clay, marble—and dinosaurs. In 1877, a geologist found fossilized remains of several Jurassic-era creatures in its southwest-facing rocks, including the venerable stegosaurus, Colorado's state fossil. In 2006, a researcher discovered some hatchling stegosaurus footprints in a boulder taken from the side of the road.

Red Rocks in winter from Morrison Slide

Red Rocks in winter from Morrison Slide

From the plateau, foothills views stretch southward to the horizon. Spectacular red rocks appear as you reach the end of the shelf and descend into them. While you are camera-clicking in the valley, look for **Red Rocks Trail** branching right. It runs beneath an overhanging, pockmarked red cliff that looks like a dwelling from a Dr. Seuss book. You can follow this tempting trail into the adjacent Red Rocks Park if you wish. Otherwise, return to the car by branching left on **Red Rocks Trail** and climbing through a notch. The trail continues beneath the drop-off to rejoin **Cherry Gulch Trail** back to old Mount Vernon.

In the cemetery, two chiseled headstones stand among several wooden markers. One dates to 1860, when the town functioned as the capital of the would-be territory of Jefferson. Back then, Colorado lay in the remote corners of four other territories. Desiring a more responsive government to safeguard gold claims and punish murderers, pioneers drafted a constitution and elected Mount Vernon resident Robert W. Steele governor. Having no capitol building, Steele sometimes held legislative councils at Mount Vernon's Wells Fargo wagon stop.

Jefferson Territory lasted 16 months and was never recognized by the U.S. government. In 1861, on the eve of the Civil War, Congress passed a bill organizing the Territory of Colorado. Steele, an anti-Lincoln Democrat, stepped aside and moved on. Mount Vernon's population dwindled, and by 1885 a family called Matthews had it pretty much to themselves. In 1974 one of their descendants sold 353 acres to Jefferson County to help create this lovely park.

From Denver. Take US 6 and I-70 west to Exit 259, then turn left onto CR 93. Proceed 0.5 miles to the Matthews/Winters Park entrance and its large parking lot, on the right. *25 mins.*

52 Mount Falcon

THIS HIGH-FOOTHILLS HIKE THROUGH ONE OF DENVER'S ORIGINAL HILL STATIONS DELIVERS falcon-eye views of the plains to the Continental Divide and some interesting ruins of castles, both real and imagined.

At a Glance

DIFFICULTY	👫	**DISTANCE/TIME**	6 miles/2.5 hours
TRAIL CONDITIONS	👫👫	**TRAILHEAD ELEVATION** / **TOTAL HIKING GAIN**	7,800 feet / 500 feet
CHILDREN	👫👫👫	**FEATURES**	Views of plains, foothills, and high peaks; historic ruins
SCENERY	👫👫	**BEST SEASON**	All year
PHOTO	👫👫	**OTHER USERS**	Bikes, horses, dogs on leash
SOLITUDE	👫	**NOTES**	Toilets at trailhead
PROPERTY	Mount Falcon Park	**JURISDICTION**	Jefferson County Open Space

Mount Falcon is a wonderful place to wander on hilltops without having to gasp to get there. The summit is reached early in the hike; it's only 100 feet higher than the trailhead and hardly the only attraction. The park has the feel of a "hill station" of yore, a place where wealthy city dwellers chilled out in style in the summertime. And it comes replete with ruins: vestiges of mountain castles to pique imaginations of all ages.

Heritage aside, this hike is an excellent way for Denver metro residents to get

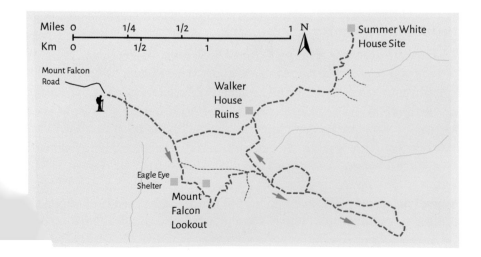

oriented. Expansive views in all directions put into perspective where "home" lies in the scheme of things.

From the trailhead, follow **Castle Trail** along a wooded ridge, dipping and ascending toward a large meadow. The mule deer here barely acknowledge you as they graze. Branch right on **Meadow Trail** and right again on **Tower Trail** as the plains come into view. The Eagle Eye shelter appears on the right, a former summer home with views of snowy peaks. Continue an easy ascent to the tower, a refurbished fire lookout, about a mile into the hike. Children will delight in this hilltop fort and its king-of-the-mountain views of Denver. "Something red" is a challenge for a game of "I Spy"; tiptoes might be required to spy it (Red Rocks).

Mule deer near the Walker House ruins in Mount Falcon Park

Descend east to rejoin **Meadow Trail**. Make a right, then another right onto **Old Ute Trail** to proceed on a lovely counterclockwise loop along the wooded ridge called Devil's Elbow. You could skip this portion and trim 1.5 miles from the hike, but you'd miss some nice views of graceful hogback ridges rolling up from the plains.

Onward to the ruins! Descend **Meadow Trail** through a field favored by bluebirds, and move up through pines and junipers to rejoin **Castle Trail**. You'll soon see why it's called this, for here are the remains of the Walker home, which was indeed a castle befitting an extraordinary man.

Meadow Trail, Mount Falcon Park

Walker House Ruins, Mount Falcon Park

John Brisben Walker once owned all of Red Rocks, Mount Falcon, and 1,600 acres north of Denver. He was a man who dreamed big and lived large. Among his many local accomplishments were to introduce alfalfa as a cash crop and produce the first concerts at Red Rocks. Before coming to Colorado in 1879 he attended West Point, soldiered in China, and managed newspapers in Cincinnati and Washington, D.C. Between stints in Colorado, he moved to New York, bought and revamped *Cosmopolitan* magazine, and manufactured early automobiles. His Mount Falcon mansion burned down in 1918, perhaps struck by lightning, and Walker left Colorado for good.

After you've explored the stone ruins of the house—it once had 10 bedrooms and eight fireplaces—continue east down the ridge to wonderful views of Red Rocks, Dakota Ridge, and Green Mountain. Turn left on **Walker's Dream Trail**. What dream, you ask? Five switchbacks over a nob hint at the answer, revealing powerful views of Mount Evans, the Indian Peaks, and the tip of Longs Peak. But that's not all. Continue along the ridge to arrive at the "Summer White House." Bits of foundation support a gleaming-white marble cornerstone inscribed: *Summer Home for the Presidents of the United States.* Though the Bavarian-style castle Walker dreamed of never materialized here, the presidential view lives on for all to enjoy.

As you return to the car on **Castle Trail**, be sure to turn around to enjoy the views out to the plains one more time. It's easy to see how this immortal landscape might inspire big dreams.

From Denver. Take US 6 and I-70 west to CO 470 east. After 5.5 miles, take Exit 5A nto US 285 south. Continue 4.5 miles and turn right onto Parmalee Gulch Road. ntinue 2.7 miles and turn right on Picutis Road. Follow signs for 2 more miles to est Trailhead entrance to Mount Falcon Park and its large parking lot. *45 mins.*

53 Plymouth Mountain

THIS HIKE OFFERS A SURPRISING WILDERNESS EXPERIENCE IN DENVER'S BACKYARD.
Beginning in shrubland, it continues into a thickly forested valley, and then pops
out atop a foothill with commanding views of the city and plains.

At a Glance

DIFFICULTY	👥	**DISTANCE/TIME**	5.5 miles/2.5 hours
TRAIL CONDITIONS	👥👥	**TRAILHEAD ELEVATION** **TOTAL HIKING GAIN**	6,100 feet 1,200 feet
CHILDREN	👥👥	**FEATURES**	Shrubland, forested valley, views of plains and foothills
SCENERY	👥👥	**BEST SEASON**	All year
PHOTO	👥👥	**OTHER USERS**	Bikes and horses on portion, dogs on leash
SOLITUDE	👥	**NOTES**	Toilets at trailhead
PROPERTY	Deer Creek Canyon Park	**JURISDICTION**	Jefferson County Open Space

The smooth, hikers-only **Meadowlark Trail**
ascends amid shrubs and yucca, then curves
to find a faceoff: to the right, an impressive
red rock formation, and to the left, a gleaming silver Lockheed Martin office building.
The latter appears to be a product of bygone
zoning rules: attractive, but something that
probably wouldn't be permitted there now.
The futuristic-looking building wasn't built
by Lockheed; it began life as the headquarters
of Johns-Manville, a roofing and building materials manufacturer that specialized in some
products containing asbestos. By the 1980s,
personal injury lawsuits forced the company
into bankruptcy protection, and the site was
sold to what became Lockheed Martin.

After some switchbacks, downtown Denver appears through a slot in the hogback. On
the third switchback the trail flirts with Deer
Creek Canyon before traversing south amid
oaks and mahogany shrubs toward a deep

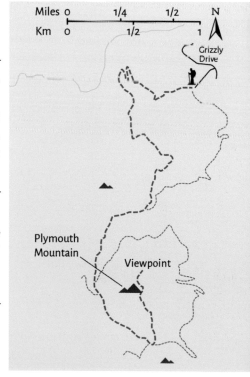

Meadowlark Trail to Plymouth Mountain

forested gully. The juxtaposition of the bramble-covered south-facing hillside with the thick green trees on the opposite slope makes for interesting photographs. Descend into shade and turn right onto **Plymouth Creek Trail**.

When a man named John Williamson left Plymouth, England, in the 1870s, he was deeply afflicted with tuberculosis and seeking a drier climate. He came to these fertile foothills, built a house, and established the Glen Plym farm. Williamson lived in prosperity here with his family for 25 more years. The park today contains portions of his homestead, along with two others.

The trail steepens along Plymouth Creek, which often runs dry, and becomes quite rocky. Mountain bikers relish the rugged path, which includes a wooden staircase. Soon the trail mellows in lush forest, a particularly welcome respite on

hot days. Keep straight when Plymouth Mountain Trail joins from the left, and straight again to *stay* on **Plymouth Mountain Trail** when Plymouth Creek Trail branches right. The path remains lovely in mixed forest, passing a rich green meadow on the right before curving uphill through tall, somber firs. When Homestead Trail branches right, continue straight for a few hundred feet and then turn left toward what is marked as "Scenic View," i.e., the top of Plymouth Mountain.

Here the trail meanders through

Plymouth Creek Valley, from Meadowlark Trail

oaks and then gains 100 final feet in a push through conifers. You'll pass the true summit on the left and continue 0.2 miles to a little rock-castle viewpoint. The vista is dominated by the sudden reappearance of the city to the east. Looking peakward, the view is mostly of foothills, although the tip of Longs Peak shows itself to the keen observer. The water shining on the plains to the southeast is Chatfield Reservoir.

This reservoir will be even more visible come 2019, when a 75 percent (by volume) expansion is completed. The dam, which was built after the deadly Denver flood of 1965, was designed to tower 100 feet over normal lake level to allow for surges. Its main purpose remains flood control, but the working level will rise by 12 feet to ac-commodate increased storage needs. All features of lakeside Chatfield State Park will be replicated to accommodate the expanded shoreline—except the land lost to the lake, of course.

Trail Runner on Plymouth Creek Trail

On the return trip, you can extend the walk 1.3 miles by turning left instead of right on Plymouth Mountain Trail and making a loop. You can also trim half a mile by staying on Plymouth Creek Trail all the way to the parking lot. For a coda, consider visiting South Valley Park across Deer Creek Canyon Road. It offers an easy 3-mile loop through red rock formations: a mini Roxborough Park qua Gar-den of the Gods.

From Denver. Take US 6 and I-70 west, then CO 470 east to Exit 10 (Ken Caryl Avenue). Turn right onto West Ken Caryl Avenue, continue 0.3 miles, then turn left onto South Valley Road. Drive 2.4 miles, turn right onto West Deer Creek Canyon Road, and continue 0.7 miles. Turn left onto Grizzly Drive and continue 0.4 miles to Deer Creek Canyon Park and its large parking lot, on the right. *40 mins.*

54 Carpenter Peak

A WONDERLAND OF TILTED RED SANDSTONE GREETS YOU ON THIS HIKE JUST SOUTHWEST of Denver, and a climb to the top of a foothill gives you a dramatic perspective unseen by most park visitors.

At a Glance

DIFFICULTY	🧍🧍🧍	DISTANCE/TIME	8 miles/3.5 hours
TRAIL CONDITIONS	🧍🧍🧍	TRAILHEAD ELEVATION TOTAL HIKING GAIN	6,200 feet 1,000 feet
CHILDREN	🧍🧍🧍	FEATURES	Red rock formations, geological perspective, plains and mountain views, forest
SCENERY	🧍🧍🧍🧍	BEST SEASON	All year
PHOTO	🧍🧍🧍🧍	OTHER USERS	Bikes and horses on small portion
SOLITUDE	🧍🧍🧍	NOTES	Entrance fee, no dogs, toilets at visitors center, confirm park hours if hiking early or late
PROPERTY	Roxborough State Park, Pike National Forest	JURISDICTION	Colorado Parks & Wildlife, U.S. Forest Service

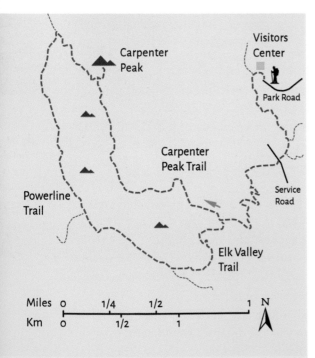

You'll get some great views of Roxborough's extraordinary red rocks as you pull into the parking lot. Is there any need to venture from the car? Yes! This hike up Carpenter Peak will take you above the formations for an even more interesting look.

Carpenter Peak Trail begins with a walk toward red cliffs through a tunnel of Gambel oaks, which are ubiquitous here at the northern limit of their range. Soon you'll come into a broad valley where more red sandstone formations jut into the sky. As you cross a service road and begin ascending, you may think you are leaving the rocks behind, but at the first switchback, serrated red ridges will stare you in the eye. As you continue climbing through shrubland alternating with dense stands of pines, a pod of hazy Denver skyscrapers appears to the northeast, followed in a bit by views of Indian Peaks to the north.

The exposed layers of upthrust earth to the east present themselves in roughly 20 million-year increments. The bedrock of Carpenter Peak, on which you are standing, is the Fountain Formation—about 300 million years old. Farther east are the red slices of Roxborough's Lyons sandstone, formed from sand dunes about 280 million years ago. Beyond them are the yellower

Gambel oaks near start of Carpenter Peak Trail

hogbacks of the Lykins and Morrison Formations, compressed about 260 million years ago from mudflats and the bottom of the once-great Western Interior Seaway.

At 1.8 miles, keep right when Elk Valley Trail branches left. The grade eases as the trail wraps a shoulder, where you can see Carpenter's summit along the ridge. Descend through a wooded gully and continue on a gentle uphill traverse to a spur branching right, at 3 miles. From here it is only minutes to Carpenter's rocky top. A little mountain goat impersonation gets you to the highest point.

Looking down, the true picture of Roxborough Park emerges: a set-aside valley walled in by the red rocks, with private mansions populating the western side of the "fence." What is now the state park

View from Carpenter Peak Trail

would have been developed, too, had the original owner had his way. Henry Persse acquired it in the 1880s, named it Roxborough after his family's estate in Ireland, and set about luring Denver's elite to what he dreamed would be an exclusive hotel and golf resort. Some guests were not hip to the idea, including Denver

Mayor Robert Speer, who wrote in Persse's guestbook that the area "should be owned by the city for the free use of the people."

Persse died before his resort came to fruition, but others pursued the same dream. As you can see from Carpenter Peak, much prized terrain is now taken by luxury homes and the shockingly green Arrowhead Golf Course. Although the public isn't allowed to enjoy the western side of Roxborough's formations from below, here on Carpenter Peak you get the exclusive view from above. Why, you could almost toss your apple core down into those posh backyards.

Continue north on Carpenter Peak Trail, then turn left onto **Powerline Trail** (FS 800) to continue through cool forest. The trail bottoms out alongside a creek amid tall evergreens before ascending southward close to power lines, then rising over a hump and into a sunny gulch. Halfway down, you'll branch left onto **Elk Valley Trail** to return to **Carpenter Peak Trail** and the visitors center.

For a coda, you can stroll in those dazzling red rock formations. The **Fountain Valley Trail** is an easy and popular loop, with side branches leading to several dramatic overlooks.

From Denver. Take I-25 south to Exit 207B, then US 85 (Santa Fe Drive) south 14.4 miles to the Titan Parkway exit. Turn right and proceed on West Titan Road for 2.9 miles, passing through a traffic circle. Continue as the road curves left and becomes North Rampart Range Road. Proceed 3.8 miles to the road's end, turn left on Roxborough Park Road, then make an immediate right onto Roxborough Drive. From here it is 2.25 miles to the visitors center, where there is a large parking lot. *45 mins.*

Roxborough's Fountain Valley from Carpenter Peak Trail

55 Evergreen Mountain & Three Sisters

A GENTLE FOREST ASCENT TO THE 8,500-FOOT SUMMIT OF EVERGREEN MOUNTAIN IS THE warm-up for a nice stroll through a family of bizarre rock formations.

At a Glance

DIFFICULTY	🚶🚶🚶	**DISTANCE/TIME**	8 miles/4 hours
TRAIL CONDITIONS	🚶🚶🚶	**TRAILHEAD ELEVATION**	7,700 feet
		TOTAL HIKING GAIN	1,200 feet
CHILDREN	🚶🚶🚶	**FEATURES**	Forest, summit views, rock formations
SCENERY	🚶🚶🚶	**BEST SEASON**	Fall, winter, spring
PHOTO	🚶🚶🚶	**OTHER USERS**	Bikes, horses, dogs on leash
SOLITUDE	🚶🚶	**NOTES**	Toilets at trailhead
PROPERTY	Alderfer/Three Sisters Park	**JURISDICTION**	Jefferson County Open Space

As you pull into the parking lot, look east past the huge old ranch house. See those lumpy, lobed rock formations poking through the trees? Those are the Three Sisters, and you'll walk through them on the final stretch of this hike, which takes you on a counterclockwise tour through this many-trailed park. Be sure to pick up a park brochure at the trailhead; its route map comes in handy.

To begin, cross the road and turn right onto the **Wild Iris Loop**. After 0.6 miles, turn right again on **Evergreen Mountain West Trail** and head uphill through dense lodgepole pines whose trunks creak in the breeze. The bike-friendly switchbacks are unnecessarily gentle and might be annoying to hikers if the woods weren't so lovely. At 1.4 miles, branch right onto **Summit Trail**. After crossing a shoulder, views of green foothills open up to the south. More switchbacks lead to another woodsy traverse, where at 2 miles a sign entices you to a scenic overlook to the right. Take that path for views of Evergreen Reservoir and the Three Sisters formations.

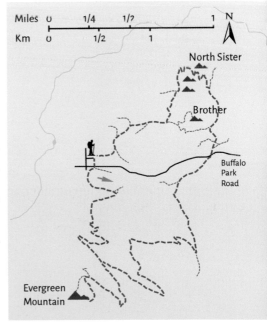

West Evergreen Mountain Trail

Back on the main trail, a comfortable half-mile climb takes you to the rocky 8,542-foot summit of Evergreen Mountain, where you'll have great views west to Mount Evans and its kindred peaks. Mount Evans and the Three Sisters are vastly different-scaled versions of the same geological process: hard rock cooled from magma that pushed upward to form the foundation of the Rockies. All were once covered with softer rock, which wore away over eons to expose these natural, in-progress sculptures.

Heading back down on Summit Trail, you have a choice: turn left back onto Evergreen Mountain West and retrace your steps 1.4 miles to your vehicle, or turn right onto **Evergreen Mountain East** to hike 4 miles to the same place via the Three Sisters.

Descending on East Evergreen, ignore the trails entering from the right and arrive at the road and the park's east trailhead. Follow the signs to **Sisters Trail**, where the lobed tops of the Sisters peek over the trees. Soon the trail branches left to make six switchbacks up into the weird, bulbous hills. It's fun to look for faces in the rock as the trail gains a pass just below the North Sister, where the lumpy spire makes a pleasant backdrop for a pause and a snack.

Mount Evans from Evergreen Mountain

The North Sister from Sisters Trail

Continue down the trail, traversing along the west flanks of the other Sisters. Keep left at a junction and you will soon arrive at **Ponderosa Trail**. You can turn left here for an optional half-mile round-trip to **Brother Lookout**. This 7,800-foot promontory offers nice views; it's nothing you haven't already seen from Evergreen Mountain, but you will have visited all the relatives.

From the Sisters/Ponderosa trail junction, proceed west on **Silver Fox Meadow Trail**. It's an easy walk to the car through a meadow named for the silver foxes that were once raised around here. In the early 20th century, fox furs were all the rage, and it was common for landowners in Colorado's mountains to spend several thousand dollars on a breeding pair of silver foxes. That's what E. J. and Arleta Alderfer did when they moved here from Denver in the 1930s. But after World War II, Russian breeders glutted the market with pelts. Prices plummeted, and many folks released their foxes into meadows like this one, where they have mixed with their native red fox brethren.

The attractive meadow has nice views of Mount Evans and a good perspective back to the Three Sisters. It's also a fine place to lie down and have a victory snooze.

From Denver. Take US 6 and I-70 west to Exit 252, then CO 74 south to Evergreen. Turn right onto CR 73 south, proceed 0.5 miles, and turn right onto Buffalo Park Road. Continue 2.2 miles, past the east entrance to Alderfer/Three Sisters Park, to South Le Masters Road. Turn right and right again to Alderfer Ranch Trailhead and its parking lot. *45 mins.*

56 Maxwell Falls

TWO MURMURING STREAMS AND A SERIES OF LOW FALLS BID YOU "STAY AWHILE" ON THIS peaceful, kid-friendly forest hike outside Evergreen. The ridgetop view is a bonus.

At a Glance

DIFFICULTY	👥	DISTANCE/TIME	4.5 miles/2 hours
TRAIL CONDITIONS	👥👥	TRAILHEAD ELEVATION TOTAL HIKING GAIN	7,700 feet 1,000 feet
CHILDREN	👥👥👥	FEATURES	Forest, creeks, small waterfalls, rock formations
SCENERY	👥	BEST SEASON	Spring and fall
PHOTO	👥	OTHER USERS	Bikes, horses, dogs on leash
SOLITUDE	👥	NOTES	No toilets at trailhead
PROPERTY	Arapaho National Forest	JURISDICTION	U.S. Forest Service

This tranquil slice of woodland is terrific during fall colors and also in the cool, moist spring when higher elevations remain caked in snow. The deep-nature feel of the hike is its main attraction, so avoid summer weekends when the trails are crowded. Modest length and elevation gain make this an enjoyable nature walk for children. There are waterfalls, too, but don't expect Niagara: the little cascades are lovely but not powerful, in keeping with the serenity of the scene.

You'll begin **Maxwell Falls Trail** (FS 111) along a seasonal stream and ascend through soothing mixed forest, where bulbous rock formations poke out of the hillside. At 0.75 miles cross the stream and follow the steepening trail to gain a ridge. From here, views expand across the lush pine-forested valley and down to aspens populating its floor. It's easy to see how the nearby community of Evergreen got its name. This is an eastern finger of Arapaho

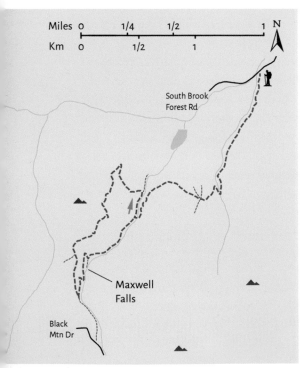

National Forest, established by President Theodore Roosevelt in 1908.

Sixty years earlier, this was Ute Indian territory, officially set aside by an 1849 treaty following the Mexican War. The treaty did not define the Utes' boundaries, but nevertheless ordered the Indians to remain within them, live in pueblos, cultivate the soil, and "cease the roving and rambling habits that have hitherto marked them as a people." Ute authority over this region went out the window when gold was struck nearby in 1859. Lumberjacks arrived and cut large tracts of forest for log cabins, barn wood, railroad ties, mine shaft supports, and fuel.

At just under a mile, you'll arrive at a saddle and a confusing five-way junction. Ignore the branches to the left and right and go straight to descend through more forest and odd rocks. This is the only section of trail where you might encounter road noise, from the unseen Brook Forest community through the trees to the right.

Maxwell Falls in Spring

Maxwell Creek gurgles at the bottom of the next valley. Cross a footbridge and turn right onto **Cliff Loop Trail**. After a hundred yards veer left, away from the stream, and ascend a forested ridge. At the top there's an awesome view rock on the left with a nice perspective of Maxwell Creek's valley. This is the place to have your picnic if you brought one.

The trail snakes along the ridge and tops out in an open area amid ponderosas. You'll descend left at a fork, and turn left again at creekside to rejoin the **Maxwell**

Ridge crest on Maxwell Falls Trail

Maxwell Creek's Valley from Cliff Loop Trail

Falls Trail. The cliffs of Cliff Loop loom above the trees as the path zigzags downstream. To reach the waterfalls, look for a spur branching right at the second of two downward switchbacks. After about 50 yards you'll reach a series of cascades tumbling over boulders. You can park yourself on one of the rock seats to gaze at them as they gush in spring or trickle in fall.

Back along the trail, the creek burbles and blue spruces join the forest mix. After a third of a mile look for the footbridge on the right which will take you back to the trailhead.

The town of Evergreen is worth a visit on the return drive. Now mostly a bedroom community for Denver, with a good crop of ostentatious houses, it has an old center of 23 buildings—including the original lumberjack bunkhouse—that is listed in the National Register of Historic Places.

From Denver. Take I-70 west to Exit 252, then CO 74 south to Evergreen. Turn right onto CR 73, proceed 1 mile, then turn right on South Brook Forest Road. The parking lot for Lower Maxwell Falls Trailhead is 3.6 miles down the road on the left; more parking is available farther along on the left. *50 mins.*

57 Chief Mountain

THIS SHORT, KID-FRIENDLY TRAIL WEST OF GENESEE PARK GETS TO THE TOP OF AN 11,700-foot peak with supreme views in all directions. Add some nearby attractions, and you've got a full, fun-filled day.

At a Glance

DIFFICULTY	🥾🥾	DISTANCE/TIME	3 miles/1.5 hours
TRAIL CONDITIONS	🥾🥾🥾🥾	TRAILHEAD ELEVATION	10,700 feet
		TOTAL HIKING GAIN	1,000 feet
CHILDREN	🥾🥾🥾🥾	FEATURES	Short hike to summit, 360-degree views
SCENERY	🥾🥾🥾🥾	BEST SEASON	Early summer
PHOTO	🥾🥾🥾	OTHER USERS	Horses, dogs
SOLITUDE	🥾	NOTES	No toilets at trailhead, thunderstorm exposure above tree line
PROPERTY	Arapaho National Forest	JURISDICTION	U.S. Forest Service

This is a great first summit for all ages. From the pullout above Echo Mountain ski area, look for **Chief Mountain Trail** (FS 58) slanting up the embankment across the road. Follow it through trees for a quarter mile to arrive at a junction with a wide dirt path, the Old Squaw Pass Road. If you parked at the second pullout, you can walk this old road from there back to this junction.

The modest ski hill below you dates to the era of mom-and-pop ski operations that sprang up close to cities in the mid-20th century. By the 1970s, Clear Creek County boasted seven such places. This one operated from 1960 until 1975, two years after the Eisenhower Tunnels improved access to the big resorts west of the Continental Divide. In the winter of 2006–2007 it reopened with a triple chairlift

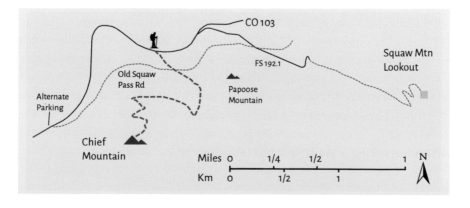

Chief Mountain Trail

scavenged from Lake Tahoe's Heavenly Valley, and it continues to operate, albeit sporadically.

On the uphill side of the old road, find the Chief Mountain signboard and proceed on a left-hand ascent through Douglas fir forest. After a switchback you will arrive at an overlook with nice views of the Divide—a good resting point for small hikers. From here you can look uphill and see your rocky destination above the tree line. As you make four more switchbacks through ever-stubbier trees, Mount Evans presents itself to the southwest and the plains appear to the east. Near the top, you'll arrive at a notch framing Evans along with Mount Bierstadt, which peers over its left shoulder. From here it's a short, fun scramble over sparkly boulders to the summit and its 360-degree panorama: a view fit for a chief.

The biggest thing around, of course, is Evans, the tallest of the Chicago Peaks dominating the skyline above Denver. From here you can see the access road leading to its summit. Completed in 1930, it was the highest paved road in the western hemisphere for a long time (a road in Peru now has this honor). The sce-

Chief Mountain Trail

nic byway is a byproduct of a failed campaign in the early 1900s to make Mount Evans a national park. The road was built using steam shovels that operated at about half their usual efficiency, due to altitude, and the final 600 feet were dug largely by hand.

Are the kids tired yet? If not, you can extend this hike to reach a wonderful old fire lookout atop Squaw Mountain, Chief's partner to the east (a lower apex, Papoose, lies between them). To get there, head back down to **Old Squaw Pass Road Trail**, turn right, and turn right again to follow the dirt road, **Forest Road 192.1**, about a mile to Squaw's summit. Completed in the 1940s by the Civilian Conservation Corps, the stone-built lookout was staffed for 29 seasons. Nowadays the Forest Service rents it to the public as a cozy guesthouse-with-a-view: four beds, a kitchen with fridge, heat and electricity—but no water. You don't need a reservation to enjoy the superb views from its wraparound deck.

Back in your vehicle, consider driving to the top of Mount Evans. The turnoff is 5.5 miles farther along the road you came in on. There's no charge to drive the

Chief Mountain Summit

spectacular 15-mile route each way so long as you don't stop; if you decide to park at the top and visit the summit sites, you can pay the per-car fee there, hike a quarter mile to the apex, and add bagging a fourteener to your accomplishments for the day.

From Denver. Take US 6 and I-70 west to Exit 252, then CO 74, Evergreen Parkway, south for 2.8 miles. Turn right onto Squaw Pass Road (CR 66, later CO 103) and continue 12.3 miles to a pullout parking area on the right. Chief Mountain Trailhead is on the left side of the road. If the parking area is full, continue 1 mile to the next pullout. *1 hour.*

Idaho Springs & Georgetown

Soul-restoring high rambles

As summer arrives in Denver, it's time to hop on Interstate 70 and go hiking, not skiing. The onetime mining towns of Idaho Springs and Georgetown are gateways to superb high-country roaming. Some trails, such as Herman Lake and Woods Mountain, begin right by the side of the freeway. Don't worry; as you walk, the interstate soon becomes a silent, invisible thread lost in a sea of spectacular high mountains.

It may feel like cheating to begin your hike above 11,500 feet, but it's not—it's being resourceful. Three highways lead from I-70 to magnificent high passes, where you can usually begin hiking by early to mid-June. Guanella Pass is more accessible than ever since being paved in 2012; from it you can meander to Square Top Lakes or huff your way up 14,065-foot Mount Bierstadt (if you start at dawn, you can summit this fourteener and still make it to work in the morning). Next is Loveland Pass, offering ready access to the catbird seat of Mount Sniktau. My favorite is Berthoud Pass, which puts you on the Continental Divide Trail heading west past the gorgeous Ten Little Indians Cirque.

Cirques—the amphitheater-like cliff-bowls that are gouged in the northeast faces of peaks—are a recurring feature in the mountainscape. You can gaze up a classic one from Chicago Lakes on the side of Mount Evans, and look down on many others from above on High Lonesome. The hikes in this chapter also offer some 360-degree panoramas from notable summits, such as James Peak. Highest is Grays Peak, reached via a popular old tourist trail, which tops out at the highest point of both the Front Range and the entire Continental Divide.

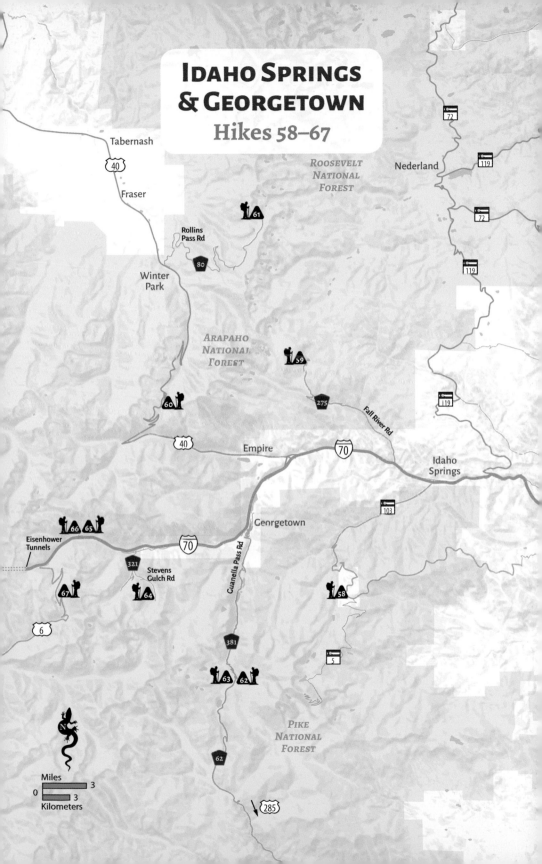

IDAHO SPRINGS & GEORGETOWN
Hikes 58–67

Tabernash

40

Fraser

ROOSEVELT NATIONAL FOREST

Nederland

72

119

72

119

119

Rollins Pass Rd

61

80

Winter Park

ARAPAHO NATIONAL FOREST

59

275

Fall River Rd

60

40

Empire

70

Idaho Springs

103

Georgetown

66 65

70

Eisenhower Tunnels

321

Stevens Gulch Rd

58

67

64

Guanella Pass Rd

6

381

5

63 62

N

62

PIKE NATIONAL FOREST

Miles
0   3
                 3
Kilometers

62

285

View from the summit of Mount Bierstadt, Hike 62

58 Chicago Lakes

THIS HIKE OUTSIDE IDAHO SPRINGS LEADS TO TWO LAKES BENEATH A GORGEOUS HIGH mountain cirque that has inspired landscape painters for over 150 years.

At a Glance

DIFFICULTY	🚶🚶🚶	**DISTANCE/TIME**	9.5 miles/4 hours	
TRAIL CONDITIONS	🚶🚶🚶🚶	**TRAILHEAD ELEVATION** **TOTAL HIKING GAIN**	10,600 feet 1,800 feet	
CHILDREN	🚶🚶🚶	**FEATURES**	Mostly gentle trail, lakes, creek, mountain views, cirque	
SCENERY	🚶🚶🚶🚶	**BEST SEASON**	Early summer	
PHOTO	🚶🚶🚶🚶	**OTHER USERS**	Bikes and vehicles on portion, horses, dogs on leash	
SOLITUDE	🚶🚶	**NOTES**	Toilets at trailhead	
PROPERTY	Echo Lake Park, Idaho Springs Reservoir, Mount Evans Wilderness	**JURISDICTION**	Denver Mountain Parks, City of Idaho Springs, U.S. Forest Service	

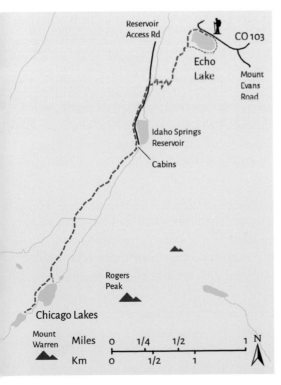

This hike's loveliness begins at the trailhead, where distant craggy peaks reflect in the waters of Echo Lake. These peaks form a cirque above two high unseen lakes which are your destination.

Start by turning right to walk around the north edge of Echo Lake. After a quarter mile, branch right onto **Chicago Lakes Trail** (FS 52) and continue through forest with good views of the cirque in the distance. Chicago Creek rushes below you on the right; soon the trail turns and descends 300 feet to meet it.

"Chicago" is Algonquian for "wild garlic," but the creek was named for its source in the Chicago Peaks, which were in turn

Chicago Lakes Trail

named for the Midwestern city. In the 1880s, Chicago architects began experimenting with steel-frame construction. By 1885 the city had two buildings that were 10 stories high—the first "skyscrapers." This range of peaks scraping the sky above Denver was named after buildings that were 130 feet tall, but the highest of these peaks—Mount Evans—tops out at 14,271 feet!

Cross the creek, turn left on an **access road**, and continue to the spillway of the Idaho Springs Reservoir. This reservoir is over 100 years old, and like many with earthen dams, it has sprung leaks over time. In the early 2000s, sheets of geosynthetic clay were rolled down the inner dam surface to seal it, which seems to have done the trick.

After passing two cabins at the end of the reservoir, continue on Chicago Lakes Trail into Mount Evans Wilderness. The valley opens up with good views of its impressive eastern wall, which comprises the lower sections of Mount Warren and Rogers Peak. Continue on a gradual upslope into a higher basin, where dead trees are evidence of a 1978 blaze caused by an abandoned campfire. Squirrels scold loudly from bleached dead branches, and abundant wildflowers add color to the setting.

As you cross a tributary creek in shrubland, the cirque shows up in nearer view, asking you to pause. It is truly breathtaking. Continue onward, and Lower Chicago Lake will soon appear on the left. At 4 miles, this is a fine turnaround point, but if you want to see what blew the 19th-century landscape painter Albert Bierstadt away, keep going to the upper lake. Follow a path set back from the shore to the lower lake's south end. Beneath a field of gigantic boulders, duck through willows and ascend a gully. In early summer you might have to kick steps up through a small snowfield to arrive at the sparkling tarn.

Above the lake, the cirque's headwall looms. Another word for this amphitheater formation is "corrie," which comes from a Scottish Gaelic word for "cauldron."

Upper Chicago Lake

In the northern hemisphere, cirques are found mostly on northeastern faces—as in this case—which give maximum shelter from the sun and prevailing winds. When glaciers occupied these mountainsides, their upper sections accumulated more ice each year than they lost, and the lower portions less. Consequently, the glaciers flowed. Freeze-thaw action in the upper interfaces caused big hunks of rock to be "plucked" and entrained in the glaciers, creating a sandpaper effect as they flowed. Often an over-scoured section was gouged at the bottom of a cirque, leaving a tarn when the glacier retreated, like the one you see here.

On the return, keep a sharp eye out for the right-hand turnoff from the access road back to Echo Lake—and save some juice in your legs for the 300-foot climb back to the car.

Marmot near Lower Chicago Lake

From Denver. Take US 6 and I-70 west to Exit 240, Mount Evans. Turn left onto CO 103 and continue 13 miles south to Echo Lake Park. The parking area for the trailhead is on the right; additional parking is available in a lot a quarter mile farther down the road. *1 hour.*

59 James Peak from Saint Mary's

LEAVE THE TOURISTS BEHIND AS YOU MARCH UP A FAMOUS SNOWFIELD OUTSIDE IDAHO Springs, then shift gears and stroll through high tundra meadows to the top of James Peak. It's a bucket-list adventure in the heart of the Front Range.

At a Glance

DIFFICULTY	🚶🚶🚶🚶	**DISTANCE/TIME**	8.5 miles/4 hours
TRAIL CONDITIONS	🚶🚶🚶	**TRAILHEAD ELEVATION** **TOTAL HIKING GAIN**	10,300 feet 2,900 feet
CHILDREN	🚶🚶	**FEATURES**	Year-round snowfield, high meadow, 13,200-foot peak, views
SCENERY	🚶🚶🚶🚶	**BEST SEASON**	Summer
PHOTO	🚶🚶🚶🚶	**OTHER USERS**	Horses and bikes on portions, dogs on leash
SOLITUDE	🚶🚶🚶	**NOTES**	Parking fee, toilets at trailhead, significant snow walking (hiking poles and/or traction cleats suggested), thunderstorm exposure above tree line
PROPERTY	Arapaho National Forest, James Peak Wilderness	**JURISDICTION**	U.S. Forest Service

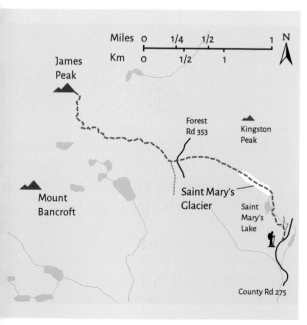

Don't worry about the crowds along the first part of this hike; most folks have come to visit St. Mary's Lake and its snowfield, and you'll soon leave them behind. Begin the **Glacier Hike** on a hewn-boulder jeep road, turning left at successive junctions to arrive at the lake within half a mile. The popularity of this picturesque setting is justified. Cliffs and fingers of snow seem to tumble to the shore; across the way, the white hump of St. Mary's Glacier rises.

Make your way to the snowfield's base. Most of the visitors will stop here, throw a snowball or two, take some selfies, and turn around; you,

Saint Mary's Lake and Glacier

on the other hand, will kick steps into the snow and keep going. The first part is the steepest, and none of it is difficult; traction cleats and hiking poles can help. After about a quarter mile you can walk on dirt and scree to the right of the snow if you prefer, but I think it's easier to "snow-walk" right up the center.

Incorrectly called a glacier, this snowfield remains year round to a varying extent, despite the relatively low elevation. It doesn't flow or have crevasses, but care must be taken at the edges to avoid "post holing" through soft or thin snowpack. Like the other 140-odd named semi-permanent snow and ice bodies in Colorado, St. Mary's shrank in the 1940s, fluctuated in size through the '60s, grew into the '80s, and since the '90s has retreated quite a bit. It remains to be seen whether future summer hikers will have snow to walk on at all.

Hiking Saint Mary's Glacier

In early summer, the snow extends farther than you might expect. You may see ski tracks and even some summer skiers and boarders. St. Mary's was one of the birthplaces of Colorado skiing and it remains popular year round.

On leaving the snow, you'll continue on an unnamed but clear path through a vast meadow of yellow tundra flowers. Ahead, James Peak displays its signature dorsal fin. Mount Bancroft rises on its left, nearly equal in height. James's northeast face is severe; some of its climbing routes are called Bailout, Sky Pilot, and Superstar. You'll take the easier southeast route instead, called the **Continental Divide Trail**.

Continue toward the peak, cross a jeep road (Forest Road

Descending from James Peak's summit

Summit marmot, James Peak

353), and look for cairns marking the Continental Divide Trail as it joins from the right. This fine path climbs to a notch that stares at Bancroft, with views down to enchanting lakes. From here you'll continue climbing and curving, steeply at times, amid tiny violet primroses which provide a welcome distraction through the final pitch.

No false summit here! Once you're there, you're there. Views northward are to the Indian Peaks. To the south, Mounts Evans and Bierstadt appear benign, unlike Grays and Torreys to their west, which look intense. At the summit's western edge you can peer down at Winter Park Ski Resort, where double-black-diamond runs look tame from above. As you survey the scene, be mindful of your lunch sack. The resident marmots are quite bold.

This peak was named for Edwin James, a Middlebury College–educated botanist who summited Pikes Peak in 1820. In fact, Pikes Peak was called James Peak for a while. The name is now assigned to this lesser summit which, when viewed from north Denver, is impressive nonetheless. You've likely admired its snowy fantail from a distance; now you're standing on it!

On the way back, have fun stepping down St. Mary's Glacier. Use big steps and sink in your heels. It goes by quickly.

From Denver. Take US 6 and I-70 west to Exit 238 in Idaho Springs. Drive north on CR 275, Fall River Road, for 9 miles to a large parking lot on the left, just before St. Mary's Glacier Trailhead; there is more parking just beyond the trailhead. *1 hour.*

60 Berthoud Pass West

THIS HIKE FROM HISTORIC BERTHOUD PASS IS A TREAT AMONG TREATS. YOU CAN MAKE IT short and sweet to a mesmerizing promontory, or extend your wander along the Continental Divide, deep into the Vazquez Peak Wilderness.

At a Glance

DIFFICULTY	🚶🚶	DISTANCE/TIME	4 miles/2 hours
TRAIL CONDITIONS	🚶🚶🚶🚶	TRAILHEAD ELEVATION TOTAL HIKING GAIN	11,300 feet 1,100 feet
CHILDREN	🚶🚶🚶🚶	FEATURES	Historic pass, high mountain and cirque views, tundra ridge walk
SCENERY	🚶🚶🚶🚶🚶	BEST SEASON	Summer
PHOTO	🚶🚶🚶🚶🚶	OTHER USERS	Horses, bikes on portion, dogs on leash
SOLITUDE	🚶🚶🚶	NOTES	Toilets at trailhead, thunderstorm exposure above tree line
PROPERTY	Arapaho National Forest, Vasquez Peak Wilderness	JURISDICTION	U.S. Forest Service

For some high-mountain soul time, drive up to Berthoud Pass on a long summer day and start walking. You can even do this hike after work; in fact, the landscape is achingly beautiful in late afternoon. Fine views begin in the parking lot and stay with you most of the way.

Take care crossing the road, then find the **Continental Divide Trail** cutting left of the old ski runs. As you walk through the trees you can almost hear the shouts and laughter of bygone ski kids.

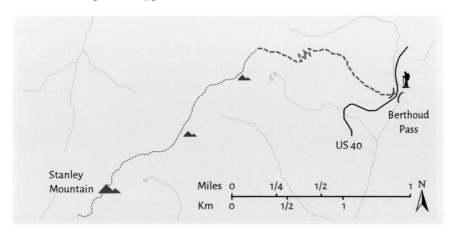

Ten Little Indians Cirque

A toll road opened here in 1874, 13 years after Edward Berthoud surveyed the area and deemed it unsuitable for a railroad. The wagon route was later upgraded for automobiles and, beginning in the 1930s, was kept open during the winter. No better place to try the burgeoning sport of skiing! Just zip down the slopes and have a car drive you back up for the next run. Colorado's first public rope tow opened here in 1937, right where this trail begins. Ten years later, the country's first double chairlift was built here. As you can see, there are no longer any lifts, but Berthoud Pass continues to be a popular car-shuttle area for backcountry skiers.

As you traverse up through spruce and fir, you'll get some fabulous views through the trees. The mountains are especially gorgeous in the first half of summer when they retain fingers of snow. The trail wends through meadows and over rocks, then levels on a ridge where the ski lift used to end. A big green hill of switchbacks rises ahead and invites you onward.

To the right, a cirque appears. It's hard to take your eyes off it, especially as you rise higher and see how it is gouged from the tundra above. This is Current Creek Cirque, also known as Ten Little Indians, a name given for the approximate number of its extreme-skiing chutes. You get to enjoy it from many different angles on this walk, so keep your camera at the ready. Fun Fact: a 1902 aqueduct delivers its meltwater to Denver faucets via a tunnel that runs under the lot where you parked.

View from Continental Divide Trail west of Berthoud Pass

Ten Little Indians Crique from Continental Divide Trail

A stiff climb takes you to the next ridge. There are 14 switchbacks, and it's understandable if you want to stop halfway to sit and soak up the panorama of the cirque and lofty peaks. When you reach the top, a grassy bowl and a pair of tarns appear down the other side.

Keep going! From here the trail continues along a ridge to a higher, unnamed hilltop. At 2 miles this is a dazzling turnaround point, but even small hikers might find it hard to resist continuing along the Continental Divide. Three successive temptation points present themselves along the Divide ridge; the third is Stanley Mountain, a 12,500-foot hill two miles away.

If you make it to Stanley Mountain you can gaze west to Vasquez Pass and Vasquez Peak, which Berthoud named during an 1861 scouting trip. Berthoud was guided by veteran mountain man Jim Bridger, who had been trading post partners with another veteran, Louis "Old Vaskiss" Vasquez.

Also visible from Stanley Mountain is the huge scar of the Henderson molybdenum mine, in operation since 1976. In 2010 the billionth pound of moly was mined there, and about half that much remains underground. You don't see any ore being transported because everything goes beneath the Continental Divide through a 10-mile rail tunnel to a mill in a remote valley farther west. Ute Peak Trail (Hike 69) has views of this mill and its tailings pond.

From Denver. Take US 6 and I-70 west to Exit 232, then US 40 west 15 miles to the large parking lot on the east (right) side of Berthoud Pass. The trail begins across the road on the west side of the pass. *1 hour, 20 mins.*

61 High Lonesome

AFTER THE GRUELING DRIVE TO ROLLINS PASS, THE REWARDS ARE IMMENSE: A WALK ON the high lonely Continental Divide with magnificent views of cirques and dozens of lakes, all in an historic—and prehistoric—setting.

At a Glance

DIFFICULTY	🚶	**DISTANCE/TIME**	6 miles/2.5 hours
TRAIL CONDITIONS	🚶🚶	**TRAILHEAD ELEVATION** **TOTAL HIKING GAIN**	11,600 feet 600 feet
CHILDREN	🚶🚶🚶🚶	**FEATURES**	Historic railroad pass, prehistoric hunting relics, tundra, cirque and high lake views
SCENERY	🚶🚶🚶🚶🚶	**BEST SEASON**	Summer
PHOTO	🚶🚶🚶🚶🚶	**OTHER USERS**	Horses, dogs on leash
SOLITUDE	🚶🚶🚶🚶🚶	**NOTES**	Very rough road for final 11 miles to trailhead, 4WD highly recommended; no toilets at trailhead; thunderstorm exposure above tree line
PROPERTY	James Peak Protection Area	**JURISDICTION**	U.S. Forest Service

The drive up to Rollins Pass is rough, but the wondrous scenery of **High Lonesome Trail** (FS 7), a portion of the **Continental Divide Trail**, is worth it. For starters, a gorgeous headwall and cirque rise north of the pass. Farther northeast are the Arapaho Peaks.

A trench curves through the center of the pass, recalling a bygone era when trains ran through here beneath wooden snow sheds and stopped at a nearby hotel. Debris from these structures now lies scattered on each side of the pass. The railroad was a temporary route across the Continental Divide. Expensive to operate due to the steep grade and heavy snows, it ran only from 1903 to 1927.

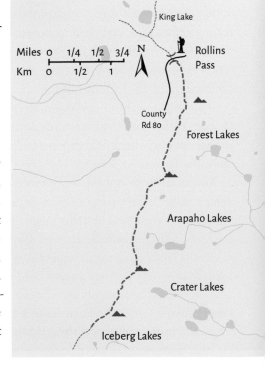

Rollins Pass

This trail is so lonesome there isn't really a trail. Just cross the train trench and follow post markers up the hillside heading south. When you reach a saddle, you'll get your first dizzying look down into a cirque; this one drops precipitously to the Forest Lakes. Route markers continue just below the ridge's western slope, but the rim is fine for walking and its views are spectacular.

An interesting man-made feature sits in the saddle. At first glance it doesn't appear to be much, just a rock-lined pit near the drop-off, but it is archaeologically significant. Native people practiced communal hunting along the Divide for thousands of years, and 12 prehistoric hunting complexes have been found in and around Rollins Pass. The Olson Game Drive, one of the largest sites, is located on the opposite shoulder of the hill you just crossed. There, lines of cairns and low rock walls converge in a V-shape upslope from a grazing area that attracted big game, likely bighorn sheep and elk. During the fall migration, animals could be hazed toward this funnel point, where hunters, hidden in blinds like this rocky pit, readied their bows and arrows or, in earlier epochs, their atlatls and darts. The animals may have been field-dressed up here, and then brought down to lakeside camps for further processing.

Farther along the not-trail is a high point requiring a 200-foot ascent through tundra. At the top, James and Parry Peaks will greet you from the south; to the north you'll have a view of Rollins Pass Road snaking up from the east side and disappearing into the old Needle's Eye Tunnel. This tunnel was closed in 1990 when rock fell from the ceiling and injured someone badly. Since then, the only way to drive all the way to Rollins Pass has been from the Winter Park side.

Soaking up the energy of this high special place, it's easy to commit to walking across the next few knobs. Each delivers a stunning view of a chain of lakes; they are, in order of appearance: the Arapahos, Craters, and Icebergs. It feels like cheating to enjoy these lakes from this easy raptor's-eye-view walk, as visiting

High Lonesome Continental Divide

them from the east would require days of walking and thousands of calories. Travel the ridge as far as you wish; you can't get lost, and the trail becomes more prominent the closer you get to James Peak.

Back at Rollins Pass, you might consider exploring the wonderlands north. A short path drops to King Lake, where trails continue to Betty and Bob Lakes. After expending the time and effort to reach this high, historic, and lonesome place, it seems a shame to hurry up and leave it.

From Denver. Take US 6 and I-70 west to Exit 232, then US 40 west another 25 miles to Winter Park. Turn right onto CR 81 and continue 2.9 miles. Turn right onto CR 80 (Rollins Pass Road), and proceed 11 miles to the pass on a road best handled by a high-clearance, four wheel drive vehicle. Parking is at the pass. *2 hours, 45 mins.*

View into a cirque from High Lonesome Trail

62 Mount Bierstadt

THIS POPULAR, ACCESSIBLE, AND EASY FOURTEENER DELIVERS GLORIOUS HIGH MOUNTAIN scenery. Do it early in the morning on a summer weekday and get a great start to your day.

At a Glance

DIFFICULTY	🚶🚶🚶🚶	**DISTANCE/TIME**	7 miles/4 hours
TRAIL CONDITIONS	🚶🚶🚶	**TRAILHEAD ELEVATION** **TOTAL HIKING GAIN**	11,700 feet 2,500 feet
CHILDREN	🚶🚶🚶	**FEATURES**	Tundra wetland, boulders, expansive views, 14,000-foot peak
SCENERY	🚶🚶🚶🚶🚶	**BEST SEASON**	Summer
PHOTO	🚶🚶🚶🚶	**OTHER USERS**	Horses, dogs on leash
SOLITUDE	🚶	**NOTES**	Guanella Pass Road closed winter to late May, toilets at trailhead, thunderstorm exposure
PROPERTY	Mount Evans Wilderness	**JURISDICTION**	U.S. Forest Service

How nice to begin with such a clear view of the task at hand! From the car park on 11,670-foot Guanella Pass, Mount Bierstadt displays its entire route. Also in view is the aptly named Sawtooth, a jagged, three-pronged ridge to its left.

Start the climb by descending **Mount Bierstadt Trail** (FS 711) toward sparkling Deadman's Lake. This is seasonal wetland and though there are boardwalks, stretches of the route are often puddled and muddy. It's no fun getting wet feet at the start of a hike, but it's important to stay on the trail in this heavily used and fragile area, which is prime habitat for white-tailed ptarmigans.

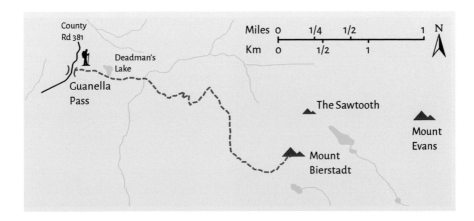

The trail bottoms out at 0.8 miles, where you'll cross Scott Gomer Creek and head uphill amid willows. The expansive basin falls away, and there are good views to peaks on the other side of the pass. Guanella is a fairly recent name, honoring a mid-20th century road commissioner who spearheaded the campaign to upgrade the 1860s wagon route to a dirt road for autos. The pavement you enjoyed coming in was completed in 2012, making Bierstadt more accessible than ever; it is probably the best fourteener to climb before work in the morning. It's also an excellent choice for a kid's first fourteener. You might meet "Bier

Mount Bierstadt Trail

runners" on the trail who first climbed it when they were little—and dozens of times since.

After about 1.5 miles, you'll reach a shoulder where Sawtooth and Bierstadt stare in your face. Just two miles to go, on a no-nonsense route toward a notch west of the summit. Set a steady pace and ascend amid grass and lichen-covered rocks or, in early summer, atop snowfields. As you get higher, pay attention to how your body is handling the altitude and respond accordingly. This could

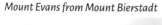

Mount Evans from Mount Bierstadt

mean descending and trying again a different day.

From the notch prepare for the final push to the top. Though it requires some boulder scrambling, the route is less steep than below. Cairns mark the route and views are superb along the way. Looking west, little obstructs the panorama of central Rockies peaks: Square Top, Grays, Torreys, and many others. Southeast lies the vast basin of South Park, and north are Mount Bancroft, James Peak, and the Indians. Soon you're on the ridgetop with nothing to do but walk along it and enjoy the thrill. The

Summit ridge, Mount Bierstadt

big mound in front is Mount Evans, of course, displaying a lesser-known western face that is steep and mostly snow-free. From the summit you literally peer into "the Abyss": a deep cut in the earth separating two mountains, where a lake of the same name shimmers.

Bierstadt is German for "Beer City," but the mountain is named after Albert Bierstadt, one of America's foremost landscape painters. Bierstadt first came to the Rockies in 1859, made sketches, and later painted many large, romanticized, gleaming-light paintings from his studio in New York City. These were the only views many Easterners had of these mountains at the time. By the 1900s, Bierstadt's work had fallen out of critical favor. It's easy to see why. In my opinion, the Rockies are not as "beautiful" as Bierstadt depicted them, and yet they are far more beautiful.

It's possible to climb Mount Evans on the same day as Bierstadt, on a fun route that drops partway into the Abyss and traverses a thrilling ledge across Sawtooth. This trek is advisable only after snow has melted, and it makes for a long day. Alternatively, you could drive to the top of Evans and be done with it.

From Denver. Take US 6 and I-70 west to Exit 228, and turn left into Georgetown. Turn right at the roundabout and proceed 0.8 miles to the other end of town. Turn onto Guanella Pass Road (CR 381) and continue 10.5 miles to Mount Bierstadt Trailhead and its large parking lot, on the left. *1 hour, 20 mins.*

63 Square Top Lakes

THIS EASY HIKE THROUGH THE TUNDRA IS GORGEOUS ALL SUMMER, AND ESPECIALLY LOVELY in early September when the scrubby shrubs turn gold. The views, of course, are for all seasons.

At a Glance

DIFFICULTY	👥	DISTANCE/TIME	4.5 miles/2 hours
TRAIL CONDITIONS	👥	TRAILHEAD ELEVATION TOTAL HIKING GAIN	11,700 feet 1,000 feet
CHILDREN	👥👥	FEATURES	Gentle grade, tundra, alpine lakes, views
SCENERY	👥👥	BEST SEASON	Summer
PHOTO	👥👥	OTHER USERS	Bikes, horses, dogs
SOLITUDE	👥👥	NOTES	Guanella Pass Road closed winter to late May, trail is muddy in spots, toilets at trailhead, thunderstorm exposure above tree line
PROPERTY	Pike National Forest	JURISDICTION	U.S. Forest Service

This hike starts high, at 11,670-foot Guanella Pass, and offers some solitude because many hikers head toward Mount Bierstadt and The Sawtooth, which soar magnificently on the *other* side of the road. Turn your back on them and step out onto **South Park Trail** (FS 600). This doesn't go to "the" South Park, the vast high basin 25 miles south that is the setting for a certain television cartoon series. Rather, it leads to a broad section of the nearby Geneva Creek Valley.

Veer right and descend into shrubland that turns lustrous gold in September. The trail loses 100 feet and crosses a marshy area before turning upward. Try to walk in the center of one of the rocky trail furrows so that you don't create an-

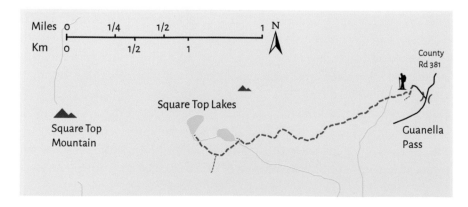

South Park Trail to Square Top Lakes

other track through the fragile vegetation. The trail gains several hundred feet before mellowing in a vegetated moonscape beneath a boulder-strewn moraine. Birds flit in the bushes here, and you might see some marmots scampering around.

As you ascend and curve around a hill, you'll find yourself staring squarely at Square Top Mountain. From this angle the pointy peak looks nothing like its name. The trail makes another 100-foot drop, this time through boulders, to the stream coming from the lakes that are your destination. Continue alongside the stream, and then cross it. Just before the trail snakes up the hillside, look for a spur going right. The first Square Top Lake is hiding calmly behind the bushes: a wide, shallow, sparkling pool ringed by tundra.

The main trail continues uphill. In the greenery below, Lake One appears as a sunlit jewel. After a quarter mile the path forks: left to continue on South Park Trail, right to Lake Two. Take the right-hand trail, which climbs a stiff stretch

Lower Square Top Lake

before leveling off and undulating through marshland that requires some fancy footwork in the mud. Try to walk through the wet spots rather than around them. Some of the bushy willows here are chest-high, and insects buzz into your eyes and mouth, but this hiking challenge doesn't last long, and in minutes the second lake appears. Tundra-ringed like the first, it couches itself in the shadow of Square Top, which rises from its western shore.

At 2.3 miles, peaceful Lake Two makes a fine destination. But if you'd like more of a go, you can climb Square Top. To get there simply do the "Square Top Scramble," i.e., ascend 1,500 feet along its eastern tundra ridge to the broad summit. You'll likely be alone up there; though just 206 feet shy of a fourteener, Square Top gets far less traffic than Bierstadt and Evans to the east and Grays and Torreys to the west.

Another option is to continue along South Park Trail. It soon traverses into what were the upper bowls of Geneva Basin, a beloved mom-and-pop ski area that opened in 1963. Sadly, lift construction claimed the life of Eddie Guanella, son of Byron Guanella, the highway commissioner who pushed for building the gravel road over the named-for-him pass in the 1950s. Stories circulated for decades of Eddie's benign but headless spirit haunting skiers at the top of Duck Creek Lift. The bargain-priced ski area rarely made money, largely because the county never paved the access road, but it remained open until 1984.

There will probably never be another Geneva Basin Ski Area, but in 2012 the Guanella Pass road got a $60 million facelift and, as you experienced, is now beautifully paved.

From Denver. Take US 6 and I-70 west to Exit 228, then turn left into Georgetown. Turn right at the roundabout and proceed 0.8 miles to the south end of town. Turn onto Guanella Pass Road (CR 381) and continue 10.6 miles to the large parking lot for Square Top Lakes Trailhead, on the right. *1 hour, 20 mins.*

Upper Square Top Lake

64 Grays Peak

THE SCENERY IS ENCHANTING AS YOU HIKE TO THE DOME OF THE CONTINENT—THE HIGHEST point on the Continental Divide—on a route that has delighted Front Range hikers for over 150 years.

At a Glance

DIFFICULTY	🚶🚶🚶🚶	**DISTANCE/TIME**	7 miles/4.5 hours
TRAIL CONDITIONS	🚶🚶🚶🚶	**TRAILHEAD ELEVATION** **TOTAL HIKING GAIN**	11,200 feet 3,000 feet
CHILDREN	🚶🚶🚶	**FEATURES**	High valley, ascent to over 14,000 feet, across-range views
SCENERY	🚶🚶🚶🚶🚶	**BEST SEASON**	Summer
PHOTO	🚶🚶🚶🚶	**OTHER USERS**	Bikes, horses, dogs on leash
SOLITUDE	🚶	**NOTES**	4WD vehicle recommended for 3-mile road to trailhead, thunderstorm exposure
PROPERTY	Arapaho National Forest	**JURISDICTION**	U.S. Forest Service

Ordinarily, a steep and rocky access road would disqualify a hike from this book. But the rewards of Grays Peak are too fabulous to pass up. This National Recreation Trail begins in a high-altitude wonderland, and in 3.5 miles reaches the highest point on the Continental Divide. It is essential Front Range walking. It's also very popular, so arrive early and avoid weekends. Or try an afternoon start on a long day in June or July, after the threat of thunderstorms has abated. Light effects at this time of day are exquisite.

Begin **Grays Peak Trail** (FS 54) in a striking peak-ringed valley that curves out of sight beneath McClellan Ridge. Cross a metal hikers' bridge over Quayle Creek and continue

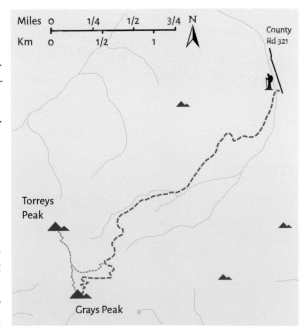

through shrubland on a well-built path. Soon the remains of a silver-mining operation appear across the valley. This area was home to Colorado's first "argentine" discoveries, back in the 1860s. The Stevens Mine, which you can see from the trail, was one of the most productive mines in the region. Several others operated on the other side of McClellan, where the ghost town of Waldorf is all that remains of a once bustling mining and tourist station that had its own narrow-gauge railway.

The grade eases as you reach a higher portion of the valley where the creek tumbles and marmots scurry. Grays appears to your left, looking easy to climb and farther away than it is. To the right, steep-faced Torreys Peak appears much more forbidding. At 1.5 miles, you'll pass an old sign-board and continue through a marmot city sprinkled with blue alpine forget-me-nots. The tundra becomes a rocky moonscape as the trail veers

Start of Grays Peak Trail
Sunset view from Grays Peak summit

up-left on a grassy flank, enters a rock-field traverse, and hooks left to gain a high shoulder of Grays. The onward switchbacks are visible; all that's left to do is climb them. Mountain goats may ogle you along the way, and even pose for photos.

Outdoors enthusiasts have long been climbing Grays and Torreys. By 1867 folks could ride horseback from Georgetown all the way to the tops. Reaching the "Dome of the Continent" became even more of a craze in 1884, when the railroad reached nearby Bakerville. The depot was built for ore and supplies, but it was called "Graymont" to attract tourists, who purchased round-trip packages from Denver that included a horse and guide.

Mountain goats along Grays Peak Trail

You may wish you had a horse as you gaze toward the summit, but keep walking. Be sure to pay attention to how your body is handling the altitude, and descend if you need to. It's really just a stroll to the top, albeit a lung-heaving one involving at least one false summit. But mountains are not infinite, and steady plodding brings you to the true summit, which is flat and broad.

Congratulations! You're standing at 14,278 feet—the highest point on not only Colorado's Front Range but also North America's Continental Divide. The view is everything you could ask for: a dreamy ocean of lofty, rocky, snowy peaks. From here a trail leads down to a saddle and up to Torreys in less than a mile, letting you bag two fourteeners if you wish.

Botanist Charles Parry named this peak for his mentor, Asa Gray, during a climb in 1861; he named the neighboring peak for Gray's mentor, John Torrey. Gray was a longtime Harvard professor and pillar of American botany. His compendium of North American plants is still an essential text. Gray made two trips west in the 1870s to collect specimens, and each time he climbed the peak Parry named for him, just as you've now done.

From Denver. Take US 6 and I-70 west about 50 miles to Exit 221. Turn left onto CR 321 (Stevens Gulch Road), a steep and rocky unpaved road best suited for 4WD vehicles that ends, after 3 miles, at the parking area for Grays Peak Trailhead. *1 hour, 20 mins.*

65 Woods Mountain

THIS HIKE WEST OF GEORGETOWN TAKES YOU TO A LOVELY PICNIC SPOT WHERE YOU HAVE plenty of time to climb to a pass, summit a mountain, or just while away the afternoon in the pretty meadows.

At a Glance

DIFFICULTY	🚶🚶🚶🚶	DISTANCE/TIME	7 miles/3 hours
TRAIL CONDITIONS	🚶🚶🚶	TRAILHEAD ELEVATION	10,300 feet
		TOTAL HIKING GAIN	2,700 feet
CHILDREN	🚶🚶	FEATURES	Forest, meadows, tundra pass and peak, views
SCENERY	🚶🚶🚶🚶	BEST SEASON	Summer
PHOTO	🚶🚶🚶🚶	OTHER USERS	Bikes, horses, dogs on leash
SOLITUDE	🚶🚶🚶	NOTES	Toilets at trailhead, thunderstorm exposure above tree line
PROPERTY	Arapaho National Forest	JURISDICTION	U.S. Forest Service

The presence of Interstate 70 cannot despoil the wild and spectacular nature of the terrain along its corridor. It's a joy to begin a hike here and have evidence of civilization fade away after the first mile. The freeway soon becomes small and quiet, then invisible and forgotten—lost in the vast mountain realm.

Begin with a short walk down **Herman Gulch Trail** (FS 98). At 0.2 miles, branch right onto **Watrous Gulch Trail** (FS 95) and traverse uphill through aspens and fallen trees. Mount Sniktau greets you from across the valley, and the tip of Torreys Peak appears as well, promising more views to come. The trail climbs into a gulch beneath the looming tundra flanks of Mount Parnassus, then eases in a meadow where a stream babbles on your right.

After crossing the stream at 1.4 miles, take the left trail fork and

Watrous Gulch and Woods Mountain

continue walking steadily up the valley on a smooth path. Ahead, the reddish wall of Woods Mountain makes its first appearance. There are many wildflowers here, and some remain into September to complement the golden color of the turning willows that fill the creek bottom.

Two miles in, the streamside meadows make a good destination for a shorter hike and picnic, and there are nice views of Torreys. But for the most spectacular views, keep going! The trail curves up-right toward the huge smooth hump of Parnassus, through steeper meadows and copses where larger trees filter into krummholz and tundra. At the tree line, you can see a pass a steep half mile away. The trail peters out along the way, but it is obvious where to go. As you rise, a quartet of peaks comes out to the south: Grays beyond Torreys; Grizzly between them and Sniktau. Also, on the left beyond Woods Mountain, a jagged section of Continental Divide pokes up: that's Hagar Mountain and Pettingell Peak.

At about 3 miles you'll reach the unnamed pass, where you'll have fine views north to Berthoud Pass and beyond. Woods Mountain blocks much of the view to the west, but its summit appears a stone's toss away, and a trail switchbacks up it to boot. Distances can be deceiving, so know that the top is 0.5 miles and 500 vertical feet away. As you rise, Parnassus exerts its gravitational pull, along with the impressive wall of Robeson Peak beyond it on the left.

Mount Parnassus, 13,580 feet tall, was named after a mere 8,061-foot but highly prominent peak in central Greece that shows up over and over again in Greek

Continental Divide from Woods Mountain

mythology. Sacred to both Apollo and Dionysus, the Greek Parnassus is home to the Muses, as well as the winged horse Pegasus. As you can see, the Colorado version would make a great Pegasus launching pad as well.

The summit of Woods Mountain offers an uninterrupted vista of a huge swath of the Continental Divide, arcing from Grays Peak to Jones Pass to Berthoud Pass, and continuing to James Peak and the Indians. What a sweep! Before heading down, you might like to take a seat here and relax a while in the ruddy tundra, where grasshoppers rasp their wings loudly in late summer.

From Denver. Take US 6 and I-70 west about 54 miles to Exit 218. Turn right, and right again, then proceed a few hundred yards to the large parking lot for Herman Gulch Trailhead. *1 hour.*

Watrous Gulch

66 Herman Lake

THOUGH IT STARTS NEXT TO INTERSTATE 70, THIS HIKE SOON TAKES YOU FAR FROM THE RAT race into a pristine wilderness valley. There are snowy Continental Divide peaks and a sparkling alpine lake for your lunch stop.

At a Glance

DIFFICULTY	🚶🚶	DISTANCE/TIME	7 miles/3 hours
TRAIL CONDITIONS	🚶🚶🚶🚶	TRAILHEAD ELEVATION TOTAL HIKING GAIN	10,300 feet 1,700 feet
CHILDREN	🚶🚶🚶	FEATURES	High lake, peak views, meadows, creek, forest
SCENERY	🚶🚶🚶🚶	BEST SEASON	Summer
PHOTO	🚶🚶🚶🚶	OTHER USERS	Bikes, horses, dogs on leash
SOLITUDE	🚶🚶	NOTES	Toilets at trailhead
PROPERTY	Arapaho National Forest	JURISDICTION	U.S. Forest Service

This kid-friendly hike to a beautiful lake has the added attraction of a striking transition in its first mile. Begin alongside the whooshing traffic of Interstate 70, then after a few minutes, turn left on **Herman Gulch Trail** (FS 98) to slant uphill toward the pyramid of Mount Bethel. Across the freeway, the tundra slopes of Mount Sniktau rise above the timberline. Soon you'll arrive at a roaring creek that drowns out the traffic noise. Then the grade mellows, and so does the creek roar. It's as if you've teleported: all sights and sounds of civilization are gone, replaced by birdsong in wilderness.

Continue through Douglas fir forest into a long meadow with views to Continental Divide peaks ahead. Plentiful clumps of yellow sulfur flowers decorate the grass-scape and, after passing through forest into a higher and rockier meadow, it's a party of little sunflowers. The trail remains gentle

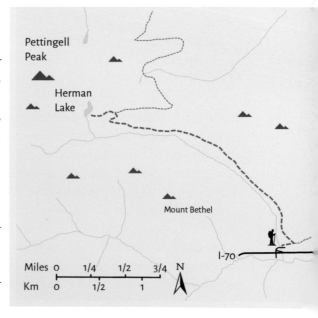

Continental Divide from Herman Lake Trail

most of the way, steepening only when it turns away from the creek to make the final climb to the lake. At this point you can tell the kids, "We're almost there!"

Two switchbacks are your clue that the lake is nearby. Immediately after them, you'll arrive at a junction: left to Herman Lake, right to continue on the Continental Divide Trail. Turn left and proceed an easy third of a mile through tundra to arrive at a pretty glacial puddle nestled beneath cliffs. Plenty of good sitting rocks make it easy to stay awhile and stare across the lake and up to the slopes of Pettingell Peak.

The lake is named for early logger Herman Hassell. The peak is named for Jake Pettingell, who came to Colorado in 1880 for health and wealth and became a fixture in Grand County. He got into politics, became a judge, and went on to serve 50 years in the same courtroom, a feat that got him into *Ripley's Believe It or Not*. From the lakeshore, two more beautiful thirteeners appear to the left of Pettingell: Hagar Mountain and an unnamed middle peak.

Back at the trail junction, the question arises: What would it take to reach the Continental Divide on this namesake trail? The answer is: 2.5 miles and a thousand vertical feet. As a compromise, you can walk an easy mile from the junction to a grassy saddle with pleasing views north across the Woods Creek Valley. From there the trail wraps northward, up to the Divide proper.

The **Continental Divide Trail** was designated a National Scenic Trail in 1978, but that doesn't mean it was built yet. Rather, a 100-mile-wide swath between Canada and Mexico was designated for the trail to run through. Now about 75 percent complete, it is walkable from end to end via different routes that include some roadways. In New Mexico, volunteers place caches of water along the way. In Montana, the trail crosses Triple Divide Pass, where a drop of water has three choices where to go: Atlantic, Pacific, or Hudson Bay.

Together with the Pacific Crest Trail and the Appalachian Trail, the Continental Divide Trail makes up what is called the Triple Crown of Hiking. To date, more than 300 people are recorded as having completed the Triple Crown, a feat that entails about 8,000 miles and well over a million

Herman Lake and Pettingell Peak

vertical feet. Among the Triple Crowners is Oregon native Reed Gjonnes, who was 13 years old when she finished it with her dad over three consecutive seasons.

From Denver. Take US 6 and I-70 west to Exit 218. Make two quick right turns and continue a few hundred yards to the large parking lot for Herman Gulch Trailhead. *1 hour.*

Continental Divide Trail near Herman Lake

67 Mount Sniktau

SCOTTISH HIGHLANDS TIMES FIVE, WITH SUPREME VIEWS ALL AROUND, THE ROUTE TO THIS 13,240-foot tundra summit gets a head start by beginning from Loveland Pass. Bring a picnic and the whole family.

At a Glance

DIFFICULTY	🚶🚶🚶	DISTANCE/TIME	3.5 miles/2.5 hours
TRAIL CONDITIONS	🚶🚶🚶	TRAILHEAD ELEVATION	12,000 feet
		TOTAL HIKING GAIN	1,300 feet
CHILDREN	🧍🧍🧍🧍	FEATURES	Panoramic high mountain views, tundra, 13,240-foot peak
SCENERY	🧍🧍🧍🧍🧍	BEST SEASON	Summer
PHOTO	🧍🧍🧍🧍🧍	OTHER USERS	Bikes, horses, dogs
SOLITUDE	🧍🧍🧍	NOTES	No toilets at trailhead, parking allowed at pass until 7 p.m., thunderstorm exposure above tree line
PROPERTY	Arapaho National Forest	JURISDICTION	U.S. Forest Service

Hello, top of the world! It's always nice to begin at a high pass with ready-made views, and at 11,990 feet, Loveland Pass delivers. All that's left is to walk eastward on **Mount Sniktau's trail**—uphill, 1,250 vertical feet to the summit. It's a wide-open route above tree line, and the views only get bigger as you go.

Until 1973 Loveland was *the* pass for motorists crossing Colorado, hairpin turns and all. Before cars, supply wagons plied the route. The pass is still an artery of choice for oversize trucks, hazmat vehicles, and bicyclists, since they aren't allowed to use the Eisenhower Tunnels.

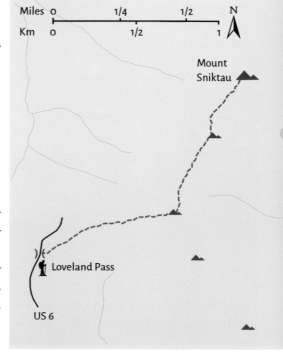

After a steep initial stretch, you'll get a brief reprieve in a saddle. It's easy to see where to go: straight up, through tundra. Small hikers might need some coaching and encouragement, and everyone will do well to set a very slow and steady pace. The good news is that the steep part doesn't last long—less than a mile—and the rewards are worth every huffing-and-puffing step.

As you climb, miniature alpine flowers appear at your

Heading down from Mount Sniktau

feet to entertain you. Look down to the south and you'll see Arapahoe Basin ski area, which might even still be open. Its latest-ever closing date was August 10 in 1993, though lift-served skiing usually wraps up by mid-June. Keep climbing and you'll reach the first of three ridge points. Here you're just shy of 13,000 feet, and the hard work is over; what's left is a delightful high mountain stroll. Look for Torreys Peak rising to the southeast, and Grays Peak peeking behind it.

Descend to a saddle and head up alongside a pretty snow cornice that usually remains into July. The route continues to the second ridge point, which at 13,150 feet is still not quite Sniktau. But it's a thirteener nonetheless, and a fine turn-around point if your group is feeling tuckered or if afternoon storms are brewing. From here you get great views of the Eisenhower Tunnels and the powerful line of Continental Divide peaks above them.

It's easy to see why engineers routed the interstate through the mountains instead of over them—not that tunnel construction was cheap or easy. The two bores were drilled sequentially, beginning in 1968. By the time the second tunnel was finished 11 years later, the project was way over schedule and budget. The biggest problems encountered were fault lines not revealed by pilot bores, and drilling equipment that didn't perform as well at high altitude as bidders had promised.

From the second hill you can see the real Sniktau summit. Getting there requires descending 150 feet to a saddle, and then climbing 240 feet to the high point. The reward is an unimpeded view northward, completing the 360-degree panorama. A cute tarn sits in a deep pocket to the southeast; to the northwest, tundra slopes drop away gracefully. These slopes almost became the giant slalom and downhill runs of the 1976 Winter Olympics. That was the plan when Denver

View northward from Mount Sniktau Trail

was awarded the games in 1970, but plans changed, Colorado voters rejected public funding, and the games went to Innsbruck, Austria.

The peak you're on was named for popular Georgetown journalist E. H. N. "Sniktau" Patterson. "Snik" claimed that Native Americans had given him his nickname, and that it meant "equal to any emergency." It should be noted, however, that there is a creek in California named Sniktaw, after fellow journalist W. F. "Sniktaw" Watkins, who never pretended his nickname was anything other than his surname spelled backwards.

From Denver. Take US 6 and I-70 west to Exit 216, then continue on US 6 west for 4.5 miles to Loveland Pass. The trailhead and parking area are on the east side of the pass. *1 hour, 15 mins.*

Looking south from Mount Sniktau

Summit County

Cradle of alpine beauty across the Great Divide

From Denver it's only an hour's drive on I-70 to reach the Eisenhower Tunnels and punch through the Continental Divide. Then comes the hard part: choosing from the myriad summer hiking opportunities waiting on the other side. Here the Gore and Tenmile Ranges beckon, north and south respectively, magnificent mountains tucked behind the Front Range and yet still easily reached for day hiking from Denver.

The majestic and craggy Gore is a huge tract of pure wilderness where you could put on a backpack and walk for weeks. Day trippers do have choices, however. Three wonderful long trails to alpine lakes are featured here, each well worth the miles; there is also a short stiff climb up Buffalo Mountain above Silverthorne that will kick your butt. The Gores best views perhaps come in panorama from a little-traveled ridge to their east that is crowned by Ute Peak.

The smooth and pyramidal peaks of the Tenmile Range jut up on the south side of I-70, less jagged than the Gores but equally majestic. These peaks and their rivers were important sources of gold and silver in the mining days; they were also seemingly made for skiing, as Breckenridge Ski Resort can now attest. The walk up Victoria Peak, which could also be called Peak Zero, begins in the town of Frisco. Once you get there it's hard to stop: Peak 1 urges you onward, as do Peaks 2 through 10. You don't need to cross them all to get to their apex, Quandary Peak; you can hike this fourteener on its own trail. Looking for a little less vertical action? Head for magnificent McCullough Gulch, in Quandary's northern shadow: a vast, high wandering place with a lovely waterfall.

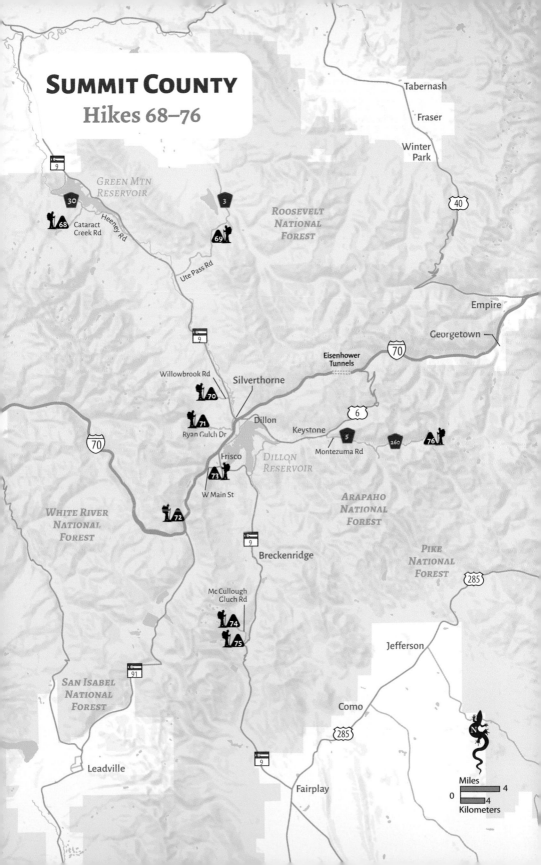

SUMMIT COUNTY
Hikes 68–76

Green Mtn Reservoir

9

30

68 Cataract
Creek Rd

Heeney Rd

3

69

Ute Pass Rd

Roosevelt National Forest

Tabernash

Fraser

Winter Park

40

Empire

Georgetown

9

Eisenhower Tunnels

70

Willowbrook Rd

Silverthorne

70

71

Ryan Gulch Dr

Dillon

Keystone

6

5

260

76

Montezuma Rd

Frisco

73

Dillon Reservoir

W Main St

72

White River National Forest

Arapaho National Forest

Pike National Forest

285

9

Breckenridge

McCullough Gluch Rd

74

75

Jefferson

91

San Isabel National Forest

Como

285

9

Leadville

Fairplay

Miles

0   4

0   4

Kilometers

Mountain goat on Quandary Peak, Hike 75

68 Upper Cataract Lake

THIS LOVELY FOREST TREK IN THE LESS-TRAVELED GORE RANGE LEADS TO SOME PRETTY lakes and culminates in rewarding views of Eagles Nest Peak, which offers an interesting geological snapshot.

At a Glance

DIFFICULTY	🚶🚶🚶🚶	DISTANCE/TIME	11 miles/4.5 hours
TRAIL CONDITIONS	🚶🚶🚶	TRAILHEAD ELEVATION	8,600 feet
		TOTAL HIKING GAIN	2,500 feet
CHILDREN	🚶🚶🚶	FEATURES	Moist forest, lakes, high granite cliffs, peak views
SCENERY	🚶🚶🚶🚶	BEST SEASON	Summer
PHOTO	🚶🚶🚶🚶	OTHER USERS	Horses, dogs on leash
SOLITUDE	🚶🚶🚶	NOTES	Toilets at nearby Cataract Creek Campground
PROPERTY	White River National Forest, Eagles Nest Wilderness	JURISDICTION	U.S. Forest Service

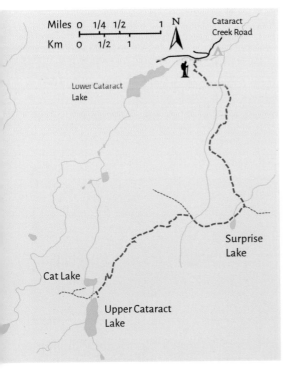

Mists rise over placid water as you start out on **Surprise Trail** (FS 62) and cross Cataract Creek. "Cataract" derives from a Greek word meaning "down-rushing," but this stretch of the stream is in no rush at all.

The trail climbs through aspens and meadows awash in lavender asters and enters Eagles Nest Wilderness, where the forest is untouched (so far) by the pine beetle infestation that has affected much of the Gore foothills. A steady uphill grade takes you through conifer forest with intermittent aspen groves, where white trunks gleam in the sunshine. Be ready to walk through

Cataract Creek at Start of Surprise Trail

lots of spider webs if you are the first on the trail in the morning.

The path levels off and descends a little, crossing streams, to reach a junction at 2.7 miles, where you'll turn right onto **Gore Range Trail** (FS 60). A quarter mile later, Surprise Lake materializes through the trees, decked out in lily pads. It's a peaceful spot with views south to the headwall of Dora Mountain, and makes a fine destination for a shorter hike or if the kids are tired. But if you have time and willing companions, keep walking! Most of the elevation gain is now done.

The soft dirt trail continues through woods kept moist by streams and summer afternoon rainfall. At 3.5 miles, turn left onto **Upper Cataract Lake Trail** (FS 63) and enjoy an easy mile before beginning an ever-steepening descent. As the trail drops to a field of rouge boulders, powerful cliffs emerge, along with the sharp point of Eagles Nest Peak to the southwest. This peak is aptly but figuratively named; its isolated apex would make a great aerie for raptors should any care to nest at 13,432 feet (but none do).

The tree-lined lake below you on the right is Cat Lake, and it is not your destination. Look for a path branching left, which will quickly take you to Upper Cataract Lake, a large and glistening oblong that fills a gorgeous cut high in the mountainside.

Upper Cataract Lake

Now is a good time to kick off your boots and—if you can muster the courage—take a chilly dip. Or just recline lakeside and soak up the wonderful view. Above the far end of the lake, the cliffs of Eagles Nest are a magnificent example of the tilted fault-block formation that characterizes the Gore Range. As in the Tetons and Sierra Nevada, massive underground pressure forced the Earth's crust apart eons ago. After the crust broke, one side rose and the other side sank. From the lakeshore it's pretty easy to see which side is which.

It's difficult to find a worthy namesake for mountains as resplendent as the Gore, and sadly funny that the honor went to an Irish baronet-playboy who came to Colorado in the 1850s on an extravagant animal-slaughtering adventure. But Sir George arrived early and caused a stir, and his name became entrenched. Gore enjoyed excellent hunting in Colorado's Rockies before continuing to Yellowstone with his guide, servants, horses, dogs, wagons, and hundreds of guns (which his servants loaded for him). He killed thousands of buffalo, elk, and deer, and more than 100 bears, all purely for sport. Local Native Americans were deeply offended, but no one stopped him, and now we have Gore Range, Gore Pass, Gore Canyon, Gore Mountain, and Gore Lake.

After enjoying the lake, the walk back might feel long. But it's pleasant to be in the forest and, if you're not thinking about it too much, the miles flow past quickly underfoot.

From Denver. Take US 6 and I-70 west to Exit 205, Silverthorne. Bear right onto CO 9 north and continue for 16.7 miles. Turn left onto Heeney Road (CR 30), continue 5.5 miles, then turn left onto Cataract Creek Road. Proceed 2.3 miles on the dirt road to the parking lot at Surprise Trailhead. *2 hours.*

Upper Cataract Lake

69 Ute Peak

THIS RIGOROUS, LONELY WALK UP A FORESTED RIDGE LEADS TO A DAZZLING TUNDRA SUMMIT. Rarely is the sharp side of the Gore Range seen in such panoramic splendor.

At a Glance

DIFFICULTY	👤👤👤👤👤	**DISTANCE/TIME**	11.5 miles/5.5 hours
TRAIL CONDITIONS	👤👤👤	**TRAILHEAD ELEVATION** **TOTAL HIKING GAIN**	9,600 feet 3,000 feet
CHILDREN	👤	**FEATURES**	Gore Range views, forest, meadows, valley view, ridge walk, summit climb
SCENERY	👤👤👤👤	**BEST SEASON**	Summer
PHOTO	👤👤👤👤	**OTHER USERS**	Bikes, horses, dogs
SOLITUDE	👤👤👤👤👤	**NOTES**	No toilets at trailhead, thunderstorm exposure above tree line
PROPERTY	White River National Forest, Arapaho National Forest	**JURISDICTION**	U.S. Forest Service

A sweeping view of the jagged Gore Range greets you as you step out of your car. From the parking lot, which may be otherwise empty, you'll cross a meadow and ascend into thick woods on **Ute Pass Trail** (FS 31). As you round the hillside into a clearing, the Gore Range reappears across the valley. This is the last you'll see of these mighty mountains for several miles, because the trail reenters woods and moves to the east side of the ridge.

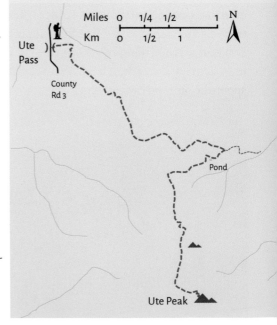

Some maps depict a shortcut trail heading directly up the ridge spine, but in reality you'll have to hike a V-shaped route, heading east into the next valley and then turning sharply right at an un-signed junction with **Ute Peak Trail** (FS 24), at 2.5 miles, to climb west and regain the ridgetop. The first leg involves a 350-foot descent through forest and delightful meadows in full flower in summer. The second is a steep uphill climb via switchbacks, past a pond in the trees to the ridgetop. From here you can see the remaining wooded ridge to be climbed before reaching green tundra.

About 4.5 miles from the start, you'll break out of the trees into a steep meadow covered in lavender daisies. The path becomes faint as it zigzags uphill, so look for cairns. To the east, the Williams Fork Valley comes into view, along with the Henderson ore mill and its vast, diseased-looking tailings pond.

Subalpine meadow, Ute Peak Trail

The world's once-leading producer of molybdenum may or may not still be in operation when you see this, and extensive land reclamation may or may not be in progress. The ore body had about five years left in 2017, but molybdenum prices at that time could not cover the cost of extraction and processing. The ore is not mined here, but rather east of the Continental Divide; it is then sent 10 miles through a tunnel to this secluded spot to be purified by froth flotation.

Gore Range from the Ute Peak Trail

The Gore Range reappears in full majesty as the route wraps west, prompting possible shouts of joy. What remains is an exhilarating ridge walk. Ahead is a rocky knob easy to mistake for Ute Peak, beautiful in its own right and a nice prelude to the summit. The trail remains faint through the tundra, but even without cairns it would be easy to find your way. Slant up and around the knob to reach a park on its southwest side. From here Ute Peak is in clear sight, the wooden cross marking its summit only minutes away. The entire Gore Range is now in view and, to the far northeast, the back side of the Front Range presents itself, including Longs Peak.

It's a straightforward climb to the 12,303-foot promontory, which gives a perspective on the world from an in-between place. You are standing at a high point in the Williams Fork Mountains, which along with the St. Louis Divide fills in the space between the Gore and the Continental Divide.

Ute Indians had trails crisscrossing the Rockies that took advantage of passes like the one you set out from, which later became routes for wagons and railways. These Native Americans didn't call themselves "Utes," of course; that is an Anglicized version of their Spanish moniker *Yuta*, a word whose meaning is unclear. The Utes called themselves *Noochee*, or "people."

Bird on a cairn, Ute Peak Trail

On the way back, you get to enjoy the trip along Ute's high ridge before diving back into the trees. Remember to save some energy for that 350-foot ascent on the final V-leg!

From Denver. Take US 6 and I-70 west to Exit 205, Silverthorne. Bear right onto CO 9 north and continue for 12.6 miles. Turn right onto CR 3 (Ute Pass Road) and proceed 5.2 miles to the parking lot for Ute Pass Trailhead, on the east side of Ute Pass. *1 hour, 45 mins.*

70 Willow Lakes

A LONG BUT GENTLE TRAIL OUTSIDE SILVERTHORNE TAKES YOU INTO THE HEART OF THE Gore Range, where some quiet, steady walking pays off in lofty granite peaks, jagged ridges, mountain cirques, and a string of alpine lakes.

At a Glance

DIFFICULTY	🚶🚶🚶🚶	**DISTANCE/TIME**	12.5 miles/5.5 hours
TRAIL CONDITIONS	🚶🚶🚶	**TRAILHEAD ELEVATION** **TOTAL HIKING GAIN**	9,000 feet 2,400 feet
CHILDREN	🚶	**FEATURES**	Rejuvenating forest, flowers, meadows, alpine lakes, stone cirques and spires
SCENERY	🚶🚶🚶🚶	**BEST SEASON**	Summer
PHOTO	🚶🚶🚶🚶	**OTHER USERS**	Horses, dogs on leash
SOLITUDE	🚶🚶🚶🚶	**NOTES**	No toilets at trailhead
PROPERTY	Willow Creek Open Space, White River National Forest, Eagles Nest Wilderness	**JURISDICTION**	Summit County Open Space & Trails Department, U.S. Forest Service

Backpackers love the Gore Range, not only for its spectacular peaks, but also for its vast roadless area, where it is possible to hike many days in untrammeled wilderness. It takes some trekking to reach the heart of these craggy mountains, and much of their core remains empty, untracked, and wild. That said, a handful of great day hikes are available for those willing to burn some shoe leather. In this hike, the 2,400-foot gain is spread out over the distance, making the long walk fairly easy. The reward is classic Gore: a high valley dead-ending at an alpine lake in a magnificent cirque.

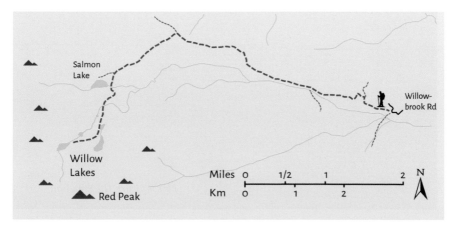

Red Peak from Willow Lakes

From the trailhead, be sure to turn right onto **Ditches Trail**. Ascend past backyards up a hillside of small aspens. You'll soon enter a forest where two out of three trees have been killed by pine beetles. The beetles have long been part of the Colorado forest ecosystem, thinning out densely grown stands of trees in 30- to 50-year cycles. The beetles burrow into tree bark in vertical channels, laying eggs and depositing a fungus that clogs the trees' water and nutrient transport systems. Healthy, uncrowded trees resist by increasing their sap flow, thus drowning and expelling the beetles. Many dead trees are down here, and many are still standing, resulting in a kind of ghost forest. But look around and you'll see new growth emerging amid grasses and wildflowers, soaking up the newfound sunshine—evidence that the forest is rejuvenating itself.

At 0.6 miles turn left onto **North Willowbrook Trail**. Climb steeply and con-

Upper Willow Lake

tinue through treefall so heavy that
some hillsides appear to be covered
in giant matchsticks. Turn left again
at the next junction. As you descend
to North Willow Creek, you will cross
into Eagles Nest Wilderness. At the
subsequent junction, at 1.3 miles,
continue straight on what is now
called **Gore Range Trail** (FS 60), making your way through more beetle-
scarred forest alternating with bright
meadows and wildflowers. The hump
of Red Peak's ridge appears in the
distance on the left, guarding the
destination valley. Opposite it, a
stark stone spear soars into the sky:
another rocky sentinel.

Fly fishing at Upper Willow Lake

At 3 miles turn left onto **Willow Lakes Trail** (FS 36). You'll ascend the right side
of a shoulder, then swerve left and traverse on a level path toward Red Peak's
shark-tooth ridge. At 4.5 miles you'll arrive at a junction with Salmon Lake Trail.
This side trail takes you a nice half mile to the namesake lake, which is nestled
beneath cliffs and surrounded by salmon-colored boulders, but a better prize
awaits straight ahead on Willow Lakes Trail.

The continuing path takes you on a mellow jaunt through lush woods and
flower meadows to the first of several ponds. As you curve left around the pond,
gray "camp-robber" jays might boldly glide down from the branches and land in
front of you. From here the path steepens toward Red Peak's breathtaking cliffs.
You'll pass Lower Willow Lake but won't see it until it is below you, then you'll find
another Willow Lake peeking at you from the left. You are now 6 miles into the
walk and may be ready to turn around, but press on another third of a mile for a
dazzling reward. After winding through trees and past a small green-hued lake
you'll arrive at the valley's terminus: Upper Willow Lake, set in a gouged-stone
bowl beneath awesome spires.

"Wow," is all that really needs to be said, but fly fishermen also say the little
trout here bite like crazy.

From Denver. Take US 6 and I-70 west to Exit 205, Silverthorne, then CO 9 north
for another 3 miles. Turn left on Willowbrook Road and continue 1 mile to Willowbrook Trailhead and its small parking area, on the left. *1 hour, 20 mins.*

71 Buffalo Mountain

GET YOUR LUNGS AND LEGS PUMPING ON A STEEP CLIMB UP A GRANITE HUMP STANDING sentinel in central Summit County. From the top you'll get an intimate look into the Gore Range and expansive views of the middle Rockies.

At a Glance

DIFFICULTY	🚶🚶🚶🚶🚶	DISTANCE/TIME	6 miles/3.5 hours
TRAIL CONDITIONS	🚶	TRAILHEAD ELEVATION	9,700 feet
		TOTAL HIKING GAIN	3,000 feet
CHILDREN	🚶🚶	FEATURES	Steep climb, talus, tundra, 360-degree views
SCENERY	🚶🚶🚶🚶	BEST SEASON	Summer
PHOTO	🚶🚶🚶🚶	OTHER USERS	Horses on portion, dogs on leash
SOLITUDE	🚶🚶🚶	NOTES	Very steep with talus in places, some obscure portions of trail, no toilets at trailhead, thunderstorm exposure above tree line
PROPERTY	White River National Forest, Eagles Nest Wilderness	JURISDICTION	U.S. Forest Service

Many Gore Range peaks remain unnamed, but not Buffalo Mountain, which rises above Interstate 70 like a giant reclining mammal. It's unclear whether Utes or settlers gave it this name, but either way, it's a distinctive hump. This hike takes you 3,000 feet up to its summit.

Begin on **Buffalo Mountain Trail** (FS 31) alongside a former forest that was decimated by pine beetles and cleared by humans. You'll soon enter woods and continue into Eagles Nest Wilderness, where most of the trees remain healthy.

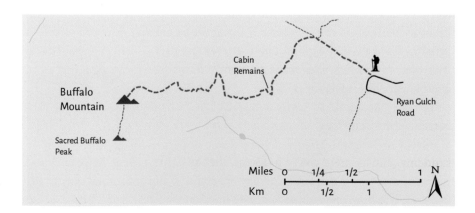

Dillon Reservoir from Buffalo Cabin Trail

At 0.5 miles turn left at a four-way junction onto **Buffalo Cabin Trail** (FS 31). This wide trail feels like an old wagon road and it is. A steep hairpin turn takes you to the remains of two log cabins, likely used by prospectors during a short-lived silver boom.

Skirting left, the trail reverts to a hikers' path and gets serious about gaining altitude. This section of trail, built in 2004, could use some TLC. Sometimes the path heads straight uphill, where wayward feet and erosion have fuzzied the route. Keep going for a reprieve on a long, albeit steep, traverse right. Then turn left and do it again, this time gazing at the sailboats down on Dillon Reservoir.

The town below is mostly Silverthorne, where thousands of people live below the earthen dam. Begun as a workers' camp during reservoir construction in the 1960s, Silverthorne now has hotels, outlet stores, and a very low sales tax. Dillon, on the northeast shore, has a longer history. It's also in its fourth location. Incorporated in 1883 on the Snake River, Dillon moved twice to be closer to rail lines, and a third time to avoid being flooded by the reservoir. If you visit "Old New Dillon" these days, you'll find vintage buildings including a church, a town hall, and the Arapaho Café, which were moved to their current locations at their owners' expense.

After the long traverse, the timberline comes suddenly: one moment you're in forest, then it's

Peeping mountain goat on Buffalo Mountain

Red Buffalo Pass as viewed from Buffalo Mountain

all talus. The next section is very steep on a beveled path through rocks marked with cairns. If you find yourself "rock climbing," pause, look for the cairns, and get back on the staircase trail. With the right attitude, the climb is a lot of fun, and not dangerous if you take care where you put your feet (some rocks are loose). If you feel a set of eyes on you, it's a mountain goat.

Wrap north when the talus ends and try not to be dismayed. The summit is still 30 minutes away, but it's a gentler stroll now through tundra, krummholz trees, and rocks where pikas squeak. When you reach the top, you'll have a western view into the heart of the Gore Range: Red Peak, Red Buffalo Pass, and the green meadows leading to Eccles Pass. Take in the long view down the Vail Valley and the seemingly endless vista of Rockies.

The pristine South Willow Creek Valley below you almost became the I-70 corridor, complete with a tunnel beneath Red Buffalo Pass. This route would have been 10 miles shorter than the one eventually built over Vail Pass; it would also have bisected what was then the Gore–Eagles Nest Primitive Area. Fortunately, the U.S. secretary of agriculture refused to grant the easement, and so the highway engineers went with Vail.

For a thrilling coda, walk a quarter mile south to a sub-summit called Sacred Buffalo. On the way, you'll cross a narrow ridge with dizzying plummets east down to Salt Lick Cirque and west toward Willow Creek.

From Denver. Take US 6 and I-70 west to Exit 205, Silverthorne. Turn right on CO 9 (Blue River Parkway) and make an immediate left at the stoplight onto Wildernest Road (or, perhaps more safely, turn right from the parkway on Rainbow Drive, turn around, and go straight back through the stoplight). Continue straight on Wildernest through two more stoplights onto Royal Buffalo Drive. After the second stoplight, proceed 1.7 miles and turn left on Twenty Grand Drive. Continue 0.2 miles and turn right on Ryan Gulch Drive. Proceed 1.1 miles to a parking lot, on the left, that is shared by Buffalo Cabin Trailhead (north end) and Lily Pad Lake Trailhead (south end). *1 hour, 20 mins.*

72 Wheeler & Lost Lakes

THE TRAILHEAD IS RIGHT BY THE INTERSTATE, BUT CIVILIZATION FALLS AWAY ON THIS SOUL-restoring hike that leads through woods, green hills, and meadows to a series of lovely lakes with smashing views.

At a Glance

DIFFICULTY	🚶🚶🚶	**DISTANCE/TIME**	11 miles/5 hours
TRAIL CONDITIONS	🚶🚶🚶🚶🚶	**TRAILHEAD ELEVATION** **TOTAL HIKING GAIN**	9,700 feet / 1,900 feet
CHILDREN	🚶🚶🚶	**FEATURES**	Forest, meadows, lakes and ponds, high terrain, views
SCENERY	🚶🚶🚶🚶	**BEST SEASON**	Summer
PHOTO	🚶🚶🚶🚶	**OTHER USERS**	Bikes on small portion, horses, dogs on leash
SOLITUDE	🚶🚶🚶🚶	**NOTES**	No toilets at trailhead
PROPERTY	White River National Forest, Eagles Nest Wilderness	**JURISDICTION**	U.S. Forest Service

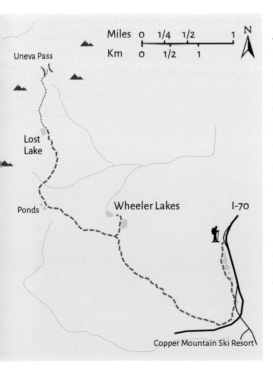

This hike requires a leap of faith. As you begin walking right alongside the roar of Interstate 70, rest assured that this will be one of the prettiest hikes in the book. In the meantime, wildflowers and some trout action in the reclaimed gravel pits along the start of **Gore Range Trail** (FS 75) offer distraction from the screaming traffic.

The trail curves with the interstate opposite Copper Mountain ski resort, whose black diamond runs look tame in the green summertime. As the name suggests, Copper Mountain was never a source for highly prized gold and silver, but long before there was a Super Bee chairlift there was a hopping town called

Gray Jay along Gore Range Trail to Lost Lake

Wheeler Junction at its base. Established in the 1870s by a man of that name, the town was a busy shipping station and supply depot, and a popular spot for miners working elsewhere in Ten Mile Canyon to get drunk.

Soon you will turn your back on I-70 and climb a gully, making switchbacks among lavender asters. At 1.75 miles you'll enter Eagles Nest Wilderness, where traffic sounds are much fainter and Jacque Peak appears, west of Copper, looking beautiful. Ascend a steady grade through forest on a smooth and foot-friendly path. At 2.5 miles you'll skirt to the right of a huge flat meadow, and half a mile later arrive at the turnoff for Wheeler Lakes. These attractive shallow lakes, set in greenery a stone's toss off to the right, make for a fine destination. But most of the elevation gain is done, and the onward miles are a joy to walk. Continue as far as your legs and time allow; it's all good.

At 4 miles you'll arrive at two ponds in a meadow on your left, beneath a snow-patched ridge. This is also a fine place to stop but continuing onward is even finer. Ahead are more natural gardens and forest, where gray mountain jays swoop to ogle you trailside. The trees seem tall for the 11,500-foot elevation, and you

Lost Lake

might spy a marmot scurrying between trunks and do a double take. Yes: marmots sometimes live below tree line.

In moist summers you'll see bright red-orange mushrooms with white spots growing in the grass beneath pines, looking like something out of a fairy tale. Note that no animals have nibbled them. If a snake or frog were such a color, you'd know it was poisonous. These iconic toadstools are *Amanita muscaria*, commonly called "fly agaric," a reference to their long history of use in fly poison. An average fungal cap contains an active dose of muscimol, a psychoactive compound that can kill you. A fatal dose is around 15 caps, which may be why there have

Amanita muscaria mushroom, along Gore Range Trail to Lost Lake

been few reported deaths. People get too sick from them first.

Descend into a green basin and cross a shrubby marsh on a well-built wooden bridge. After crossing a boulder field, you'll curve upward to find Lost Lake, a gorgeous pea-green lake reflecting the verdant tundra hillside above it. It's a rewarding destination, 100 percent worth the 5.5 miles of walking.

Would you like to go to Uneva Pass? If you've got the time and legs for it, I strongly recommend it. It's just a mile farther and 300 feet higher, a bit above timberline. The higher you go, the more awesome the granite pyramids of the Tenmile Range appear beyond Copper Mountain, especially when lit up in sunshine. From the pass there's a remarkable view northward into the heart of the craggy Gore Range.

From Denver. Take US 6 and I-70 west past Frisco. Immediately after passing Exit 198 (Officers Gulch), take the unnumbered exit to the large parking lot for Gore Range Trailhead, on the right. If you reach Exit 195, you've gone too far. *1 hour, 30 mins.*

73 Mount Victoria

THIS CLIMB TO A GATEWAY PROMONTORY OUTSIDE FRISCO GIVES MAGNIFICENT VIEWS across Summit County and the Gore Range. It just might lure you farther and higher into the enticing peaks of the Tenmile Range.

At a Glance

DIFFICULTY	🚶🚶🚶🚶	DISTANCE/TIME	6 miles/3 hours
TRAIL CONDITIONS	🚶🚶🚶	TRAILHEAD ELEVATION	9,100 feet
		TOTAL HIKING GAIN	2,500 feet
CHILDREN	🚶🚶	FEATURES	Steep trail, mining relics, aspens, pine forest, views from above tree line
SCENERY	🚶🚶🚶🚶	BEST SEASON	Summer
PHOTO	🚶🚶🚶🚶	OTHER USERS	Bikes, horses, dogs on leash
SOLITUDE	🚶🚶	NOTES	Toilets at trailhead, thunderstorm exposure above tree line
PROPERTY	Summit County Recreational Pathway System, White River National Forest	JURISDICTION	Summit County Sheriff, U.S. Forest Service

The Tenmile Range begins next to the freeway in Frisco, its peaks marching south in numbered succession, Peaks 1 through 10, before switching to names. Victoria could be called "Peak Zero." From the parking lot, cross Tenmile Creek and turn left onto a paved recreation path, formerly a narrow-gauge railway. You'll hike among bikers and joggers for half a mile before turning right on **Mount Royal Trail**.

As you traverse the aspen-covered hillside, relics appear: a scrap of rusted metal, a hump of mine tailings, the red brick foundation of a bygone smelter. These are remains of a mining camp centered on the Victoria silver vein. Aban-

Red Mountain in the Gore Range, from Mount Victoria

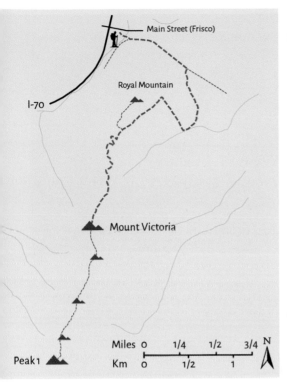

doned soon after discovery in the 1860s, the mine was revived twice over the decades amid changing politics and roller-coaster silver prices, only to close again with the silver crash of 1893. Ten years later, the Masontown Mining & Milling Company took over the camp, installed a smelter, and undercut the vein with a tunnel. It turned a profit the first year but closed the next. Later, during Prohibition, the camp was revamped as an illicit moonshine production site.

Curve right on Masontown's "Main Street" and continue uphill through conifers. Curve again into a long traverse, where the town of Frisco and Dillon Reservoir come into view. Unlike the nearby town of Dillon, Frisco didn't need to relocate when the reservoir was built in the 1960s. Instead it got a shoreline and a marina. The town was incorporated in 1880, when promoters were wooing the St. Louis–San Francisco ("Frisco") Railway to come through, and that's how it got its name.

Make a switchback and traverse on a steeper grade to reach a junction. The right-hand trail leads to Royal Mountain but there is no need to go there; you will see everything and more by continuing straight on **Mount Victoria Trail**. More cabin relics appear over the next mile as the soft pine-needle trail zigzags upward, affording expansive views north to the Gore Range. As you break from the trees, you'll see the radio hut atop Mount Victoria; beyond that soars Peak 1.

Steady marching brings Victoria's rocky knob in short order, and from here the views are stupendous. Peak 1 calls and sings, "Come climb me!" Can you resist going at least part of the way? It's a thrilling and straightforward walk with three satisfying knobs along the way, each of which makes a fine destination if you decide to extend your hike. But if you reach the top of Peak 1, watch out: you might feel compelled to go farther. Some people continue the scramble across Peaks 2 through 10, and then stagger down to Breckenridge. The way to Peak 4 requires some tricky rock-walking, but the rest is mostly a tundra trek.

Mount Victoria (right) and Peak 1 (left)

The Tenmiles were formed during the same geological events that crafted the craggy Gores, but they received less glaciation. Consequently, they are smoother cones and make better ski resorts (Breckenridge's lifts extend almost to the summits of Peaks 6 and 8). Also unlike the Gores, which remain pristine today, the Tenmiles sit astride the Colorado Mineral Belt and so were heavily mined.

Mount Victoria was named for the silver vein, which in turn was named for Victoria, the British monarch and queen of the pound sterling. Victoria held Britain's title of longest-reigning royal until 2015, when great-great-granddaughter Elizabeth II shattered her record. A lesser-known fact is that Victoria was near full-blood German, and may never have achieved complete English fluency.

From Denver. Take US 6 and I-70 west to Exit 201, Frisco. Turn left onto West Main Street and proceed 0.2 miles to the large parking lot for the county trail system, on the right. *1 hour, 25 mins.*

Hiking up Peak 1 from Mount Victoria

74 McCullough Gulch

THIS HIKE TAKES YOU ABOVE A POPULAR WATERFALL TO A VAST UNTRAVELED BASIN OF tundra and tarns surrounded by lofty gray peaks. Paradise. Really.

At a Glance

DIFFICULTY	🚶🚶🚶	**DISTANCE/TIME**	6.5 miles/3 hours
TRAIL CONDITIONS	🚶🚶	**TRAILHEAD ELEVATION** **TOTAL HIKING GAIN**	11,000 feet 1,400 feet
CHILDREN	🚶🚶🚶	**FEATURES**	Waterfalls, tundra, alpine lakes, mountain views
SCENERY	🚶🚶🚶🚶	**BEST SEASON**	Summer
PHOTO	🚶🚶🚶🚶	**OTHER USERS**	Bikes, horses, dogs on leash
SOLITUDE	🚶🚶🚶	**NOTES**	No toilets at trailhead, thunderstorm exposure above tree line
PROPERTY	White River National Forest	**JURISDICTION**	U.S. Forest Service

At the trailhead, this hike might seem as popular as its next-door neighbor, Quandary Peak. But almost everyone on **McCullough Gulch Trail** (FS 43) is going to White Falls, at 1.7 miles, and then turning back, leaving you to walk the impressive high valley in near or complete solitude.

As gulches go, McCullough is a big one, with the mighty cliffs of Quandary plummeting thousands of feet on the south side and a powerful ridge of Pacific Peak doing the same on the north. The torrent between them, McCullough Creek, is captured in a tunnel that runs under the road you came in on and conveyed beneath the Continental Divide to Colorado Springs. You can see a cement appurtenance of this tunnel sticking out of the hillside across the way as you walk

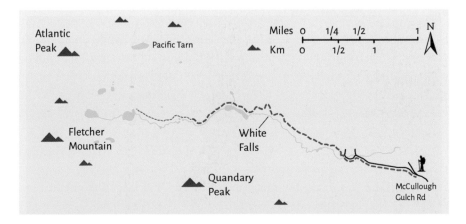

McCullough Gulch Trail

Upper McCullough Gulch

the gated road toward the soaring valley.

At 0.6 miles turn left onto an old wagon road, ascend to cross the creek on a metal bridge, and continue up the gulch. After passing a well-preserved cabin, the road is fenced off and the trail branches uphill left. The path is stony and steep, hardly user-friendly despite its heavy use. The grade eases through pine forest, but roots and rocks continue to make it hard going.

Soon White Falls arrives to delight you: a frothy stream tumbling down a granite hillside. Many people may be posing for photos, and 99.5 percent of them will stop here and miss out on the treasures above. A rest break may be in order, especially if you have tired kids with you, but then it's worthwhile to press on.

And a press it is! The ongoing trail is steep and grueling in trees to the right of the falls, but after only a half mile you'll break out of the trees to reach a stone basin with a quiet oblong lake. Here your only company may be white-crowned sparrows flitting in shrubs along the shoreline. At 2.2 miles, this is a nice place to lounge before turning back, but if you can handle another mile, you'll be glad you kept going. Continue along the tarn's north shore, scrambling a bit over rocks to reach the west end, where boulders break the surface of the shallow waters. Hop a little inlet stream, enter a meadow, and then head for the next granite rise. The trail is faint, especially where it passes through shrubs—a testament to how few people come this far.

Marmots eye you as you ascend steep natural gardens to arrive at the next level of the basin. The views from here are truly gasp-worthy. Ahead, across the tundra, Fletcher Mountain dominates the skyline with its jagged-tooth northern ridge. Uphill to the left—1,800 feet uphill—is the summit of Quandary Peak. To the north is a graceful cliff-arm of Pacific Peak.

You can hang out here or wander farther into the tarn-dotted basin. Trails are faint to nonexistent, but it is hard to get lost. More challenging would be to ascend 2.5 miles northwest and reach Pacific Tarn. At 13,420 feet it's the highest lake named by the U.S. Board on Geographic Names (beating out Lake Waiau, on Mauna Kea in Hawaii, by 400 feet). Pacific Tarn was named in 2004 after a guy from Boulder visited it with friends, took some measurements, and wrote a pseudoscientific paper promoting it.

Wherever you go, spend some time enjoying the scenery. There's no hurry. In fact, if you wait until four or five o'clock before heading back, you might have White Falls all to yourself.

From Denver. Take US 6 and I-70 west to Exit 203. At the traffic circle, take the fourth exit onto CO 9 south and continue 18 miles, through Breckenridge. Turn right on Blue Lakes Road (Forest Road 850), make an immediate right on McCullough Gulch Road (Forest Road 851), and continue 1.6 miles to a gated fork in the road. Parking is along the road; the hike begins at the gate. *1 hour, 55 mins.*

Upper McCullough Gulch

White Falls, along McCullough Gulch Trail

75 Quandary Peak

WHETHER YOU'RE LOOKING TO CLIMB YOUR FIRST FOURTEENER OR ARE A VETERAN OF stratospheric slopes, the Big Q doesn't disappoint. You'll also get thrilling views of other snow-clad giants in all directions.

At a Glance

DIFFICULTY	🥾🥾🥾🥾	**DISTANCE/TIME**	7 miles/4 hours
TRAIL CONDITIONS	🥾🥾🥾	**TRAILHEAD ELEVATION** **TOTAL HIKING GAIN**	10,900 feet 3,400 feet
CHILDREN	🥾🥾🥾	**FEATURES**	Fourteener, meadow, talus, mountain goats, vast views of peaks and high lakes
SCENERY	🥾🥾🥾🥾🥾	**BEST SEASON**	Summer
PHOTO	🥾🥾🥾🥾🥾	**OTHER USERS**	Bikes, horses, dogs on leash
SOLITUDE	🥾	**NOTES**	No toilets at trailhead, thunderstorm exposure above tree line
PROPERTY	White River National Forest	**JURISDICTION**	U.S. Forest Service

This exhilarating and accessible fourteener gets lots of action, especially on summer weekend mornings. Crowds diminish after 1 p.m. for good reason—thunderstorms—but if skies are clear or storms have passed, afternoons are good times to try. You'll meet fewer humans but plenty of mountain goats, which tend to follow you.

From the access road, **Quandary Peak Trail** (FS 47) gets serious right away, heading up steeply through woods. After a brief respite the steepness returns,

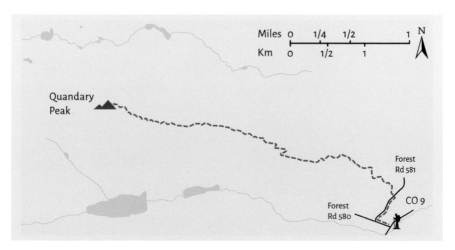

Quandary Peak and trail

and views of North Star Mountain open up to the south along the Continental Divide. After you break into a tree-dotted meadow and climb to a ridgetop, Quandary's summit appears. Distances can be difficult to judge, and the destination may seem either near or far. On a busy day the procession of ant-like people peppering the route provides a visual reference.

The gouged valley between Quandary and North Star is eye-catching, particularly the headwall in the distance. Soon you'll be above timberline and have a talus trail for the rest of the hike. This is why you buy (and wear) good hiking boots! Though the loose rock can be tiresome, the trail is well built, having received lots of attention from volunteers working with the nonprofit Colorado Fourteeners Initiative.

Zigzag along the ridgetop, then enjoy a gentle stretch straddling two dazzling valleys. You'll want to take your time here and prepare for the last push, which is a doozy: nearly a mile and 1,000 more vertical feet. The quickest way to the top is to walk very slowly but not stop. A good strategy for the highest portions is to pause briefly with each step. Along the way you can enjoy some glittery mica in the rocks.

First-time fourteener climbers Kathy and Elise Timme on Quandary Peak's summit

The summit crest often retains a stripe of snow into July. Cross it and you'll arrive on a broad mountaintop with space for everyone. At 14,265 feet this is the highest point in the Tenmile Range, which is contiguous with the Mosquito Range on the other side of the Continental Divide. Everything is beautiful from up here, not least the glimmering lakes in McCullough Gulch to the north. The highest and iciest of these sits beneath a dramatic, serrated-knife ridge north of Fletcher Mountain.

Quandary was named, so the story goes, for the puzzlement miners felt when they came looking for gold here in 1859. They found some strange outcrops on this peak but couldn't identify the ore, which later proved to be silver.

Plenty of gold was discovered as well, in the sediments of Blue River which flows near the trailhead and in its tributaries. The town of Breckinridge was established to service this boom, which evolved into hard-rock mining and river dredging and yielded over 1 million troy ounces. The town's name was chosen to flatter John Breckinridge, then vice president of the United States. Residents became less enthusiastic about this moniker two years later, when the Civil War broke out and the VP sided with the South. What to do? They changed an "i" to an "e," and it has been Breckenridge ever since.

If you didn't meet mountain goats on the way up, you likely will on the way down. There is some debate whether these shaggy white creatures should even be here. Colorado pushes the southern limit of their range, and some wildlife biologists believe they were never native. After six individuals were moved here from Montana in 1948, followed by several dozen more in the ensuing decades, the population boomed to over 2,000. No longer a protected species, mountain goats are now a managed species, which means some hunting is allowed.

On top of Quandary Peak

From Denver. Take US 6 and I-70 west about 70 miles to Exit 203. At the traffic circle, take the fourth exit onto CO 9 south and continue 18 miles, through Breckenridge, and turn right on Blue Lakes Road (Forest Road 850). The parking lot is just past the intersection, on the right; additional parking is available along CO 9. Quandary Peak Trailhead is reached on foot by turning right on McCullough Gulch Road (Forest Road 851) and walking half a mile. *1 hour, 50 mins.*

76 Argentine Pass

THIS SUPER SCENIC TRAIL OUTSIDE KEYSTONE ASCENDS THROUGH AN HISTORIC SILVER-mining district to a high-altitude pass that was once essential to the flow of people and goods across the Continental Divide.

At a Glance

DIFFICULTY	🚶🚶🚶	DISTANCE/TIME	5.5 miles/2.5 hours
TRAIL CONDITIONS	🚶🚶🚶🚶	TRAILHEAD ELEVATION / TOTAL HIKING GAIN	11,100 feet / 2,100 feet
CHILDREN	🚶🚶🚶	FEATURES	Historic wagon route to a high pass, mine relics, tundra basin, peaks
SCENERY	🚶🚶🚶🚶	BEST SEASON	Summer
PHOTO	🚶🚶🚶🚶	OTHER USERS	Bikes, horses, dogs
SOLITUDE	🚶🚶🚶🚶	NOTES	4WD vehicle recommended but not required for access road, no toilets at trailhead, thunderstorm exposure above tree line
PROPERTY	White River National Forest	JURISDICTION	U.S. Forest Service

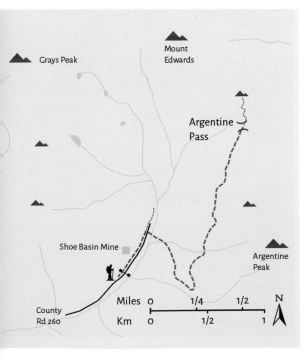

You can tell that this remote and beautiful place used to be much busier. Near the parking area are the remains of some cabins, and a short distance along the gated road ahead of you, a rusted ore hopper sticks out of the hill. This was silver-mining country, set in beautiful Horseshoe Basin. Observing the soaring Continental Divide above, you can imagine how badly the miners wanted a route from here to Georgetown. Which notch is the pass?

Walk 0.4 miles up the road from the gate, then branch right onto **Argentine Pass Trail** (FS 77) and cross a bridge above the streambed of Peru Creek, where rocks gleam silver. It's pretty, but it's pollution. The sheen is

Shoe Basin Mine at start of Argentine Pass Trail

a metallic precipitate that results when acidified, heavy metal-laden water from abandoned mines partially neutralizes on dilution with cleaner water. Peru Creek might have been inhospitable to life even before the mining era due to natural leaching, but 150 years on it is entirely devoid of fish and insects. Some of this water eventually ends up in Denver sink faucets, so cleanup efforts have been made, and with some success. From 2013 to 2016, remediation work was done at one of the biggest polluters, the Pennsylvania Mine, which is about a mile down-valley from here. The stream below the mine no longer turns reddish-orange several times a year.

As you ascend toward timberline, you'll enter a tundra basin where power lines run up the south flank of Argentine Peak and disappear over the Divide. Soon the trail swoops left on a steep uphill section of loose rock, where you can almost hear the crack of whip, the yells of wagon drivers, and feel the nervousness of passengers descending in top-heavy stagecoaches.

The trail traverses left, high above the gorgeous, tranquil basin. Gazing into it, it's clear that it would make a delightful stroll on a different day. Closer examination reveals many tracks of handcart trails and yellow-orange scars of mine tailings—clear evidence that it was once a hive of mining activity.

The moonscape traverse above tree line is graced with occasional high-altitude plants, such as sulfur flowers and alpine thistles. Ahead the destination notch is visible, but there's a deceptive amount of climbing left to do to get there. The trail is excellent for feet if not for stagecoaches, but it keeps you huffing! As you curve along the contours, you expect to arrive at the pass at any moment—but you don't. Just keep trudging, and eventually it comes: a welcome gateway at 13,200 feet.

On the other side of the pass, a jeep road snakes down through tundra toward unseen Georgetown, passing a tarn sparkling below Mount Wilcox. This route was important to local miners who worked these hills, but it was also a trans-

Precipitate-coated rocks in Peru Creek, Argentine Pass Trail

Divide artery. A toll road operated here by 1869, and by the mid-1870s it was the main route from Georgetown. In 1883 the county purchased the road for a public highway, but traffic plummeted when the railroad to Breckenridge was completed elsewhere later that year.

After you catch your breath (or even before), the Divide ridge will beckon. It's all yours in both directions. If nothing else, walk 250 feet up the hump northwest of the pass. From there Mount Edwards appears a stone's toss away, inviting willing feet to come visit. From Edwards you might be tempted to continue rambling all the way to Grays Peak, only 1.25 miles farther, as people often do. It's a lovely and crowd-free alternative to the standard route described elsewhere in this book.

From Denver. Take US 6 and I-70 west to Exit 216, then continue on US 6 west 12.7 miles over Loveland Pass to Keystone. Turn left onto East Keystone Road, make an immediate left onto Gondola Road, and after 0.3 miles turn right onto CR 5 (Montezuma Road). Continue 4.4 miles and make a sharp left onto CR 260. Proceed 4.6 miles on the bumpy dirt road to the parking area for Argentine Pass Trailhead, on the left. *2 hours, 15 mins.*

Mountain goat hunters at Argentine Pass

Conifer & Bailey

Civilization gives way to wilderness

From the southwest edge of the Denver metro, Highway 285 provides another thoroughfare into the wilds. Season dictates how far to drive, and the whole gamut of terrain is reached within two hours.

South of the town of Conifer, wooded foothills give way to year-round mountain views at Eagle's View and Pine Valley. The region feels delightfully remote, and is traversed by the excellent Colorado Trail, which was built by hikers, for hikers. Forest walks on its South Platte and Little Scraggy sections are wonderful before the higher country even begins to melt. And when it does, wow! Just continue farther west along the southern flanks of Mount Evans to sideroads and trailheads leading to the remarkable high wonderlands of Pegmatite Points, the Abyss, and Gibson Lake.

Keep going over Kenosha Pass and a different zone of the Front Range emerges. Here the vast high grassland of South Park stretches on and on, dotted by small settlements. Ringing the park's eastern edge are the Tarryall Mountains with their amazing rock formations. The trail to Bison Pass takes you up into the thick of them. Bordering South Park to the west is the Continental Divide, where several passes vied in the later 1800s to be "the" way to get across. Probably the prettiest and most forgotten of them is French Pass, the trail for which begins on a nondescript bend of a backcountry road. From the South Park hamlet of Jefferson, the majestic pyramid of Mount Guyot grabs the eyes and commands you to walk toward it. And you can! Just take West Jefferson Trail to its northern edge.

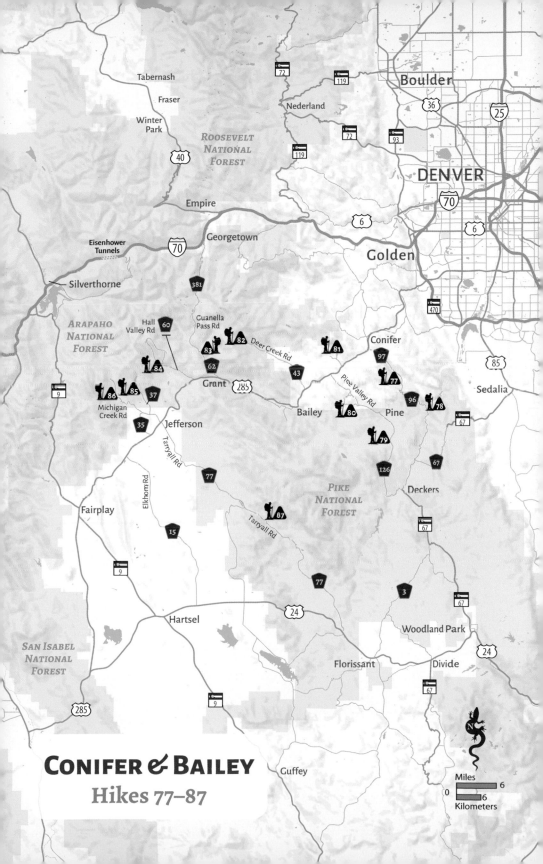

CONIFER & BAILEY
Hikes 77–87

77 Eagle's View Loop

A LOVELY HIKE IN REYNOLDS PARK TAKES YOU THROUGH FOREST TO A RIDGETOP WITH wide-angle views of Pikes Peak, then back down to the site of an historic guest ranch.

At a Glance

DIFFICULTY	🚶🚶	DISTANCE/TIME	5 miles/2.5 hours
TRAIL CONDITIONS	🚶🚶🚶🚶	TRAILHEAD ELEVATION	7,300 feet
		TOTAL HIKING GAIN	900 feet
CHILDREN	🚶🚶🚶	FEATURES	Creeks, forest, mountain views
SCENERY	🚶🚶🚶	BEST SEASON	Fall, winter, spring
PHOTO	🚶🚶🚶	OTHER USERS	Horses, dogs on leash
SOLITUDE	🚶🚶	NOTES	Toilets at west trailhead
PROPERTY	Reynolds Park	JURISDICTION	Jefferson County Open Space

This delightful mountain walk can be done all year round, weather permitting. For the best experience, begin from the east parking lot on **Songbird Trail**, crossing a footbridge and following Casto Creek through pretty meadows for a half mile before joining the main trail network. This level stretch is a great place to get the legs primed for the uphill trek to come. Alternatively, you can park in the west lot and skip Songbird Trail by walking to the junction of Elkhorn and Oxen Draw Trails.

From the end of Songbird Trail, turn left onto **Elkhorn Trail** and make a clockwise loop by keeping left at each trail junction. The trail name changes each time once you leave Elkhorn. You can shorten the loop by turning right at any of the junctions, but if you do you'll miss the expansive views from the ridgetop.

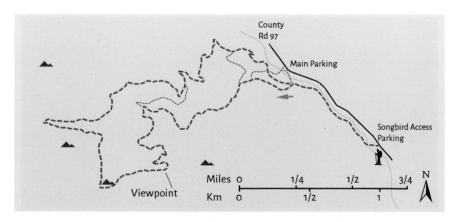

Left: Crossing the North Fork South Platte on Gibson Lake Trail, Hike 84

Songbird Trail

On Elkhorn you'll enter pine woods and begin to ascend. Two branches arrive in quick succession, the second left putting you onto **Oxen Draw Trail**. From here the path steepens through a gully amid tall trees for a half mile before arriving at another fork, where you turn left onto **Eagle's View Trail**. The trees get shorter and the grade mellows as the path traverses uphill and makes some easy switchbacks. The feeling that you are nearing the ridgetop becomes palpable.

When the crest appears ahead between the trees, you may be flooded with anticipation: What kind of view is it going to be?

The reward is a sweeping vista south to Pikes Peak and west across lower lands to ridges of the Continental Divide. The supreme view demands a pause, and it remains with you for an entire half mile as the trail follows the grassy crest before dropping beneath the eastern lip among trees. Listen for the high-pitched screeches of raptors and look for wide wingspans drifting above the forest and along the cliffs ahead.

Save some energy—the trip is not all downhill yet! After making a level excursion into a deep gully, the trail widens onto what was once a road and climbs steeply to regain the ridge. There it levels off for a ways before beginning to de-

Pikes Peak from Eagle's View Trail

Raven's Roost Trail section of Eagle's View loop

scend. On the way down, keep left at each branch of the trail to remain on the outer loop. The path descends into a pretty meadow, where wildflowers abound in spring.

Gone are the cabins of the old Idylease Ranch, a high-end resort opened in 1913 by a Mr. and Mrs. Reynolds. The ranch house still stands; it is now the park operator's residence. The Reynolds pair, former theater people from New York, moved west when Mrs. Reynolds developed tuberculosis (a common Colorado immigration story back then). They purchased this spot along a wagon road that was the primary route for pack trains traveling between Denver and the mining boomtown of Leadville. Conveniently, a narrow-gauge railroad from Denver also passed by just a few miles south, where it made a stop along the South Platte River. This allowed Mr. Reynolds to pick up his fancy guests and ferry them over the hill to his ranch, where they enjoyed horseback riding, formal dining, dances, and a Sunday night wiener roast alongside Casto Creek.

On reaching the west parking lot, the trail network can be a little confusing. Just keep left until you arrive at the familiar junction with **Songbird Trail**, and enjoy a peaceful final stretch along Casto Creek (wieners not included).

From Denver. Take US 6 and I-70 west to CO 470 east. After 5.5 miles, take Exit 5A onto US 285 south and continue 14 miles to Conifer. Turn left on South Foxton Road (CR 97) and continue 5.5 miles. Drive past the first Reynolds Park lot on your right, then turn right to park in the small second lot at the east trailhead. *50 mins.*

78 Colorado Trail from South Platte

FROM A SECLUDED BANK ALONG THE SOUTH PLATTE RIVER, THIS TRAIL CLIMBS TO A wilderness ridge with spectacular views. You feel you're far from Denver, but you're not, and you can easily hike the trail in a morning or an afternoon.

At a Glance

DIFFICULTY	🚶🚶🚶	**DISTANCE/TIME**	5.5 miles/3 hours
TRAIL CONDITIONS	🚶🚶🚶🚶	**TRAILHEAD ELEVATION** **TOTAL HIKING GAIN**	6,100 feet 1,200 feet
CHILDREN	🚶🚶🚶	**FEATURES**	River, forested hillside, views of craggy peaks and snowy mountains
SCENERY	🚶🚶🚶🚶	**BEST SEASON**	Fall, winter, spring
PHOTO	🚶🚶🚶	**OTHER USERS**	Horses, bikes, dogs
SOLITUDE	🚶🚶🚶🚶	**NOTES**	Toilets at trailhead
PROPERTY	Pike National Forest	**JURISDICTION**	U.S. Forest Service

This hike's high solitude rating comes with a qualifier: you have to go in the off-season (late fall through early spring), when it's off the beaten path. In summer it is a thoroughfare for long-haul hikers on the **Colorado Trail** (FS 1776), which runs almost 500 miles from Denver to Durango. This section starts at a charming backwater spot on the South Platte's south fork and climbs to superb views on the well-maintained trail.

From the parking area at the Gudy Gaskill Bridge, head in the other direction to snake up through grassland opposite some impressive red walls. As the trail steepens, dry-country vegetation—prickly pear, yucca, and juniper—gives way to ponderosa forest. The switchbacks here are wonderful, built by hikers, for hikers who want to get places. Soon the views of rocky peaks begin: southwest to Long Scraggy, due west to Raleigh Peak and

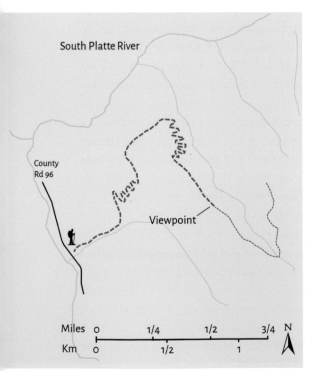

South Platte River

County Rd 96

Viewpoint

Miles 0   1/4   1/2   3/4   N
Km   0   1/2   1

Long Scraggy Peak from the Colorado Trail

Chair Rocks, and in the distance to the northwest, to the pointy Cathedral Spires (a rock climbers' playground). Across the valley is the eastern extent of the 1996 Buffalo Creek Fire, which turned the 20 miles of the Colorado Trail west of here into a barren trudge.

After a dozen switchbacks the trail shifts to the north-facing hillside, which is more densely forested. Enjoy a brief, level respite, and get ready to climb again! If you like to keep track, you can reset your mental switchback counter to 12, and count them down as you climb through the lovely lodgepole pines. On reaching zero you will arrive on the spine of Russell Ridge, where the snowy Mount Evans massif joins the stupendous view. The trail eases along the ridgetop to reach a campfire ring at 2.75 miles.

The pristine valley below, through which the South Fork South Platte River runs, came close to being filled with a reservoir. In the latter 20th century, Denver Water bought up water rights and land in the area and planned a dam that would have flooded the valley upstream for six miles—all the way south to Deckers. In 1990 the Environmental Protection Agency refused to issue a permit for the dam, stating that it would cause unacceptable environmental damage. Thus the beautiful valley remains a backwater, and not lake water.

The view campsite is a lovely stopping point, but you are welcome to go farther. The next 1.5 miles is a pleasant traverse up through the left-hand valley, around a hillside, and into deep forest. The trail feels remote and lonely, but suburban Denver's Roxborough Park and Waterton Canyon are actually less than a day's trek away.

After enjoying all the zigzags back downhill, it's nice to wander out onto the hikers' bridge and admire the beautiful river. The bridge was installed in 1999

Cathedral Spires from the Colorado Trail

and honors intrepid outdoorswoman Gudrun Gaskill, onetime president of the Colorado Mountain Club. For 30 years Gudy, as she was fondly known, led legions of volunteers to construct the Colorado Trail.

Just north of the bridge, the South Platte's main forks converge to flow down the mountains and then northeast through Nebraska. The placid waters on the plains gave the river its name, conferred by French trappers, but up here the Platte is decidedly turbulent. It's still moving fast at the base of the mountains where Cherry Creek joins it, at a spot the Arapaho called *Niinéniiniicíihéhe*. This sonic mouthful was too much for pioneers, who renamed the spot in honor of their territorial governor James Denver, in hopes of having the new settlement made a county seat.

From Denver. Take US 6 and I-70 west to CO 470 east. After 5.5 miles, take Exit 5A onto US 285 south and continue 14 miles to Conifer. Turn left onto South Foxton Road (CR 97), proceed 8.2 miles, then make a sharp left onto CR 96 and continue another 6.4 miles. The South Platte River Trailhead and its parking lot are on the right, shortly after crossing the river. *1 hour, 20 mins.*

South Fork South Platte River, from the Gudy Gaskill Bridge

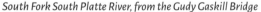

79 Little Scraggy

THIS ROLLING TRAIL DEEP IN PIKE NATIONAL FOREST MAKES FOR A MESMERIZING HIKE along a stretch of the Colorado Trail, and it can be as long or as short as you wish. The silence is awesome and so are some of the rock formations.

At a Glance

DIFFICULTY	🚶🚶	**DISTANCE/TIME**	12.5 miles/5 hours
TRAIL CONDITIONS	🚶🚶🚶🚶	**TRAILHEAD ELEVATION** **TOTAL HIKING GAIN**	7,900 feet 1,000 feet
CHILDREN	🚶🚶	**FEATURES**	Gentle portion of the Colorado Trail, forest, rock formations
SCENERY	🚶🚶🚶	**BEST SEASON**	Fall, winter, spring
PHOTO	🚶🚶🚶	**OTHER USERS**	Bikes, horses, dogs
SOLITUDE	🚶🚶🚶	**NOTES**	Parking fee, toilets at trailhead
PROPERTY	Pike National Forest	**JURISDICTION**	U.S. Forest Service

This forest trail meanders in a gentle up-and-down fashion at elevations mostly ranging in the upper 7,000s. It is a great choice even in midwinter, as it is often mostly free of snow.

Little Scraggy Trail is part of the well-tended **Colorado Trail** (FS 1776), which runs from Denver to Durango, so it is smooth and easy to follow. This section is also popular with mountain bikers, the first 3.4 miles being part of a cycling loop that circles Little Scraggy Peak to the south. These are good reasons to visit this trail in the off-season. Take a personal day on a sunny Wednesday in February and you'll experience some true solitude in the deep woods. Aside from the usual delights of the forest—pine scent, birdsong, encounters with mule deer—many interesting rock formations will come into view along the way.

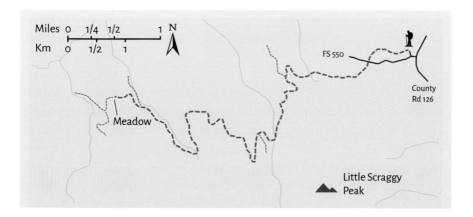

Stone sentinels in the forest along the Little Scraggy Trail

Biker on the Little Scraggy Trail

Within minutes of leaving the trailhead, the first of those rock formations appears on the right: a group of stacked and tilted boulders on a knoll. As you walk, be on the lookout for other weathered protrusions peeking through the trees. Some are towering castles; others look like sentinels standing in the woods—natural versions of the stone statues of Easter Island.

After half a mile, cross the extension of the road you came in on (this is the last time you will see it), and continue down the rolling path through the woods. The valley of Buffalo Creek is visible through the trees to the right. The trail gains the spine of a ridge and opens into a meadow with good views of the snowy humps of western peaks. To the south are the promontories of Little Scraggy, a ridge of rocky summits topping out at about 9,200 feet.

From here the trail hooks south and the Shinglemill Trail branches to the right. Keep left and continue into the valley beneath Little Scraggy's towering granite walls. Soon aspens join the forest mix. After making a hairpin turn to cross a burbling creek, the trail ascends to a shoulder with impressive cliff views. At the crest, the trail forks: right to stay on the **Colorado Trail**, left to the mountain biking loop. At 3.4 miles, this fork makes a good turnaround point, especially if you are hiking with kids.

Alternatively, continue your relaxing walk through the forest for as long as you wish before turning back. Revel in the silence, which of course isn't silence at all, as you learn the longer you are surrounded by it. Listen and you'll hear pine cones falling, birds calling in the distance, trees shifting their branches. There are other vibrations, too—forest frequencies inaudible to the human ear that contribute to the gentle deep-woods hum that surrounds you.

When you reach the junction with Tramway Trail branching right, you've gone 5.75 miles. If you press on another 10 minutes, you'll find a lovely meadow dotted with ponderosas. When you finally turn around, enjoy the views coming back, which tend to be quite different from the ones coming in.

As you drive back toward Denver, take a second look at the burn area on each side of CR 126 south of the town of Buffalo Creek. A wildfire jumped the road here in May 1996, torching a swath of forest a couple miles wide and nearly a dozen miles long. The damage was compounded two months later when a thunderstorm dumped several inches of rain over the burned soil in just a few hours, flooding Buffalo Creek and the South Platte with black sludge. Now you can see how the land is recovering and appreciate, even more, the beautiful forest you walked through, which was spared.

From Denver. Take US 6 and I-70 west to CO 470 east. After 5.5 miles, take Exit 5A onto US 285 south and continue 21 miles to Pine Junction. Turn left onto CR 126 (Pine Valley/Deckers Road), drive 13.6 miles, and turn right on FS 550. Little Scraggy Trailhead and its large parking lot are immediately on the right. *1 hour, 15 mins.*

Cliffs of Little Scraggy's Ridge

80 Pine Valley & Strawberry Jack

A DEVASTATING 2000 FOREST FIRE REVEALED SOME SURPRISING PINK ROCKS ALONG THIS forest trail outside Pine, which also offers an historic ranch and expansive views.

At a Glance

DIFFICULTY	🚶🚶	DISTANCE/TIME	5.5 miles/2.5 hours
TRAIL CONDITIONS	🚶🚶🚶🚶	TRAILHEAD ELEVATION / TOTAL HIKING GAIN	6,800 feet / 1,000 feet
CHILDREN	🚶🚶🚶	FEATURES	Forest and forest burn, views
SCENERY	🚶🚶🚶	BEST SEASON	Fall, winter, spring
PHOTO	🚶🚶🚶	OTHER USERS	Bikes, horses, dogs on leash
SOLITUDE	🚶🚶	NOTES	Toilets at trailhead
PROPERTY	Pine Valley Ranch Park, Pike National Forest	JURISDICTION	Jefferson County Open Space, U.S. Forest Service

This hike begins in a popular county park but exits during the first mile and enters National Forest land. Each additional step brings more solitude. The hike is unusual in that it crosses a major burn area, offering a stark and haunting landscape surrounded by lusher stands of pine forest.

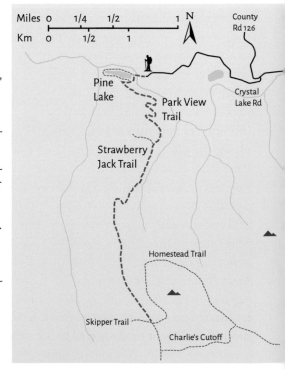

From the trailhead, cross the bridge over the South Platte River and turn left. After a few minutes, branch left onto **Park View Trail** and ascend through woods to reach the crest of a ridge. Continue on the ridge through singed ponderosas past the park boundary at 0.8 miles. The settlement of Pine comes into view, along with some pointy hills to the southeast.

Lumber was once big in this valley. The town got a boost in 1878 when the narrow-gauge railroad came through. Pine was the first fueling stop west of Denver and a base for helper engines that pushed trains over the high passes. Downhill cars carried wood from Pine to timber-starved Denver. After most of the accessible forest was cut, the industry largely died. As you can see, a more recent event has taken out the forest again.

At 1.1 miles, turn left to enter the burn area on **Strawberry Jack Trail** (FS 710). Ahead, the hillsides are covered with charred trunks, some standing and many fallen like pick-up sticks. An interlude of unscathed forest brings some shady respite before you return to the burn on a rocky hill.

The Hi Meadow fire that occurred here in June 2000 was probably ignited by a cigarette, and it burned nearly 11,500 acres.

Park View Trail, Pine Valley Ranch

As you can see, the forest is not regenerating. This trend is seen all along the Front Range in lower-elevation burned pine woods, which might convert to grass and shrubland in the coming decades. Increased temperatures could be playing a role; the average temperature here has increased by 2 degrees Fahrenheit since the 1980s.

The charred landscape takes a little getting used to, but it is otherworldly in its desolate beauty. Rouge rocks appear all around,

Forest burn on Strawberry Jack Trail

exposed by fire. The path climbs through a little valley where the only sound might be distant bird squawks, then reaches a barren crest. Here, ever-expanding views include the Mount Evans massif to the northwest. In nearer view, some of the trailside rocks glow pink.

Red rocks and pointy peaks, Strawberry Jack Trail

Continue uphill toward a distant line of living trees. They look far away, but steady marching brings their shade soon enough. The subsequent forest walk is all the more delightful for its contrast with the burn.

At 2.7 miles you will arrive at a four-way junction. This is a fine rest stop and turnaround point, but if you are up for more forest walking, an easy up-and-down 3.5-mile loop beckons. To take it, turn left on **Homestead Trail** (FS 728) and wrap around a hill. Keep right as Raspberry Ridge Trail joins from the left, and turn right on **Charlie's Cutoff** to complete the loop.

Heading back to Pine Valley Ranch, enjoy the shady woods before returning to the wasteland of pink rocks, toppled trees, and wide views.

Back at the ranch, a few things are worth checking out. One is Baehrden Lodge, a circa-1927 summer mansion built by a tycoon in the style of a German Black Forest manor. The building's pink granite facade is impressive, and tours of the interior are offered on summer weekends. You can also visit the tycoon's stargazing observatory, located on a hill downriver, and a 0.6-mile trail circles lovely Pine Lake, which is good for ice skating in winter.

From Denver. Take US 6 and I-70 west to CO 470 east. After 5.5 miles, take Exit 5A onto US 285 south and continue 21 miles to Pine Junction. Turn left onto CR 126 (Pine Valley Road) and drive 5.8 miles. Turn right onto Crystal Lake Road and Pine Valley Ranch Park. The trailhead and its large parking lots are a mile ahead. *1 hour.*

81 Staunton's Elk Falls

IN 2013, AN AMAZING NEW STATE PARK OPENED OUTSIDE CONIFER. THIS TRAIL TAKES YOU through its expansive grasslands, forests, and stream corridors. You'll see majestic cliffs much of the way, plus, there's a plunging waterfall.

At a Glance

DIFFICULTY	🚶🚶🚶	**DISTANCE/TIME**	11 miles/4.5 hours	
TRAIL CONDITIONS	🚶🚶🚶🚶🚶	**TRAILHEAD ELEVATION** **TOTAL HIKING GAIN**	8,300 feet 1,300 feet	
CHILDREN	🚶🚶🚶	**FEATURES**	Cliffs, rock formations, waterfall, forest, meadow, mountain views	
SCENERY	🚶🚶🚶🚶	**BEST SEASON**	Spring and fall	
PHOTO	🚶🚶🚶🚶	**OTHER USERS**	Bikes, horses, dogs on leash	
SOLITUDE	🚶🚶🚶	**NOTES**	Entrance fee, toilets at trailhead	
PROPERTY	Staunton State Park	**JURISDICTION**	Colorado Parks & Wildlife	

You know you're in for something special when you arrive at this new state park, which opened in 2013. The soaring red cliffs of Black Mountain greet you at the trailhead and continue in a ridge of spires and domes. Begin **Staunton Ranch Trail** by curving closer to these hills, then swing left to follow their base. The striking vertical drop to the west is Lions Head; beyond it is the distant snowy peak of Rosalie.

The easy trail meanders through meadows dotted with ponderosas and

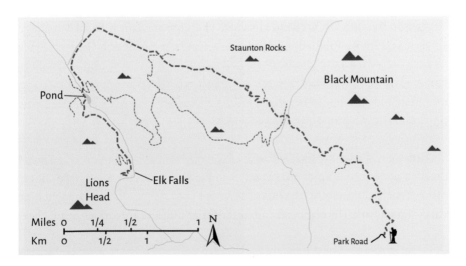

Lions Head with Rosalie Peak in distance, from Staunton State Park trailhead

bleached-trunk aspens. Keep straight at 1.7 miles, where a climbers' trail for Red Wall cuts right. Farther along you will see some cabins downhill to the left; some were part of the old Staunton Ranch. After crossing Black Mountain Creek, continue straight through a four-way junction.

The wavy red cliffs remain with you as the trail reaches Staunton Rocks, another climbing area, and switchbacks that hug their base. If you look behind you, you'll see Pikes Peak in the distance to the south. At 3 miles the trail merges with the old ranch road, and a few minutes later continues through a four-way junction, where its name changes to **Bugling Elk Trail**. You'll surmount a hump in shady pines, and curve down into meadows hemmed by forested hillsides. Look for an old plow sitting in the grass on the right, and farther along, some pretty red rock outcroppings. Elk Creek gurgles beside you, and in the distance Elk Falls Pond appears, often holding a glistening white sheet of ice into April.

A fine spring day in Staunton State Park

A refurbished cabin sits pondside, at 4.4 miles. Once a private sportsmen's retreat, it is now a park facility. Just past it, you'll branch left onto **Chimney Rock Trail** to traverse a steep hillside. Now you are in a gorge; cliffs rise across the valley and others soar right next to you. The trail itself is a marvel here, a beautiful work of stone craftsmanship.

At 5.1 miles, branch left onto **Elk Falls Trail** and you'll soon arrive at a hitching post for horses and bikes. Get ready for the falls! From here it's a quarter mile descent through a gorgeous basin ringed by red-gray cliffs. The waterfall remains hidden until you turn sharply left, and then there it is: spilling nearly 100 feet over smooth rocks. Look the other way and the dramatic cliff of Lions Head appears almost beside you. This is a delightful place to sit a spell and rest weary feet.

On your way back, you can make a worthwhile detour by turning right after the pond onto **Marmot Passage Trail**. The route looks steep but in truth adds only 150 feet of gain (and 1 mile) to your return trip, and delivers an adventurous ridge walk with views of Mount Rosalie to the west and the Tarryalls to the south. After curving up through a notch, the trail drops to a junction with hikers-only **Scout Line Trail**; turn right here to descend a forested hillside to the main trail.

Massive thanks for this wonderful park go to Frances Staunton. Her parents, both doctors, moved to Denver in the early 1900s and fell in love with this area. Her mom "proved up" homestead land here by living on it for part of the year, raising crops and livestock while providing medical services to locals. By the 1920s the Stauntons had expanded their holdings to encompass Black Mountain. An only child, Frances donated the entire 1,720-acre parcel to the state before she died, in 1989, and now it makes up the heart of this lovely state park.

From Denver. Take US 6 and I-70 west to CO 470 east. After 5.5 miles, take Exit 5A onto US 285 south and continue about 19 miles to Shaffers Crossing. Turn right onto South Elk Creek Road (CR 83), proceed 1.3 miles, and turn right to enter Staunton State Park. Proceed through the fee station to the large parking lot at the main trailhead. *55 mins*

Elk Falls, Staunton State Park

82 Pegmatite Points

SO NEAR TO DENVER, YET SUCH A WILDERNESS EXPERIENCE! AFTER A TRANQUIL FOREST walk, you'll make a rigorous climb to a high pass with vistas galore and have, closer by, the strange company of pegmatite points.

At a Glance

DIFFICULTY	🚶🚶🚶🚶	DISTANCE/TIME	9 miles/4.5 hours	
TRAIL CONDITIONS	🚶🚶	TRAILHEAD ELEVATION	9,300 feet	
		TOTAL HIKING GAIN	2,700 feet	
CHILDREN	🚶🚶	FEATURES	Creekside forest, meadow, high pass, rock formations, views	
SCENERY	🚶🚶🚶🚶	BEST SEASON	Early summer	
PHOTO	🚶🚶🚶	OTHER USERS	Horses, dogs on leash	
SOLITUDE	🚶🚶🚶	NOTES	No toilets at trailhead, thunderstorm exposure above tree line	
PROPERTY	Pike National Forest, Mount Evans Wilderness	JURISDICTION	U.S. Forest Service	

This trek to a high saddle between Mount Rosalie and Pegmatite Points begins in shady forest along Deer Creek. If you brought some nagging demands of civilization with you, they're soon lost in the backwoods soundtrack of birdsong and rushing water.

Begin on **Rosalie Trail** (FS 603), where buttery spires of mountain golden banner pop up between tree trunks. Cross Deer Creek and then cross over a tributary, Tanglewood Creek, which remains a tumbling trailside companion for a couple of miles. At 1.2 miles keep straight to continue on **Tanglewood Trail** (FS 636), which enters Mount Evans Wilderness on a steady uphill climb through thick cool forest. The delightful setting helps to distract you from the trail, which becomes a bit of a bugger with all its rocks and crisscrossing tree roots. Soon you'll get your first views of Mount Rosalie through the trees ahead of you. These views repeat and expand, and then a ridge materializes, studded with stone mounds: the Pegmatite Points.

Cross the creek again, and leave it behind to ascend through Douglas fir forest. Broad switchbacks and narrower zigzags take you higher. A reprieve is imminent when you turn alongside some shrubs in an opening in the forest and spy the Points above. The next switchback delivers you into a beautiful hillside meadow. Now the pass is in sight beneath the Points, and as you traverse some seasonal streams, more views open up to the vast forest-clad hillsides behind you.

You still have some climbing to do. Five switchbacks ascend steeply among rocks, flowers, and twisted bristlecone pines to reach the wide grassy saddle at 12,000 feet. To the left, Mount Rosalie displays its dramatic cirque. On the right, the Pegmatite Points rise along the ridge like giant ancient burial mounds.

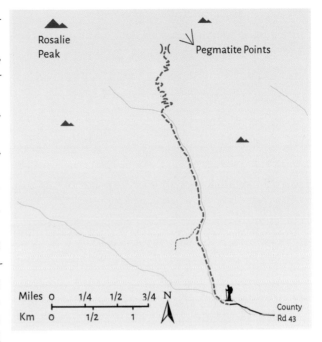

Pegmatite is igneous rock distinguished by visible interlocking crystals ranging from an inch to many feet in length. The name comes from Greek meaning "bound together." Gemstones such as aquamarine and topaz are often found in pegmatite, as are rare-earth metals and lithium. Pegmatite is difficult to analyze, chemically, because getting a representative sample could mean bringing a whole Point to the lab.

Pegmatite Points, from meadow below

Left: Mount Rosalie, from saddle at Pegmatite Points, right: Tanglewood Trail, beneath Pegmatite Points

From the pass you can see the Mount Evans Scenic Byway wrapping Mount Warren and Rogers Peak on its way to the top of Evans, whose summit is obscured here by Rosalie. In fact, Mount Evans was once called Mount Rosalie. Landscape painter Albert Bierstadt gave it that name in the 1860s in honor of the woman he would later marry. In 1895, the Colorado Legislature voted to change the mountain's name to Evans, in honor of aging former territorial governor John Evans. In recent years, activists have lobbied to change the name again, citing Evans's role in the Sand Creek massacre in 1864, in which scores of Native American women, children, and older men were murdered.

To get a good view of Evans, you'd have to climb Rosalie. While straightforward, the ascent through tundra is no pushover: it's another 1.5 miles and 1,600 vertical feet. Only on reaching the top of Rosalie will Evans reveal the cropped-off pyramid that is its summit. Also in view from Rosalie are the Sawtooth, Mount Bierstadt, Longs Peak, the Mosquito Range, and Pikes Peak—a panoply of peaks. It's a well-earned thrill for those who choose to go there, and really fun to skip upon the hills on the way down.

Alternatively, from the pass you can turn right and wander among the pegmatite. If you go far enough along the ridge, Evans will show up from behind Rosalie.

From Denver. Take US 6 and I-70 west to CO 470 east. After 5.5 miles, take Exit 5A onto US 285 south and continue 25 miles, past Pine Junction. Turn right onto CR 43A and veer right as it becomes CR 43, Deer Creek Road. Continue 6.3 miles, bear left to stay on CR 43, and proceed 2.1 miles to the road's end, where there is a large parking lot for Deer Creek Trailhead. The last 0.9 miles is on a decent-quality dirt road. *1 hour, 20 mins.*

83 Abyss

THE HARROWING NAME OF THIS HIKE IS AMUSING. YOU COULDN'T ASK FOR A MORE pleasant, gentle, user-friendly trail. But if you want to step into the Abyss, you can do it.

At a Glance

DIFFICULTY	🚶🚶🚶🚶	DISTANCE/TIME	12.5 miles/5 hours
TRAIL CONDITIONS	🚶🚶🚶🚶	TRAILHEAD ELEVATION TOTAL HIKING GAIN	9,600 feet 1,500 feet
CHILDREN	🚶🚶	FEATURES	Forest, gentle creekside walk, mountain views, alpine lake
SCENERY	🚶🚶🚶🚶	BEST SEASON	Early summer and fall
PHOTO	🚶🚶🚶🚶	OTHER USERS	Horses, dogs on leash
SOLITUDE	🚶🚶🚶🚶	NOTES	Toilets at nearby Burning Bear Campground
PROPERTY	Mount Evans Wilderness	JURISDICTION	U.S. Forest Service

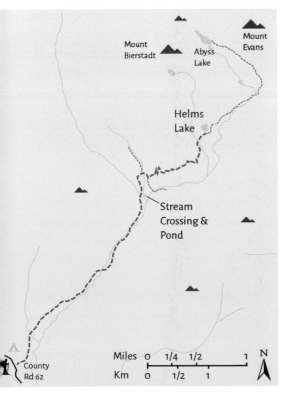

What sounds like a hike down through the Gates of Hell is really a long and gentle forest walk that rises into a lovely alpine zone. Because the grade is modest, the miles seem to melt beneath your feet and it is easy to do a lot of them. The farther you go the more varied the scenery becomes, and it does not disappoint.

After you fill out the card to enter Mount Evans Wilderness, follow **Abyss Trail** (FS 602) through an aspen grove. The rockiness mellows to smooth dirt as the trail meanders through lodgepole pines. Scott Gomer Creek, named for a logger, rushes to the right, making the final

Geneva Mountain in September, from Abyss Trail

leg of its journey from Mount Bierstadt to Geneva Creek. Soon the lower flanks of Bierstadt peer over treetops.

At 2.25 miles, cross the creek and continue along its southern bank. Here the aspens really take over, filling the valley and covering the hillsides. At 3.25 miles, cross to the north side and continue in this lovely setting, where peaks are the backdrop and flowing water the soundtrack. Soon you will arrive at a meadow and pond with more views of lower Bierstadt. At 4 miles, this is a decent turnaround point, but if your motor is still running, press onward for another two miles and enjoy many rewards.

In the next mile Rosalie Trail (FS 603) joins from the left and departs to the right, in opposite order from what is shown on some maps. Now it's time for some real uphill walking. In case you'd forgotten what a switchback looks like, several sturdy ones ascend here with views northward toward Guanella Pass and glimpses southeast toward the Mosquito Range. The trail eases over a shoulder but stays on a decent upslope as it approaches the tree line. You'll sense a lake nestled beneath high peaks and—

Abyss Trail crossing of Scott Gomer Creek

The Abyss

sure enough—at just over 6 miles you'll arrive on the shores of Helms Lake. Due north is Bierstadt's summit. An even more dramatic view appears to the east, where a cliff shoulder of Mount Evans looms beyond the drop-off of Bierstadt, and a deep cut of earth wraps into unseen territory between them. This is the Abyss. You are peering into it.

This area received special attention long before Mount Evans became a designated Wilderness Area. In 1956, the Abyss and much of its fork of Scott Gomer Creek were set aside as a Scenic Area under the U Regulations of 1939. These precursors to the Wilderness Act of 1980 marked a shift in the administration of certain National Forest lands, both in tone and practice. What had been called Primitive Areas were now deemed Wilderness and Wild Areas. No roads were permitted; no commercial logging, hotels, or resorts either. Most rights of public access remained, including—curiously—mineral prospecting, as well as some grandfathered-in grazing.

Twenty-five years later came the Wilderness Act, with its poetic definition of wilderness as "an area where the earth and its community of life are untrammeled by man, where man himself is a visitor who does not remain." In 1986 the law was reinterpreted to mean "untrammeled by man riding a bicycle," to much ongoing opposition. For this reason the long and gentle Abyss Trail is off-limits to mountain bikers.

If you want to enter the Abyss, you should do it. Less than two more miles and a thousand vertical feet deliver you to the shores of Abyss Lake, in the thrilling cut between two fourteeners. The epic scale of this now 17-mile day is tempered by the pleasure of its long, mellow walk back.

From Denver. Take US 6 and I-70 west to CO 470 east. After 5.5 miles, take Exit 5A onto US 285 south and continue 39 miles west to Grant. Turn right onto CR 62 (Guanella Pass Road/Geneva Road) and continue 5.4 miles to the parking area for Abyss Trailhead, on the right. *1 hour, 20 mins.*

84 Gibson Lake

THIS SWEET AND LIGHTLY VISITED HIGH TARN OUTSIDE GRANT IS TUCKED BENEATH PEAKS of the Continental Divide. It's a beautiful spot for a picnic among summer wildflowers.

At a Glance

DIFFICULTY	👤👤👤	**DISTANCE/TIME**	8 miles/3.5 hours
TRAIL CONDITIONS	👤👤👤	**TRAILHEAD ELEVATION** **TOTAL HIKING GAIN**	9,900 feet 2,000 feet
CHILDREN	👤👤👤	**FEATURES**	Forest, streams, tundra, alpine lakes, peak views
SCENERY	👤👤👤👤	**BEST SEASON**	Summer
PHOTO	👤👤👤👤	**OTHER USERS**	Bikes on portion, horses, dogs
SOLITUDE	👤👤👤👤	**NOTES**	Toilets at Hall Valley Campground near trailhead, thunderstorm exposure above tree line
PROPERTY	Pike National Forest	**JURISDICTION**	U.S. Forest Service

Begin this delightful hike by walking toward Hall Valley Campground from the parking area and turning right on **Forest Road 126**, a four wheel drive road. Any question about the feasibility of continuing in a passenger car is soon answered by Handcart Creek, which makes a deep cut across the road. Cross on a footbridge and continue uphill amid aspens and mountain golden banner, with the headwaters of the North Fork South Platte River rushing below to the left. The trees shift to evergreens before you reach Gibson Lake Trailhead, on the left

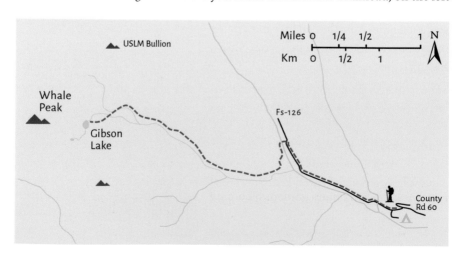

at 1.3 miles. Turn left here onto **Gibson Lake Trail** (FS 633).

You'll descend to cross the river and traverse up-left through forest. It's a steady ascent on a good-quality trail, one that feels rather old. After curving right into the next valley, the trail broadens into something more like a wagon road. Look carefully and you'll spot an aged metal trail sign nailed to a tree. The path alternates between rocky and smooth stretches as it heads up-valley through forest alongside a tributary of the Platte called Lake Fork. Higher slopes appear through the branches, displaying the tree line.

You feel you're getting close to the lake when the trail opens into shrubland and

Crossing the North Fork South Platte on Gibson Lake Trail

rocky meadows, but don't be fooled. The lake is tucked into a higher pocket reached by continuing through a stretch of tundra crisscrossed by streams. On fording a significant rivulet, you'll see a large pile of orange mine tailings. Now the aged feel of the trail makes sense: this was a miners' route. Hall Valley mines were active in the 1870s, producing a little gold and much silver. Several mines were worked by the Hall Valley Mining Company, which had a settlement at the spot where you parked that included saloons, a smelter, and a post office.

The miners were pushing the limits. Almost all of Colorado's mineral wealth is concentrated in a narrow band stretching some 300 miles from the San Juan mountains in southwest Colorado to the Front Range foothills just northwest of Boulder. The Continental Divide, which runs above Gibson Lake, demarcates the southeastern fringe of this belt. Silver mining really had its heyday on the other side of the Divide, in the Snake River and Argentine districts.

Traverse left to approach the lake, which remains hidden in tundra gardens blooming

Tundra flowers and willows on approach to Gibson Lake

Gibson Lake and Whale Peak

with mountain avens. These flowers have creamy white petals and yellow centers that look like egg yolks. When the lake finally appears, it sparkles like a precious jewel beneath the cliffs and green slopes of Whale Peak. This 13,078-foot point on the Divide was likely named for the Whale Mine, located one valley north. It's unclear how the mine got its name, but certain its diggers were hoping for a whale of a lode.

Looking down at the orange tailings you passed, you can see they are not one of a kind. In the gulch above them are several more scars in the mountainside, along with zigzags of old cart roads, culminating in a point listed on maps as "USLM Bullion" (USLM is a surveying acronym meaning "U.S. Land Marker"). Obviously this was once a heavily mined hillside.

Not anymore! With industrial activity gone, this gorgeous place has returned to its primordial role as a haven for wildlife, wandering, lounging, and possibly picnicking. For a great stroll, continue around the south shore of Gibson Lake and follow the inlet waterfalls to a higher, smaller, unnamed tarn. You may call it whatever you wish.

From Denver. Take US 6 and I-70 west to CO 470 east. After 5.5 miles, take Exit 5A onto US 285 south and continue 42 miles. Turn right onto CR 60 (Hall Valley Road). Follow this good dirt road for 5 miles, to the forks for Hall Valley Campground and Webster Pass. Parking is in a small area at the fork. The hike begins down the left fork. *1 hour, 30 mins.*

85 West Jefferson

THIS GENTLE TREK ASCENDS THROUGH FOREST AND MEADOW TO AN HISTORIC PASS ON the Continental Divide, where eager prospectors once passed through on their way to the next valley, gold pans in hand.

At a Glance

DIFFICULTY	🚶🚶🚶	DISTANCE/TIME	10.5 miles/4.5 hours	
TRAIL CONDITIONS	🚶🚶🚶	TRAILHEAD ELEVATION TOTAL HIKING GAIN	10,000 feet 1,800 feet	
CHILDREN	🚶🚶	FEATURES	Creekside forest, alpine meadow, mountain views, high tundra pass	
SCENERY	🚶🚶🚶	BEST SEASON	Summer	
PHOTO	🚶🚶🚶	OTHER USERS	Bikes, horses, dogs on leash	
SOLITUDE	🚶🚶🚶	NOTES	Access closed November to late May, entrance fee, toilets at campground near trailhead, thunderstorm exposure above tree line	
PROPERTY	Jefferson Lake Recreation Area, Pike National Forest	JURISDICTION	U.S. Forest Service	

To begin, enter the campground and find the sign for **West Jefferson Trail** (FS 643) on the right. The trail leads you through cool forest along Jefferson Creek, crossing after a mile to continue above its willow bottoms.

The creek was named in honor of the third president of the United States, when prospectors in 1859 sought to carve out a territory independent from Kan-

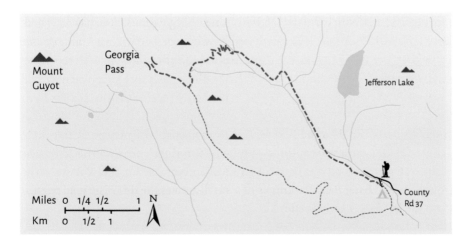

Continental Divide from West Jefferson Trail

sas to better administer to their needs. "Jefferson Territory" operated from its base at the foot of the Rockies for 16 months without federal authorization, electing officials and passing laws. In 1861, Congress put an end to it, organizing the Territory of Colorado under a different administration. The nearby town of Jefferson, a onetime stage and rail stop, keeps the name.

Ahead in the distance rises a graceful ridge of the Continental Divide. Cross back over the main creek, curve left in quiet woods, and prepare to climb. Some of the dozen or so switchbacks are long traverses, others are short zigzags; all have a modest grade. At about the 4-mile point, you'll reach a grassy shoulder with views down to South Park and up to a rim of the Divide. As you continue through meadow, you'll swoop beneath snowfields clinging inside this rim, which will be mostly reddish scree by late summer as the snow recedes.

The next saddle proves to be a vast park. Most striking is the handsome, soaring pyramid of Mount Guyot which may have caught your eye from the lowlands near Jefferson. It doesn't look anything like a "guyot," which is an underwater volcano with a flat top. Both the ocean landform and this peak were named for Arnold Henri Guyot, a Swiss-born geologist, geographer, and longtime professor at Princeton University. Guyot helped establish the scientific methods of the Weather Bureau of the United States, which was the precursor

Mount Guyot from the Colorado Trail

of the National Weather Service. He also staunchly rejected the theory of evolution.

In the park, the trail joins the **Colorado Trail** (FS 1776) coming up from the east. At about 5 miles, this is a good turnaround point, but Georgia Pass beckons and is less than half a mile away. By now some mountain bikers have probably ridden up the Colorado Trail and continued on through the moor-like landscape toward the pass. As you follow them, you get shifting views of Mount Guyot and its dramatic, knife-edge south ridge—stark contrasts to the planar tundra below.

Hiking West Jefferson

From Georgia Pass the view is northwest into the Swan River Valley, home to Colorado's earliest and richest gold-panning sites. Some prospectors from Georgia came over this pass in 1859 and struck in a side gulch several miles down, which they named Georgia Gulch. There the boomtown of Parkville sprang up. For a couple of years it was the biggest settlement in Summit County, bigger than Breckenridge. The gold flakes quickly played out, as tended to happen, but not before several million dollars were extracted. By the 1880s, soon-to-be abandoned Parkville became buried under mounds of tailings as latecomers dredged and hydraulically blasted the creek gravel for remaining flecks.

You can make a loop trip by returning via the Colorado Trail. This path is popular with mountain bikers, but less interesting for hikers since it is a dry walk in the woods with no stream or other notable features. It also makes the trip half a mile longer than the return along lovely Jefferson Creek.

From Denver. Take US 6 and I-70 west to CO 470 east. After 5.5 miles, take Exit 5A onto US 285 south and continue 45 miles, over Kenosha Pass, to Jefferson. Turn right onto CR 35, proceed 1.8 miles, then make another right onto CR 37, a dirt road. Continue 3.7 miles, through the Jefferson Lake Recreation Area fee station, to the small hikers' parking lot located at the entrance to Jefferson Creek Campground. *1 hour, 50 mins.*

86 French Pass

THIS SWEET TRAIL MEANDERS UP THROUGH FOREST AND MEADOW BENEATH GRACEFUL peaks in a little-traveled section of the Continental Divide outside Jefferson. There's plenty of solitude here, but you might have moose for company.

At a Glance

DIFFICULTY	🚶🚶🚶	DISTANCE/TIME	7 miles/3 hours
TRAIL CONDITIONS	🚶🚶🚶	TRAILHEAD ELEVATION / TOTAL HIKING GAIN	10,500 feet / 1,600 feet
CHILDREN	🚶🚶🚶🚶	FEATURES	Gentle grade, forest, alpine meadow and shrubs, high mountain pass, mountain views
SCENERY	🚶🚶🚶🚶	BEST SEASON	Summer
PHOTO	🚶🚶🚶🚶	OTHER USERS	Bikes, horses, dogs
SOLITUDE	🚶🚶🚶🚶	NOTES	No toilets at trailhead, thunderstorm exposure above tree line
PROPERTY	Pike National Forest	JURISDICTION	U.S. Forest Service

A discreetly placed numbered signpost marks the start of **French Pass Trail** (FS 651), giving no hint of the splendors to come. Begin on an old wagon road curving west on the south side of French Creek. This was one of the early routes used by prospectors going to Breckenridge, and before that, a favorite path of a trapper now known to us mainly by his first name, Pierre. According to lore, "French Pete" worked both sides of the Continental Divide, and this was one of his favorite portals for getting back and forth.

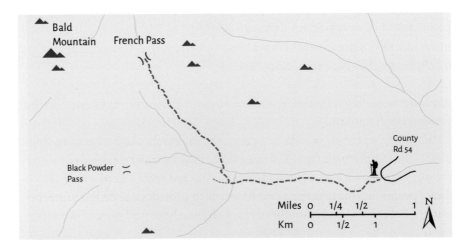

The trail enters a long flower-filled meadow along the creek. A graceful ridge of the Divide rises ahead in the distance. The grade remains gentle as the trail skirts a south talus slope and continues in lush conifer forest. Be on the lookout here for moose. These are big animals, much taller than kids in your party and probably taller than you, but they are often unseen in the foliage, chewing on twigs. It's important to keep your dog leashed, as moose don't distinguish between dogs and wolves, their onetime predators, and your canine can arouse their fight-or-flight instincts. Moose were unknown in Colorado until a few decades ago, save for a few that wandered in from Wyoming and didn't stay. Between 1978 and 1991 several score were introduced, mostly near North Park, and they have traveled and multiplied. The state's moose population now stands at several thousand, and hunting is used to control their numbers.

Shrub walk, French Pass Trail

The trail curves north in the valley among flowers, trees, and looming hills. Ahead, colorful mountainsides swoop to the pass. The designation for this section of the Rockies is a bit ambiguous: not the Front Range, and not yet the

Bald Mountain's stone bowl, from French Pass Trail

Mosquito Range. Here the Continental Divide jogs west before resuming its usual north-south orientation; consequently, French Pass has the distinction of crossing north to south.

At 2 miles the trail veers unexpectedly to the right off the old roadbed and drops to cross the creek. Resume traveling up-valley on the other side where, aside from one steep hump of meadow, all remains gentle—and pretty! Across the valley is Black Powder (meaning *gun*powder) Pass, which provides a shorter but steeper route to Breckenridge. Its southern ridge rises to beautiful Boreas Mountain, which guards the unseen valley and pass next door, the route of an old railroad.

Above timberline, the trail cuts through seemingly manicured expanses of shrubby, waist-high willows. In grassy patches between them, spires of orange Indian paintbrush light up. Ahead, a two-lobed snowfield hangs above the pass. Bald Mountain soars left of it, displaying a massive gouged stone bowl etched with magnificent horizontal striation marks.

As you make the final meander to the pass, you might get an energy boost from the beauty all around you, and even young feet will have little trouble with the grade. The wide grassy saddle arrives at 3.5 miles and just over 12,000 feet. On the other side is French Gulch, where civilization appears in the distance.

Both sides of this pass look fine for train passage. Why did the railroad choose Boreas Pass, to the south, instead?

It all came down to elevation. In 1879, when the tracks reached South Park, both passes already had toll roads. French Pass was shorter in terms of miles, but "Breckenridge Pass," as it was then called, was 565 feet lower. Even so, it was feat of 19th-century engineering to get the narrow-gauge over "the notch" which a railroad honcho renamed Boreas Pass, in honor of the Greek god of the the north wind and bringer of winter.

From Denver. Take US 6 and I-70 west to CO 470 east. After 5.5 miles, take Exit 5A onto US 285 south and continue 45 miles, over Kenosha Pass, to Jefferson. Turn right onto CR 35. Continue 2.8 miles on what becomes a dirt road, then bear right onto CR 54 (Michigan Creek Road). Proceed 2.5 miles and veer left to stay on CR 54. Continue 3 miles on a curvy but decent dirt road to an inconspicuous "651" trail marker on the left, just before a creek; there is a parking area on the right. *2 hours.*

French Pass Trail

87 Bison Pass

A BRACING CLIMB TO A PASS AND A HIGH PARK IS HUGELY REWARDED WITH SWEEPING views of the Continental Divide and close-ups of the highest peak in the Tarryalls.

At a Glance

DIFFICULTY	🚶🚶🚶🚶	**DISTANCE/TIME**	8 miles/4 hours
TRAIL CONDITIONS	🚶🚶🚶	**TRAILHEAD ELEVATION** / **TOTAL HIKING GAIN**	8,800 feet / 2,500 feet
CHILDREN	🚶🚶	**FEATURES**	Forest climb to pass, views of the Continental Divide, rock pinnacles
SCENERY	🚶🚶🚶🚶	**BEST SEASON**	Early summer
PHOTO	🚶🚶🚶🚶	**OTHER USERS**	Horses, dogs on leash
SOLITUDE	🚶🚶🚶🚶	**NOTES**	No toilets at trailhead
PROPERTY	Pike National Forest, Lost Creek Wilderness	**JURISDICTION**	U.S. Forest Service

Begin this thrilling hike in the Tarryall Mountains on **Ute Creek Trail** (FS 629) by crossing the peaceful creek for which the mountains are named. Pass through streamside meadows and skirt left of a willow bottom to reach a grassy saddle, then veer left across a ponderosa hillside into the valley of Ute Creek. The path

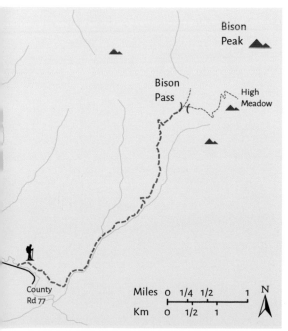

continues alongside the creek's gurgling water, enters Lost Creek Wilderness, and crosses the creek to slant up into aspen meadows. The grade steepens toward the mountainside. After one switchback, it's a stiff uphill traverse. Across the valley, the thickly forested hillside is crowned by a lower outcrop of Bison Peak, the highest in the Tarryalls.

The name Tarryall goes back to South Park's gold rush days. Rumors had circulated for decades of "color" in the upper streams of Valle Salado, which is what South Park was then called,

Dusky grouse along the Bison Pass Trail

Bison Peak from meadow above Bison Pass

but this vast high-altitude grassland was important territory to Ute Indians and therefore dangerous to enter. In 1859 a group of prospectors "tarried" on this creek's upper reaches and found gold fragments reportedly the size of watermelon seeds. Within a year, thousands more came, and many weighing scales were brought out and "tared" (zeroed). The Tarryall Diggings were nicknamed "Grab-all," because the earliest arrivals claimed more land than they could reasonably work. A nearby mining settlement was soon established called Fairplay, named in hopes of fairer competition.

At about 3 miles, the trail gains a wooded shoulder and zigzags up it. Look for dusky grouse creeping through the trees, and listen for heavy flapping wings if one is startled. You'll get your first views of the Continental Divide to the west from here, and there are more to come. After a few switchbacks you might start to wonder where the pass is. Arrival is imminent when you cross the shoulder on a long right-hand traverse, with Bison Peak's lower buttresses looming above you.

Soon you'll come to a tree-filled pass beneath rock pinnacles. This is the 4-mile mark and a good place to rest or turn around, but if you can push yourself one more mile, the rewards are stupendous. To go for it, turn right on **Brookside McCurdy Trail** (FS 607) and proceed up a reasonable grade toward the tree line. You'll traverse beneath a hunk of Bison granite and enjoy a 180-degree view of the Continental Divide. Soon Mount Evans joins the mix to make it 220 degrees. On the ridgetop is a gorgeous tundra meadow, flat and large enough to accommodate a dozen soccer fields. Above are the awesome rock spires of Bison Peak, extending to 12,431 feet. This range has some of the most jagged rocks in the Rockies, and Bison is their epicenter.

On the opposite, unseen side of the peak flows Lost Creek, for which the wilderness area is named. This perennial stream disappears and reappears nine times over its granite-bed course, an atypical drainage pattern that has created extensive underground caves. A section of Lost Creek was designated a Scenic Area and National Natural Landmark in the 1960s. The much larger wilderness area was established in 1980.

While you're in the neighborhood, consider a visit to **Lizard Rock**. The trailhead is 8 miles south on CR 77. It's only 4 miles round-trip to a view of what appears to be a mutant triceratops leaping out of the hillside in crazy bas-relief. Is the creature smiling or is he biting? Depends on your point of view.

From Denver. Take US 6 and I-70 west to CO 470 east. After 5.5 miles, take Exit 5A onto US 285 south and continue 45 miles, over Kenosha Pass, to Jefferson. Turn left onto CR 77 (Tarryall Road) and proceed 20.6 miles to the parking area for Ute Creek Trailhead, on the left. *2 hours.*

Continental Divide from meadow above Bison Pass

South of
Denver

Hike beneath a soaring mountain sentinel

As you head south from Denver, it's impossible to ignore Pikes Peak. This 14,115-foot behemoth above Colorado Springs truly dominates the southern Front Range. This book doesn't hike to the top of Pikes (you can get there on an intense toll road in your car), but it does let you in on a secret: the trail to Oil Creek Tunnel, tucked up high on the peak's north face. Two hikes, The Crags and Pancake Rocks, reach rock formations on its western flanks, and another, Barr Trail, offers a winter workout of northeastern switchbacks. On the peak's south side, you can take the Mount Rosa Challenge: the pink-rocked summit is this book's most rigorous hike.

West of Pikes you'll find lower forested woodlands and two delightful preserves for wandering. Among Mueller State Park's many well-maintained trails is the lovely hike to the mirror of Rock Pond. Next door, the trails in Dome Rock State Wildlife Area are less visited and a little rougher, as they are designed to give bighorn sheep their space. Both preserves light up gold when their aspens turn around the first week of October.

Colorado Springs' Red Rock Canyon offers rock formations just as delightful as its more famous neighbor, the Garden of the Gods. Nearer to Denver are some wonderful walks for all ages. Devil's Head is eye candy with a working fire lookout, and Mount Herman and Spruce Mountain offer easy year-round tromping with a surprising wilderness vibe next to the I-25 corridor. For a beautiful canyon with a haunting story, head into the prairie uplands of Castlewood. Wherever you go, Pikes Peak will be your steady and majestic companion.

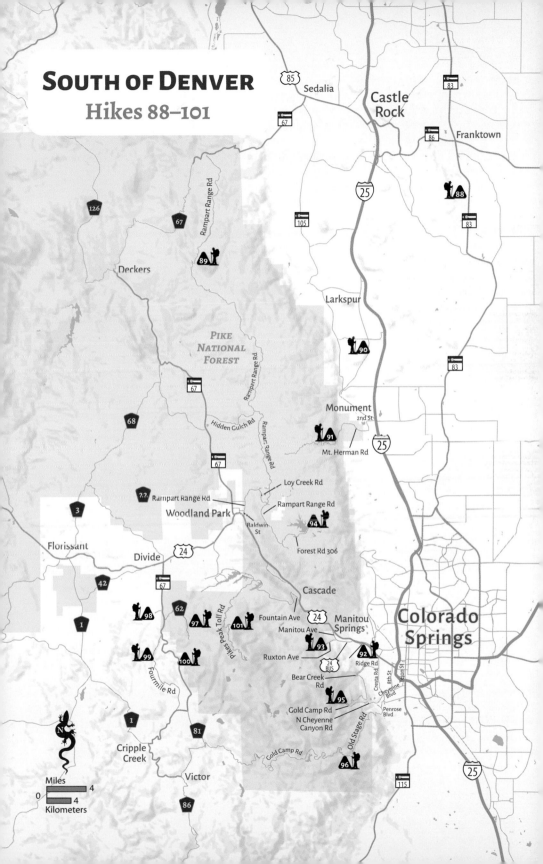

SOUTH OF DENVER
Hikes 88–101

Devils Head Fire Lookout, Hike 89

88 Castlewood Canyon

A BEAUTIFUL CANYON TRAIL LEADS PAST AN EERIE ANOMALY: THE GREEN BOWL OF A FORMER reservoir and the remains of a busted dam whose floodwaters reached Denver. A lovely return walk along the canyon rim invites you to contemplate mankind's mistakes.

At a Glance

DIFFICULTY	👤👤	**DISTANCE/TIME**	6.5 miles/2.5 hours
TRAIL CONDITIONS	👤👤👤👤	**TRAILHEAD ELEVATION** **TOTAL HIKING GAIN**	6,200 feet 600 feet
CHILDREN	👤👤👤👤	**FEATURES**	Canyon, creek, foliage, former reservoir and ruins of 1890s dam
SCENERY	👤👤👤	**BEST SEASON**	All year
PHOTO	👤👤👤👤	**OTHER USERS**	Dogs on leash
SOLITUDE	👤👤	**NOTES**	Entrance fee, toilets at trailhead
PROPERTY	Castlewood Canyon State Park	**JURISDICTION**	Colorado Parks & Wildlife

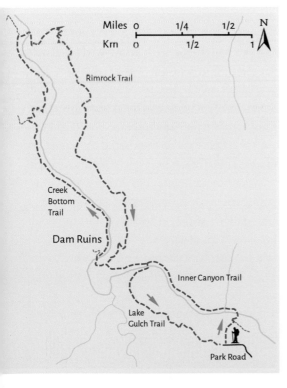

Take the paved **K Trail Access** path to start this hike, which makes a figure eight through the park. Scenery comes quickly as you join the **Inner Canyon Trail** and drop 150 feet to cross Cherry Creek amid well-watered Gambel oaks. Note that the stream flows *toward* the mountains rather than away. This is plains water, originating on a high eastern plateau and flowing 50-odd miles to meet the South Platte in downtown Denver. The creek is named for the abundant chokecherry shrubs that once lined its banks. Their bitter-sour red berries, which turn near-black when ripe, were important to Native American diets.

Castlewood Canyon

The trail continues up and down and across boardwalks over streamlets. Above you rise bulbous canyon walls, dynamite in fall colors. As you enter a wider valley, keep right at a junction to continue along the creek's northern bank. Ahead is a large bowled field which, once you're in it, might feel like the belly of a former reservoir. Such suspicions are confirmed when the path bends right and a ruined dam comes into view.

Turn left onto **Creek Bottom Trail** and cross the stream to reach the south remnant of the dam. Staring at its cross section, imagining it giving way, can be a hair-raising experience. Also impressive is the white gash in the downstream valley, made when the torrent of floodwater crashed through the canyon.

Citizens became concerned about the dam in 1890, when it began to leak soon after it was built. By 1900, large holes had developed at its base and scarcely any water could be contained for irrigation. But a succession of owners, many of whom were land speculators, made repairs, and the reservoir was full to brimming when the dam broke on a rainy August night in 1933. Once the water roared through the canyon and fanned out, it took several hours to reach Denver, where about 5,000 people living in low-lying areas were able to get out of the way. Approximately 1.5 billion gallons of mucky water containing boulders, logs, farm animals, and other debris knocked down six bridges and surged through downtown. Union Station received six inches; a log drifted into its waiting room.

The flood killed two people and created a horrible mess, but it was not as damaging as an 1864 flash

Cherry Creek in Castlewood Canyon

flood that killed about 20 folks. At that time, the new settlement of Denver was set in the streambed of Cherry Creek, contrary to the advice of local Arapaho Indians.

At 1.3 miles, the dam site is a good turnaround point for small hikers. Others can continue along Creek Bottom Trail, where the onward canyon appears well recovered from the flood—until you reach another scoured section with some pretty waterfalls. Continue farther and then branch right on **Rimrock Trail** to recross the creek and ascend the north canyon wall. At the top, the trail curves southeast to follow the rim back toward the trailhead. Here you'll have sweeping views of the Rockies from Pikes Peak to Longs, but the most exciting sight is the sheer drop-off of the canyon, in sustained view as you walk the easy trail along its rim.

The eerie feeling returns as you again approach the dam site, this time peering through its ruptured opening to the empty green bowl beyond. The trail descends to the dam's northern remnant, where you can take some haunting photos of the gap between the broken buttresses.

On reaching the canyon floor, branch right onto **Lake Gulch Trail** to cross Cherry Creek over a series of large boulders, and finish the figure eight in the oak fringes along the former reservoir's shoreline.

From Denver. Take I-25 south to Exit 184, in Castle Rock, then drive east on Founders Parkway (CO 86) for 9.2 miles. Turn right onto CO 83 and drive south 5 miles. Turn right into Castlewood Canyon State Park and proceed through the fee station to the large Canyon Point parking lot. *1 hour.*

Castlewood Dam, looking north to south

89 Devil's Head Lookout

TAKE AN EASY HIKE TO THE HIGHEST POINT IN THE RAMPART RANGE. A DIZZYING STAIRCASE takes you to an historic fire lookout that is still in operation and has unimpeded views over a huge swath of Pike National Forest.

At a Glance

DIFFICULTY	🚶	DISTANCE/TIME	3 miles/1.5 hours
TRAIL CONDITIONS	🚶🚶🚶🚶🚶	TRAILHEAD ELEVATION TOTAL HIKING GAIN	8,800 feet 900 feet
CHILDREN	🚶🚶🚶🚶🚶	FEATURES	Historic fire lookout, 360-degree views, rock formations
SCENERY	🚶🚶🚶🚶	BEST SEASON	Spring and fall
PHOTO	🚶🚶🚶🚶	OTHER USERS	Horses, dogs on leash
SOLITUDE	🚶	NOTES	10-mile drive on dirt road, access road closed Dec. 1 to about April 1; toilets at trailhead campground and near summit; stairway at top can be slippery
PROPERTY	Pike National Forest	JURISDICTION	U.S Forest Service

More than 10,000 people visit this viewpoint each summer, and for good reason. But do yourself a favor and go in spring or fall, when it is less crowded, and try to avoid weekends. You'll probably have the sunrise to yourself on a Tuesday morning in May. Mornings are great for lighting effects, and for the unlikelihood of *lightning* effects.

The trail, **Forest Trail 611**, begins beneath some towering castle-like rocks and soon enters a section of upturned trees, the result of an EF1-rated tornado that touched down here in 2015 (EF0 means "little or no damage"; EF5 means "train cars thrown a mile"). Huge uprooted aspens give way to gorgeous ones

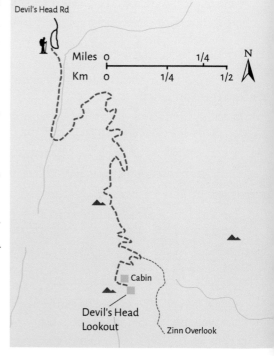

Devil's Head Observatory

still standing before the trail continues on through fir and spruce amid some jutting granite cliffs. Unlike the washboard road you came in on, this is a top-rated trail. Built in 1951 using portions of two earlier trails, it had to accommodate pack mules and a Forest Service tractor, hence the remnants of pavement you still see in places. Never steep, the trail reaches a notch at the halfway point and continues zigzagging up a ridge, with impressive stone castles and cliffs for company the whole way.

Pass through a slot in the rocks to arrive at a high little basin called Devil's Half Acre. A homey 1950s wood cabin sits on the left: the fire lookout's residence. Above, a metal stairway viaduct vaults to a watchtower perched on the apex of the granite summit. With luck, you won't have to wait your turn to climb 143 dizzying steps to the outfitted hut, where views stretch forever in every direction.

Rustic but in excellent shape, the hut is a cozy place with a wood-burning stove, instruments, and walls covered in historical photos and memorabilia. The first fire-finding equipment was installed in the open air here in 1912: just a simple instrument bolted to a rock. If a storm threatened, the lookouts could huddle in a nearby log hut. An enclosed observatory was built in 1919 and was replaced by the current hut in 1951.

Kids and adults alike will enjoy a visit inside and will be welcomed by the lookout if one is on duty. The station's centerpiece is an Osborne Firefinder, which was installed along with the 1951 hut and is still in use. The lookout scans the landscape and, when smoke is spotted, uses the instrument's rifle-like sight to pinpoint the location on a circular map. Another key piece of equipment is a stool with glass boots, where the lookout perches during lightning storms. For much of the previ-

A misty, moisty morning on Devil's Head

ous century, being a fire lookout was an important job; at one point, more than 8,000 people watched for forest fires in the U.S. In the 1970s it became more cost-effective to monitor forests by satellite and airplane, and lookout numbers dwindled. This observatory is one of few still in operation on Forest Service property; in 2017 the lookout here spotted three fires, and in 2016 he spotted seven.

When seen from the southwest, Devil's Head's summit can resemble a fiendish horned face gazing upward. From the top, many other faces and forms appear in the bizarre cliffs along its ridges. If a game of Find the Landmark is in order, Pikes Peak should be off-limits—it's too obvious!

On the way back down the trail you can take a quarter-mile side trip to **Zinn Overlook**. The woodsy path descends 120 feet to more rock formations, where it is fun to scramble around.

From Denver. Take I-25 south to Exit 207B, then continue south on US 85 (Santa Fe Drive) about 20 miles to Sedalia. Turn right onto CO 67 (Manhart Avenue). Proceed west 10 miles and turn left onto Rampart Range Road. Follow this dirt road for 9 miles. Veer left at a junction to continue 0.5 miles to the parking lot for Devil's Head Lookout. *1 hour, 30 mins.*

Pikes Peak in distance, from Devil's Head

90   Spruce Mountain

THIS TRANQUIL MESA-TOP OPEN SPACE IS RIGHT OFF I-25, YET IT SOMETIMES FEELS LIKE A forgotten corner of the prairie. An easy walk affords grand views of grassland, mesas and buttes, and venerable Pikes Peak.

At a Glance

DIFFICULTY	🚶	DISTANCE/TIME	5 miles/2 hours
TRAIL CONDITIONS	🚶🚶🚶🚶	TRAILHEAD ELEVATION TOTAL HIKING GAIN	7,100 feet 500 feet
CHILDREN	🚶🚶🚶🚶🚶	FEATURES	Gentle trail, mesa, forest, prairie, views
SCENERY	🚶🚶🚶	BEST SEASON	All year
PHOTO	🚶🚶🚶	OTHER USERS	Bikes, horses, dogs on leash
SOLITUDE	🚶🚶🚶	NOTES	Toilets at trailhead
PROPERTY	Spruce Mountain Open Space	JURISDICTION	Douglas County Open Space & Natural Resources

"Mountain" is a bit of a misnomer for this tree-covered mesa rising a few hundred feet above the prairie near the town of Larkspur. But its views are delightful, and the setting peaceful despite the nearness of Interstate 25. From the parking

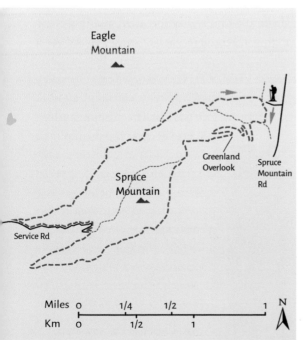

lot turn left onto **Oak Shortcut** and slant upward through Gambel oaks. Rattlesnake Butte rises out on the plains, as do other hills north and east. In spring and early summer you'll see blue chiming bells, purple larkspur, and a variety of yellow flowers all along the trail.

At 0.2 miles turn left at a sign pointing to "**Mountain Top**" and curve uphill amid ponderosas. Gentle switchbacks take you beneath an odd lobed white rock. A train might rumble through the quiet valley below on the modern tracks that replaced a narrow-gauge line laid here in 1871.

Spruce Mountain Trail

You'll enter thicker woods of Douglas fir, make a switchback, and soon reach **Greenland Overlook**, where you'll have sweeping views of grassland and foothills. The vista extends along the gray-white sandstone cliffs at the mesa's edge and on south to where Pikes Peak rises over the hills.

The overlook is a fine turnaround point for small hikers. For those wanting more, the "hard" part is over and several beautiful miles beckon. Continue along the mesa top to **Paddock's Point**, which offers a northward view to a pretty, cliff-ringed butte called Eagle Mountain. It's part of Eagle Mountain Ranch, which came into its heyday when I. J. Noe bought out a homestead in 1890 and then expanded it to 1,400 acres. The Noe family still runs the ranch, making it one of Douglas County's official "Centennial Farms"—working farms that have been in the same family for over 100 years.

At 1.3 miles, branch left for the **Mountain Top Loop**. Much of the foot traffic drops off after this point, even on weekends and holidays. Proceed along the hilltop with the mesa edge on the left and lush ponderosa forest standing at attention on the right. At the hill's southern limit, curve west and enjoy more Pikes Peak and valley views. Below is Spruce Mountain Ranch, a combination wedding event center and Angus seed stock operation. Smile! You might be a speck in someone's wedding pictures.

At 3 miles turn left on a **service road**, which will take you down into the valley west of the mesa. Turn right here onto **Eagle Pass Trail** for an enchanting walk in countryside with little evidence of human incursion. The path meanders

through grassland amid bird boxes and wildflowers, hugging the oak-and-aspen fringes of the fields. A crescent-shaped pond sparkles in a pocket below you. Across the way, foothills of the Rampart Range rise into *real* mountains. Nearby roads are concealed behind folds of earth; breeze,

Along the Spruce Mountain Trail

Eagle Mountain from Spruce Mountain

birdsong, and scraping feet are the only sounds. Ahead are the distinctive gray-white cliffs of Eagle Mountain, with Raspberry Butte in the distance to the left.

The trail curves east near the base of Eagle Mountain, where a viewing bench offers a nice place to sit and watch the light play on the mesa's corrugated walls. From here a 100-vertical-foot "climb" takes you to Eagle Pass and back to your vehicle.

Don't be surprised if you see some cows on portions of the open space. This prairie evolved symbiotically with bison, whose high-intensity, short-duration grazing pattern stimulated plant growth. Cattle are now being brought in for a few weeks each year to replicate the bison effect.

From Denver. Take I-25 south to Exit 173, Spruce Mountain Road. Drive south 5.7 miles, through the town of Larkspur, to arrive at the trailhead for Spruce Mountain Open Space and its large parking lot, on the right. *1 hour.*

91 Mount Herman

SATISFY YOUR DESIRE TO GET TO THE TOP OF SOMETHING, EVEN IN THE MIDDLE OF WINTER, with this delectable hill hike just off Interstate 25. It's a great way to start the morning, and a nice hike for adventurous kids.

At a Glance

DIFFICULTY	🥾🥾	DISTANCE/TIME	2.2 miles/1.5 hours
TRAIL CONDITIONS	🥾🥾🥾	TRAILHEAD ELEVATION TOTAL HIKING GAIN	8,100 feet 1,000 feet
CHILDREN	🚶🚶🚶🚶🚶	FEATURES	Mountain, foothills, prairie views, paraglider launch point
SCENERY	🥾🥾🥾	BEST SEASON	All year
PHOTO	🥾🥾🥾	OTHER USERS	Bikes, horses, dogs
SOLITUDE	🥾🥾🥾	NOTES	No toilets at trailhead
PROPERTY	Pike National Forest	JURISDICTION	U.S. Forest Service

Mount Herman is a hump of ridge rising over the town of Monument just north of Colorado Springs, clearly visible from the I-25 freeway. The trail climbs its

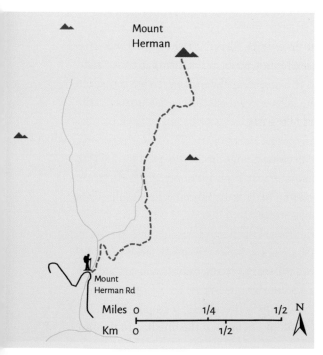

back side and has a great wilderness vibe before reaching the top, which has commanding views of plains and civilization. This easy-to-get-to, year-round hike is great for all ages looking for a mountain adventure. The ascent is brisk but short—a superb way to introduce children to the thrill of getting to the top of something. It's also a fantastic place to enjoy a sunrise.

Mount Herman Trail (FS 716) begins by ascending into an intimate valley. After a few minutes, a spur heads left to an unofficial camping spot; keep right and climb the hillside. Here it's good to practice a slow, steady pace. The steepness doesn't last long. Listen

Pikes Peak from Mount Herman

for raptor calls and enjoy copses, stands of aspen, and some weirdly-shaped rock formations as you go. Kids might have fun looking for faces and figures in the rock walls.

The trail veers right and steepens again. The route is easy to follow, and there are cairns to mark the way. Gain a notch and head left (north) as the plains come into view. There are several paths to the summit; the clearest route keeps west of the ridge spine. Soon the Pikes Peak massif presents itself behind you, to the southwest—a stunning perspective not enjoyed by those who stay down on the plains.

The high point is marked by some poles with flags. To the west are wooded tablelands; in the distant northwest rise the snowy mounts of Evans and Bierstadt. A metal box with a logbook is chained to a tree near the top. Here kids can document their achievement, and everyone is free to wax poetic, which is easy to do if you are here enjoying the first hours of the day.

You might sense you could jump off Mount Herman and fly across the prairie, and that is exactly what some people do. Just below the summit is a paraglider launch point, described by one enthusiast as a "steep grassy meadow ending at a point of no return cliff"—for experienced gliders only. From here it is 1,800 feet down to a landing spot by Mount Herman Road. A signboard lists a phone number at the nearby Air Force Academy for gliders to call to coordinate their flights with jet flyovers, in order to avoid wake turbulence.

Below your wilderness perch, I-25 hums along to the east. If you squint you will also see the train tracks you crossed on the way in. The train was Monument's raison d'être. When the Denver & Rio Grande Railroad built a stop here in 1872 its motto was "Thru the Rockies, Not Around Them," but the line had to first go all the way south through Pueblo before heading up into Royal Gorge.

Summit of Mount Herman

Another "I spy" game to play from the top is to look for Monument Rock, the town's namesake monolith. Find where Mount Herman Road becomes a dirt road, then study the fields to the southwest. You should see a tiny white stone tower. It's only a blip when viewed from here, but up close it is impressive and bizarre. Back in the car, if you are ready for more, you can go check it out. There's a trailhead on the south side of Mount Herman Road right where it becomes paved. It's a very easy 2.6-mile loop trip to admire this strange stone formation.

From Denver. Take I-25 south to Exit 161 in Monument. Turn left onto 2nd Street and drive 0.7 miles west to its end, where it crosses train tracks. Turn left onto Mitchell Street, proceed 0.6 miles, and turn right onto Mount Herman Road. After 1.5 miles the pavement ends. Continue 3.6 miles on the dirt road, bearing left when Red Rock Drive enters to stay on Mount Herman Road. The trailhead is in a hairpin turn; some parking spaces, vertical signposts for Forest Trails 715 and 716, and some spray-painted rocks mark the spot. *1 hour, 10 mins.*

Sunrise from Mount Herman

92 Red Rock Canyon

BRING YOUR CAMERA FOR THIS EASY ADVENTURE THROUGH SOME SPECTACULAR sandstone formations outside Colorado Springs, where kids of all ages will delight in some eye-popping scenery.

At a Glance

DIFFICULTY	🚶	**DISTANCE/TIME**	3.5 miles/2 hours
TRAIL CONDITIONS	🚶🚶🚶🚶	**TRAILHEAD ELEVATION**	6,200 feet
		TOTAL HIKING GAIN	500 feet
CHILDREN	🚶🚶🚶🚶🚶	**FEATURES**	Red sandstone formations, historic quarry
SCENERY	🚶🚶🚶🚶	**BEST SEASON**	All year
PHOTO	🚶🚶🚶🚶	**OTHER USERS**	Bikes, horses, dogs on leash
SOLITUDE	🚶	**NOTES**	Toilets at trailhead
PROPERTY	Red Rock Canyon Open Space	**JURISDICTION**	City of Colorado Springs Parks, Recreation & Cultural Services

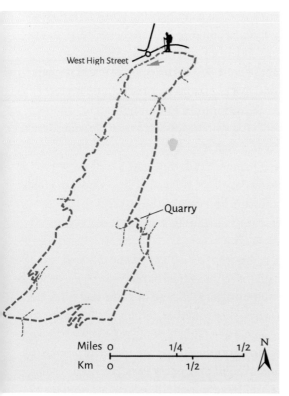

This beautiful open space is a geological extension of the rouge sandstone formations of the Garden of the Gods, the famous National Natural Landmark just north of here. Some call this "The Secret Garden of the Gods," since before 2003 few people knew what treasures lay beyond the landfill, mobile homes, and billboards that had sprung up on its perimeter. Sequestered for decades as private land with big development ambitions, Red Rock Canyon is hardly secret anymore. It was too good to be kept under wraps.

This varied route saves the best for last: a descent through the canyon, the best direction from which to view it. If you're

Red Rock Canyon

hiking in the afternoon, you're in for some dazzling lighting effects. Just allow enough time to reach the canyon before the sun dips behind the western mountains.

Begin on **Contemplative Trail** at the west end of the parking lot. As you meander and ascend 0.7 miles alongside some startling red rock walls, the traffic noise from Highway 24 fades away. Continue onto **Roundup Trail** for another steady half mile uphill in scrubland, making switchbacks left to join the wide **Mesa Trail**. Go right on Mesa and follow it as it slants up through the grassland. Looking north, you'll see you have gained some altitude and now have an eye-level perspective of the formations of the Garden of the Gods. Continue on Mesa Trail, past where the Section 16 Trail Connection branches to the right. On a different day you might take Section 16 deeper into the foothills, where it connects with the popular 6-mile Palmer–Red Rock Loop.

Turn right on Roundup Trail when it reconnects with Mesa and descend to the floor of Red Rock Canyon. Here you might see red-tailed hawks soaring above the canyon walls. In summer you'll see hummingbirds flitting in the bushes; they are surprisingly feisty with each other when they find that perfect nectar flower to sip. Follow the trail through the canyon between the stunning red rocks and keep your camera at the ready. When the sun lights the walls, they appear to be on fire.

After a half mile in the canyon, branch left on **Quarry Pass Trail** and climb a rock staircase to enter a slot in the hill. Here you might feel you've been trans-

Relaxing at the Red Rock Canyon quarry

Quarry Pass Trail

ported to ancient Egypt to inspect some monumental building project—a sphinx, perhaps, or pyramids. In truth, the quarry you see before you bustled in the late 1800s, when the advent of steam-powered equipment made it possible to carve 25-ton blocks from these walls and ship them all over the country to build banks, campus buildings, and mansions. But the bustle was short-lived. By the early 1910s, builders were chasing concrete and steel, materials that didn't erode as quickly as this gorgeous sandstone. Though it's tempting, do not climb the rocks here—or anywhere else in the park—unless you have technical expertise and a permit from the Garden of the Gods Visitors Center. It is illegal to get more than 10 feet off the ground without that permit.

Proceed through the quarry pass and descend to **Greenlee Trail**. Turn right and return to the park entrance. Along the way you'll pass a pond lit up blue by the sky. It makes a striking contrast to the ruddy rocks soaring all around you.

Now, aren't you glad this is public open space? If developers had had their way in the early 2000s, you would be looking at housing, two hotels, and an 18-hole golf course.

From Denver. Take I-25 south to Exit 141, then US 24 west 3.7 miles to Ridge Road and turn left. Continue 500 feet, turn left to enter a roundabout, and take the second exit onto West High Street to reach Red Rock Canyon Open Space. The trailhead and its large parking lot are on the right. *1 hour, 15 mins.*

93 Barr Trail

GET YOUR WINTER BLOOD PUMPING ON THIS INTRODUCTION TO A TRAIL THAT MORE ambitious hikers can take all the way to the top of Pikes Peak.

At a Glance

DIFFICULTY	🚶🚶🚶🚶	**DISTANCE/TIME**	8.5 miles/4 hours
TRAIL CONDITIONS	🚶🚶🚶🚶	**TRAILHEAD ELEVATION** TOTAL HIKING GAIN	6,300 feet 2,600 feet
CHILDREN	🚶🚶	**FEATURES**	Good steep trail, eventual solitude, Pikes Peak views
SCENERY	🚶🚶🚶	**BEST SEASON**	Fall, winter, spring
PHOTO	🚶🚶🚶	**OTHER USERS**	Bikes, horses, trail runners, dogs on leash
SOLITUDE	🚶🚶	**NOTES**	No onsite parking (shuttle service or prepaid parking only), toilets at trailhead
PROPERTY	Pike National Forest	**JURISDICTION**	U.S. Forest Service

This excellent trail starts out climbing the same flank of Pikes Peak as the Manitou Incline, the immensely popular fitness challenge course outside Colorado Springs. Unlike the Incline, which is a straight-up stairway set into an old funicular track, **Barr Trail** (FS 620) ascends by steady switchbacks on an old "burro route" and continues on along the ridge, soon leaving the crowds behind and entering a zone of silence and delightful views. It is part of a longer trail that leads to the summit of Pikes Peak, a 23-mile round-trip that is the more popular of its two main hiking routes. For this reason, this lower portion is best enjoyed during the off-season.

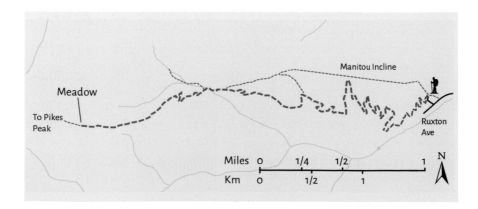

The trail doesn't waste time getting started, ascending what in summer is a hot hill with little shade. It's a fine and wide path here, as it needs to be, since it gets heavy downhill use by trail runners (it is considered bad manners to run *down* the Incline itself). Many of the switchbacks are bounded by nice wooden fences that serve as guardrails. After a little over 2 miles the trail forks left, away from the stairway, and the stream of happy downhill runners evaporates. The path narrows at the branch and a welcome solitude descends as you traverse the hill on a gentler grade. After the 2.5-mile marker you'll pass through an interesting natural tunnel beneath a slanted boulder and then almost immediately encounter a decidedly non-natural tunnel emerging from the hillside. Behind the tunnel's cement facade is a large pipe used to divert runoff water. Soon the trail reaches another fork, where you turn left.

Continue past the 3-mile marker and the trail forks yet again. Take the left branch and climb through a lovely gully filled with aspens to gain the ridgetop, at 3.5 miles. Way below, the city of Colorado Springs sprawls in silence. From here you also get a distant, bird's-eye view of the red rock formations of Garden of the Gods. The hard work is done, and the real rewards of this hike commence. The path along the ridgetop is easy going, walkable even in snow. The mountain looms through the trees. All is quiet. You soon reach the 4-mile marker, but don't turn around quite yet. Keep going a few hundred more yards to reach a meadow with fine views of the northeast slope of Pikes.

This 14,115-foot mountain was called *Tava*, or "Sun" by the Utes. Early Spaniards called it *El Capitán*. The current name honors explorer Zebulon Pike, who attempted to climb it with his team in November of 1806 but had to turn around due to waist-deep snow. The mountain was readily climbed 14 summers later by Edwin James, a young graduate of Vermont's Middlebury College. James had signed on as a botanist on Stephen Long's expedition up the Missouri and Platte

Near the start of the Barr Trail   *Barr Trail*

Two views of Pikes Peak from Barr Trail

Rivers. On the way up the peak, James described the blue columbine, which became Colorado's state flower. For a while the mountain was named after the young botanist, but nowadays James gets a less imposing (but still stunning) Front Range peak farther north.

The meadow is an excellent lunch spot and a good turnaround point, but you could keep going to the 4.5-mile marker, or the 5-mile—or farther. Pikes Peak is just 8 miles away. But you probably shouldn't try to climb Pikes Peak all in one day! It's more enjoyable when done over two days, breaking the trek at Barr Camp, at the 6.5-mile mark, where a cozy cabin with hostel-style accommodations is open all year round (reservations required).

From Denver. Take I-25 south to Exit 141, then US 24 west to Manitou Springs. Exit onto US 24 BUS/Manitou Avenue and continue 2 miles. Turn right on Old Man's Trail. Free parking with shuttle service to the trailhead, which also serves the Incline and Pikes Peak Cog Railway, is on the right. If you have prepaid for parking at the trailhead, continue 0.5 miles on Manitou Avenue to a traffic circle, veer onto Ruxton Avenue, and proceed 0.7 miles to the lot. *1 hour, 20 mins.*

94 Stanley Rim

THIS HIKE IN THE FOOTHILLS ABOVE COLORADO SPRINGS OFFERS A HUGE CLEAR-WATER reservoir, a lovely forested ridge, dramatic views of Pikes Peak, and a pretty lake where you can take a dip.

At a Glance

DIFFICULTY	🥾🥾	DISTANCE/TIME	6.5 miles/3 hours
TRAIL CONDITIONS	🥾🥾🥾🥾	TRAILHEAD ELEVATION TOTAL HIKING GAIN	9,000 feet 800 feet
CHILDREN	🥾🥾🥾	FEATURES	Reservoirs, Pikes Peak views, forested ridge
SCENERY	🥾🥾🥾	BEST SEASON	Spring and fall
PHOTO	🥾🥾🥾	OTHER USERS	Bikes, horses, dogs on leash
SOLITUDE	🥾🥾🥾	NOTES	Parking fee, cash or check only; access road closed in winter; toilets at trailhead
PROPERTY	Rampart Reservoir Recreation Area, Pike National Forest	JURISDICTION	U.S. Forest Service

This hike starts at Rampart Reservoir, where you'll get a beautiful view of Pikes Peak hovering across the cerulean waters. Climb from the lakeshore on **Backdoor Trail** (FS 723) through aspens and fragrant ponderosas, then continue on a gentle up-and-down path through this same mix of trees. At just under a mile turn right onto **Stanley Rim Trail** (FS 722), a two-track that follows the rim ridge bounding the watershed of Stanley Creek to the north.

When you arrive at the top of a bald, burnt hilltop, you'll have views of Ram-

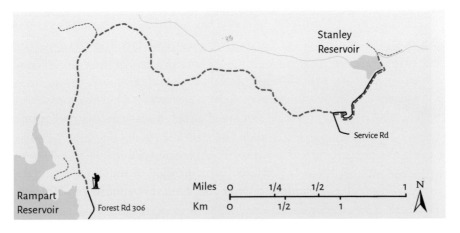

part Reservoir and beyond. This reservoir is a 13 billion-gallon storage tank supplying potable water to Colorado Springs. In dry summers, expect to see significant drawdown. The water is owned by the City, but the land is all Pike National Forest, open to the public 24/7. You can walk or ski in anytime you like, but the access road is closed to cars in winter.

The burned area extends less than half a mile along the trail; it is an isolated patch of the Waldo Canyon Fire which ignited more than 300 homes in northwest Colorado Springs in 2012. More than 18,000 acres burned, including the south shore of Rampart Reservoir, and the fire came within 1.5 miles of the city of Woodland Park after a flaming deer leaped across Rampart Range Road.

Continue along Stanley Rim, enjoying sustained views of Pikes Peak as you dip into two lovely saddles. Come fall, the aspens here blaze yellow and orange in the sun. The trail gets very quiet with just the sound of breeze and an occasional distant airplane. Don't be surprised if you meet someone from the nearby Air

Air Force Academy cadet on the Stanley Rim Trail

Force Academy huffing along; this trail leads down-mountain into the Academy's backyard and is a superb training ground for cadets, who are required to pass two fitness tests each semester.

At 2.7 miles, you'll cross a boulder-pile roadblock and turn left onto the service road for Stanley Reservoir. Descend two swooping switchbacks of the road through aspens to arrive at the shining, calm water. Continue through a yellow metal gate and walk across the dam to the splashing spillover; the trout fishing is reportedly excellent here.

Stanley Reservoir

This is a tranquil spot, great for lounging. The small, secluded reservoir is no longer used for water storage and, unlike Rampart Reservoir, you are allowed to dip your toes here—or even your whole body. You might also enjoy a half-mile stroll around the lake's perimeter, which entails some fun and creative log-walking at the opposite end to get across a marshy inlet stream.

Instead of returning to your vehicle, you could go to the Air Force Academy. It's closer—only two miles down steep and gorgeous Stanley Canyon. The problem is that the trailhead is located on a Defense Department site with ever-changing security rules, so you might get in trouble at the exit gate. Between 2001 and 2006 the Academy grounds were off-limits to the public, but since then the administration has become much more welcoming. Best to check the current situation.

All problems can be avoided, of course, by enrolling at the Academy. To do so you must be a U.S. citizen, over age 17, less than 23, unmarried, and of good moral character. You also need to be nominated by a member of Congress, and each member can only have five nominees at the Academy at a time.

From Denver. Take I-25 south to Exit 141, Colorado Springs, then US 24 west another 18 miles to Woodland Park. Turn right onto South Baldwin Street and continue as it curves right to become CR 22, Rampart Range Road. After 3 miles, turn right onto Loy Creek Road, proceed 1.5 miles, and turn right back onto Rampart Range Road, now a dirt road that is also labeled Forest Road 300; it is rough but passable if driven slowly. Continue 4 miles and turn left on Forest Road 306. Enter Rampart Reservoir Recreation Area and proceed to the trailhead and large parking lot at road's end. *2 hours.*

Pikes Peak and Rampart Reservoir from Stanley Rim Trail

95 Mount Rosa

THIS STRENUOUS LOOP TREK OUTSIDE COLORADO SPRINGS PAYS OFF IN WATERFALLS, BIG vistas, and rare close-up views of Pikes Peak from the south. Cap off the forest descent with a stroll along popular Seven Bridges Trail.

At a Glance

DIFFICULTY	🥾🥾🥾🥾🥾	DISTANCE/TIME	14.5 miles/6.5 hours
TRAIL CONDITIONS	🥾🥾🥾	TRAILHEAD ELEVATION TOTAL HIKING GAIN	7,500 feet 4,000 feet
CHILDREN	🥾	FEATURES	Long ascent, waterfalls, bridge trail, views of Continental Divide, Pikes Peak, and plains
SCENERY	🥾🥾🥾	BEST SEASON	Early summer
PHOTO	🥾🥾🥾	OTHER USERS	Bikes, horses, dogs on leash, motorcycles and ATVs on small portion.
SOLITUDE	🥾🥾🥾	NOTES	Toilets at Helen Hunt Falls, 0.5 miles before trailhead
PROPERTY	North Cheyenne Cañon Park, Pike National Forest	JURISDICTION	City of Colorado Springs Parks, Recreation & Cultural Services; U.S. Forest Service

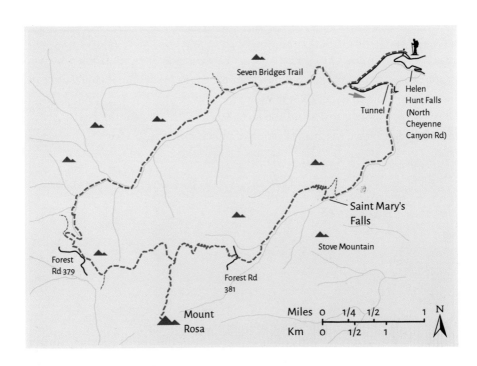

Begin this epic adventure heading west from the parking lot on a gated-off section of **Gold Camp Road**. After 1.2 miles, note Seven Bridges Trail branching right at North Cheyenne Creek; you'll return on it later. Stay on the dirt road until you arrive at a closed tunnel. Ascend left and over it to reach Pike National Forest and the start of **St. Mary's Falls Trail** (FS 624).

The aspen-and-pine woods are refreshing along Buffalo Canyon Creek. Above rises the pink granite face of Stove Mountain. On a switchback at 2.7 miles, branch left on a side-loop to ascend next to the falls, a series of attractive cascades. After gaining 300 feet, traverse away from the falls to rejoin the

Mount Rosa Trail

main trail, where a sign indicates Mount Rosa is 3 miles away. This refers to the start of the summit trail spur; the summit itself is closer to 4 miles away.

Climb, traverse, and climb again to meet a dirt road, **Forest Road 381**. You'll pass through an opening in a wire fence, turn right on the road, and 100 feet later turn left onto **FS 672** (Nelson's Trail). From here the switchbacks get serious, packing on altitude through shady trees. Behind and far below you are the radio towers atop Cheyenne Mountain and its subterranean NORAD facility. Keep a steady pace and you'll soon arrive on a hilltop for your first glimpses of Pikes Peak. Soon you will fork left onto **FS 673** (Mount Rosa Summit Trail). The climb through forest to the top—0.75 miles and 600 feet—is well worth it. After scrambling over some boulders, you'll reach a collection of pink rocks at 11,500 feet.

Pikes Peak hiding in clouds, as viewed from Mount Rosa

Mount Rosa Summit

Wow! Check out the ranges: from Mosquito to Sawatch to Sangre de Cristo. Those are the Spanish Peaks far to the south; to the east, the plains seem to go on to Texas. If afternoon clouds aren't rolling in yet, you'll also get more close-up views of Pikes Peak.

Mount Rosa could have been named Pikes Peak, since this is the mountain that explorer Zebulon Pike and his men actually went up in 1806. It was November—bad timing—when Pike sighted "Highest Mountain" and attempted to ascend it. After spending a stormy night in a cave on Rosa's southeast ridge, the team encountered waist-deep snow, saw how far they still had to go, and headed back down to the expedition's business. Rosa's summit rocks *are* rouge, but the peak is named for a woman: Rose Kingsley, who came from England in 1871 to visit her brother, one of the earliest settlers. She stayed a while and hiked around, enchanted by columbines so beautiful they made her forget her "mountain sickness."

It's all downhill from here. Return to **FS 672** and turn left to continue the circuit through deep forest to arrive at a dirt road. Turn right here onto FS 668 (Pipeline Trail), a motorcycle trail, and stay right at a fork 0.3 miles later. The trail drops farther into the North Cheyenne Creek drainage, then levels off along an abandoned water pipeline. When you turn right onto hikers-only **FS 622** (Seven Bridges Trail), you'll be on home stretch!

Continue descending on a south-facing slope, sparsely vegetated compared to the north, and you'll soon arrive at the first of seven bridges—or the last, according to the many hikers you will probably encounter coming up this trail. From here it's social hour on a popular and pleasant creekside path until the last (or first) bridge, a simple boardwalk that deposits you near your starting point.

From Denver. Take I-25 south to Exit 140 in Colorado Springs, and merge right onto South Tejon Street. Proceed 0.3 miles and make a slight right onto Cheyenne Boulevard. Continue 2.5 miles and make another slight right onto North Cheyenne Canyon Road. Proceed 2.6 miles, pass the parking lot for Helen Hunt Falls, and continue on a steep curved road 0.6 miles to a large dirt parking lot and the trailhead, on the left. *1 hour, 30 mins.*

96 Gray Back Peak

THIS PRETTY, LOW-KEY HIKE OUTSIDE COLORADO SPRINGS FOLLOWS A PINK-DIRT RIDGE TO a wooded promontory, where you'll have views of forested valleys, granite cliffs, and a sweep of eastern plains.

At a Glance

DIFFICULTY	👫	**DISTANCE/TIME**	3.8 miles/2 hours
TRAIL CONDITIONS	👫	**TRAILHEAD ELEVATION**	8,700 feet
		TOTAL HIKING GAIN	600 feet
CHILDREN	👫👫	**FEATURES**	Forest walk, views of valley, cliffs, and plains
SCENERY	👫	**BEST SEASON**	Spring and fall
PHOTO	👫	**OTHER USERS**	Bikes, horses, dogs
SOLITUDE	👫👫	**NOTES**	No toilets at trailhead
PROPERTY	Pike National Forest	**JURISDICTION**	U.S. Forest Service

You might think you're off the beaten path when you arrive at the tiny unmarked parking lot and see a hand-painted "Horse Trail" sign on a tree. But this enjoyable little path is a great family choice, and well beaten by those in the know; a sort of "Gray Back Club" exists. Begin **Gray Back Peak Trail** by ascending on

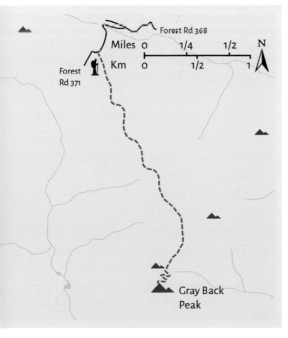

pink gravel amid spruce. Across is the lovely cliff-dome of Mount Vigil, which is about 700 feet higher than where you're going. The trail climbs the right side of a ridge with views of a wooded valley; nice shocks of color flare up there in autumn. As you gain the ridgetop, a view opens east through a V-slot to the plains.

The trail is a steady incline, sometimes in a narrow rut, which makes "Horse Trail" easier for boots than hooves. In other places the path is nearly wiped off the hillside—even more of an equestrian's challenge, but no problem for human feet.

Gray Back Peak

You know you're probably in the vicinity of Pikes Peak when the trail is made up of granular reddish dirt, similar to the crushed red brick sometimes used on sports fields. This is the "milled" version of Pikes Peak granite, the same material that makes up the massif. Pikes Peak is the tip of a body of former magma

that cooled beneath the surface about a billion years ago. Because of its composition, and because it cooled slowly, large crystals formed, sometimes a centimeter across. The resulting granite is coarse-grained, easily weathered, and crumbly.

The trail eases as you gain the ridge a second time, in aspens. Ahead is another dome-cliff; this time it's a lower appurtenance of the aptly named Gray Back. Clearly not all the granite here is pink! The trail drops a hundred feet and then rises in thicker woods, where fall aspens drop their leaves like gold coins on the path. As you meander, look for outcrops where you can get better views—and your best photos—of Gray Back.

After passing through a stand of mature aspens, the trail climbs the eastern side of the ridge. You'll make a few switchbacks and suddenly be standing at

Gray Back Peak Trail

a campfire ring on the wooded summit. It's a peaceful and pleasant place, and there are views, but you'll have to stand on boulders between the trees to see them. Children might have to go on shoulders. Best is the sweep of wavelike hogbacks and plains rolling to the east. Pikes Peak is felt but unseen to the northwest; Mount Rosa, big and pointy, does a good job obscuring it.

The pink color in many of the granite walls is due partly to iron minerals, and largely to the presence of potassium feldspar, which is mostly silicate. "Feldspar" comes from the German words *feld*, meaning "field," and *spat*, meaning "rock that does not contain ore." Indeed, though eager prospectors painted "Pikes Peak or Bust" on their wagons when they headed to Colorado in 1859, it soon became clear that Pikes Peak was a bust. Miners had to search elsewhere for gold, and some met with great success. A huge late-in-the-game strike at Cripple Creek, southwest of here, was as close to Pikes as the gold rush got.

You can't see them, and they can't see you, but a thousand feet downhill to the west guests are enjoying luxury cabins at the Ranch at Emerald Valley. This upscale resort advertises Colorado sunsets as a main attraction. But you can get a better view of the sunset—not to mention sunrise—up here on Gray Back for free.

From Denver. Take I-25 south to Exit 140 in Colorado Springs, and bear right onto South Tejon Street. After 0.3 miles, bear right onto Cheyenne Boulevard. After 1.6 miles, turn left on Cresta Road, drive 0.3 miles, and turn right onto Mesa Avenue. At the traffic circle, take the first exit to stay on Mesa. Continue 0.5 miles as the road name changes first to Park Avenue and then El Pomar Road. Turn left onto Penrose Boulevard, proceed 0.5 miles, and turn right onto Old Stage Road. After 0.8 miles, turn right to stay on Old Stage Road. Continue 5.5 miles on a good dirt road. Turn left on Forest Road 371, and continue 0.3 miles to the unmarked trailhead and its small parking area, on the left. *1 hour, 50 mins.*

Gray Back Peak summit

97 The Crags

PIKES PEAK HAS A GARDEN OF CLEFT AND PINNACLED ROCK FORMATIONS ON ITS LOWER northwest slopes called The Crags. This trail shows them off: some huge, distant, and dazzling; others up close.

At a Glance

DIFFICULTY	🚶🚶	DISTANCE/TIME	5 miles/2 hours
TRAIL CONDITIONS	🚶🚶🚶	TRAILHEAD ELEVATION	10,000 feet
		TOTAL HIKING GAIN	800 feet
CHILDREN	🚶🚶🚶🚶	FEATURES	Rock formations, forest, meadow, expansive Pikes Peak views
SCENERY	🚶🚶🚶🚶	BEST SEASON	Early summer
PHOTO	🚶🚶🚶🚶	OTHER USERS	Bikes, horses, dogs
SOLITUDE	🚶🚶	NOTES	Toilets at trailhead
PROPERTY	Pike National Forest	JURISDICTION	U.S. Forest Service

You get your first "crag" view from the parking lot: a dome-cliff, rising gracefully to the west. Take a look, and then cross the road to begin **The Crags Trail** (FS 664) by crossing Fourmile Creek and climbing through spruce. The trail soon mellows on a hillside where the extended massif of Pikes Peak comes into view. From this angle it lives up to its Arapaho name, *Heey-otoyoo*, which means "Long Mountain." The true summit remains hidden, while Sentinel Point peeks at you over the hump farther south.

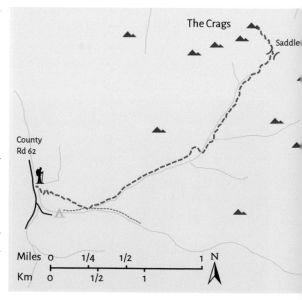

The trail descends to meet a spur coming from Crags Campground, below you on the right, and then rejoins Fourmile Creek.

Here the trail forks. The right-hand Devil's Playground Trail (FS 753) leads to the summit of Pikes Peak, 7 miles and 4,000 vertical feet away. That might sound like a lot, but it's only about half the distance— and half the elevation gain— of the far more popular route up the eastern slope. Why is

The Crags Trail

this western route so neglected? Probably because two miles of the hike are along the Pikes Peak toll road.

Go left instead, where pleasant forest gives way to meadow and many interesting rock formations appear, including a dome-wall rising on the left. The trail passes into the wide shrub-bottoms of the creek, where expanding views reveal two main sets of crags: a pointy assembly on the left, and a knobby mound on the right that has some giant's stairsteps. High up on the side of Pikes is a distinctive stegosaurus-back formation. Farther on, the trail passes a natural sculpture on the left containing many shapes and forms (see if you can spot the camel's face).

The grade remains gentle in willow bottoms alongside gurgling water, then rises slightly to pass another notable formation: a bulbous pillar with a cave. When the flats end, the trail crosses the stream and steepens through forest to a saddle. Climb left from the saddle toward The Crags, over roots and granite slabs. Here you'll have views of pillar-prongs sticking out of the northern side of Pikes. Higher up is a massive picket fence of spiky rocks. In near view, some gnarled bristlecone pines are as photogenic as the rocks: ancient deadwood with new growth that seems grafted on. The top of the rise offers even more to gawk at. Best is the perspective to the southwest, where Pikes displays contours and formations that can only be fully appreciated from this height and angle.

An erosion process called "frost wedging" is responsible for many of the formations. Particularly on lower slopes, water can seep deep into fissures in the rock, where it freezes and thaws repeatedly to wedge the rock into sheared formations and large boulders. Higher up, water is not able to penetrate as deeply, so the boulders are smaller.

Camel face along The Crags Trail

Pikes Peak is composed mostly of pink-hued granite belonging to the Pikes Peak Batholith, "batholith" being a combination of the Greek words *bathos*, meaning "deep," and *lithos*, meaning "rock." This batholith formed about a billion years ago, when magma cooled slowly deep within the Earth's crust. It has risen to the surface several times over the eons, most recently about 65 million years ago, when the modern Rockies formed. Visible portions extend north to Mount Evans, south to Cañon City, and west to South Park. What we see is just the tip of the rockberg; Pikes Peak granite has also been spotted at the bottoms of wells 80 miles out on the plains.

From Denver. Take I-25 south to Exit 141, then US 24 west another 25 miles to Divide. Turn left onto CO 67 south, continue 4.3 miles, and turn left onto CR 62. Proceed 3 miles to The Crags Trailhead, on the left; the parking lot is on the right side of the road. *2 hours.*

End of the trail, The Crags

98 Mueller's Rock Pond

A MEANDERING LOOP THROUGH OLD RANCHLAND OUTSIDE DIVIDE BEGINS ON A RIDGE with views of distant peaks and leads to a rock-reflecting pool. Vibrant aspen groves are a treat the whole way.

At a Glance

DIFFICULTY	🚶🚶	**DISTANCE/TIME**	5 miles/2.5 hours
TRAIL CONDITIONS	🚶🚶🚶🚶🚶	**TRAILHEAD ELEVATION**	9,700 feet
		TOTAL HIKING GAIN	700 feet
CHILDREN	🚶🚶🚶	**FEATURES**	Mountain views, aspens, old ranch ponds
SCENERY	🚶🚶🚶	**BEST SEASON**	Spring and fall
PHOTO	🚶🚶🚶🚶	**OTHER USERS**	Bikes, horses
SOLITUDE	🚶🚶🚶	**NOTES**	Entrance fee, no dogs, toilets at trailhead
PROPERTY	Mueller State Park	**JURISDICTION**	Colorado Parks & Wildlife

The broad west side of Pikes Peak greets you at the parking lot, looking more like "Pikes Ridge" from this perspective as it stretches south to the pink cone of Sentinel Point. Walk past the visitors center to Outlook Trailhead and begin on **Trail #7, Outlook Ridge Trail**. Like most Mueller trails, it is superbly maintained: wide and smooth as it descends the ridge through aspens, ponderosas, and meadows. Stay on Trail #7 as Trail #8 branches left and look for the high Sangre de Cristo peaks in the distance to the southwest. Pass the left-branching Trail #9 and continue downhill. That's the Sawatch Range to the west.

At just under a mile, curve right to stay on Trail #7 as Trail #10 branches left. A quarter mile later, turn left on **Trail #25, Geer Pond Trail**, and proceed downhill through delightful quiet back-country. Geer Pond glitters in a broad meadow to the left. Startled ducks might hop in and swim

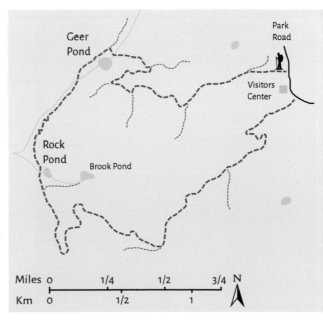

Geer Pond

Park Road

Visitors Center

Rock Pond

Brook Pond

Miles 0   1/4   1/2   3/4   N

Km 0   1/2   1

Trail #5, Mueller State Park

Rock Pond, Mueller State Park

away from this old ranch pond's marshy shoreline.

The first European "settlers" in this area were not ranchers but horse thieves who lived in the southern end of the park, where ruins of their corral are still visible. The local economy got a big boost in 1890 when gold was struck 15 miles south at Cripple Creek. Colorado's last great gold rush was a big one, yielding more than $10 billion in bullion to date. When the industry peaked in 1900, more than 32,000 people were living in and around Cripple Creek. Area homesteaders supplied them with timber, meat, and potatoes. In the 1950s, W. E. Mueller bought up many of the old homesteads and created a 12,100-acre working ranch. The Nature Conservancy acquired it in 1978 and sold it to the state; today Mueller's land is split between this state park and the gorgeous Dome Rock State Wildlife Area next door.

Turn left at Geer Pond onto **Trail #15, Rock Canyon Trail**. This more rugged path takes you down through a wooded stream valley. After some switchbacks, you'll wrap left across a grassy hillside toward this hike's centerpiece: Rock Pond. It's easy to linger here and would be a shame not to. A cleft rock wall drops into clear water where it is perfectly reflected, creating an iconic scene. Snap all the pictures you like, but be sure to savor the experience in real life, too!

After enjoying the pond, continue on the trail, now called **Trail #5, Rock**

Pikes Peak from Trail #5, Mueller State Park

Pond Trail. This two-track turns uphill to make a sustained 2.5-mile climb back to the car. It's a moderate ascent through mixed forest, including large stands of mature aspens.

Aspens are prolific in Mueller, in part because they're so good at reestablishing themselves in lands disturbed by logging and ranching. Many groves have a shared root system, which remains alive after the above-ground trees are felled, and they resprout quickly. Aspens tend to sabotage themselves, however, by nurturing evergreen competitors with their shade and decayed fallen leaves. Their root systems can live for thousands of years, but it will be interesting to see if the stands along Trail #5 get overtaken by conifers in the coming decades.

Trail #5 becomes less steep as Pikes Peak's lower reaches reappear; you'll know you're close to the car when you leave the pine forest and curve through more grassland and aspens. The last bit is a stiff uphill climb to a viewing pavilion at the edge of the parking lot, where encore panoramas of Pikes, the Sangres, and the Sawatches cap off the hike.

From Denver. Take I-25 south to Exit 141, Colorado Springs, then US 24 west another 25 miles to Divide. Turn left onto CO 67 and drive south 3.9 miles. Turn right at the entrance to Mueller State Park and continue 1 mile to the large parking lot at the visitors center. *1 hour, 40 mins.*

99 Dome Rock

FOR BEAUTY AND SOLITUDE IN A LESS VISITED PRESERVE, TRY THIS CREEKSIDE TREK OUTSIDE Divide. Snow-free by spring, gorgeous in fall colors, it reaches a promontory with a view of a startling granite dome set against a backdrop of mighty mountains.

At a Glance

DIFFICULTY	🚶🚶🚶	**DISTANCE/TIME**	11 miles/4.5 hours
TRAIL CONDITIONS	🚶🚶🚶	**TRAILHEAD ELEVATION** **TOTAL HIKING GAIN**	8,800 feet 1,400 feet
CHILDREN	🚶🚶	**FEATURES**	Creek, marsh, forest, rock formations, views of high peaks
SCENERY	🚶🚶🚶	**BEST SEASON**	Spring and fall
PHOTO	🚶🚶🚶	**OTHER USERS**	Bikes and horses
SOLITUDE	🚶🚶🚶🚶	**NOTES**	No entrance fee, no dogs, toilets at trailhead
PROPERTY	Dome Rock State Wildlife Area	**JURISDICTION**	Colorado Parks & Wildlife

   Few people ever lay eyes on Dome Rock. Unlike Mueller State Park next door, this expansive state wildlife area is a hike-if-you-are-in-the-know kind of place, with an unpretentious access road and a no-fee dirt parking lot. The centerpiece Dome is well hidden; to glimpse it you must trek five miles through a lovely creekside landscape and over hill and vale.

   To begin, cross Fourmile Creek and head down its right bank on **Dome Rock Trail**. This runoff from Pikes Peak gushes in spring beneath towering rock formations. At 0.6 miles the trail crisscrosses the creek. There is no bridge at the second

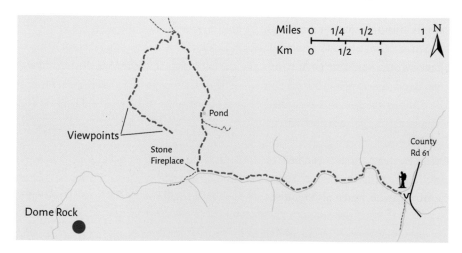

Fourmile Creek and the start of Dome Rock Trail

ford; to keep your feet dry, take the rugged side trail before the first crossing and rejoin the main trail after the second. As you continue along a hillside of shrubs and well-spaced pines you will notice that the north-facing slope is more densely vegetated in spruce and fir. That shadier slope retains more water, and temperatures on the two hillsides can differ by as much as 38 degrees Fahrenheit.

At just over a mile the valley widens into a long marshy flat populated by willows. Some sections of stream are more like lakes, where duck couples paddle and mad geese honk to protest your presence. The trail is up-and-down here, curving right below pink rocks that poke out of the forest.

At 2.5 miles, look for a large stone fireplace hiding in the bushes. This is what remains of the Jack Rabbit Lodge, a deluxe hunting cabin built in the early 1900s when this was Crescent Cattle Company land. The ranch headquarters were located near the town of Divide, and this lodge served as a place to corral stockholders for annual summer meetings. Theodore Roosevelt is rumored to have slept here during a hunting trip in the area.

The onward streamside trail, which makes a loop around Dome Rock, is excruciatingly tempting, but it is closed from December 1 to July 15 to allow bighorn sheep to lamb in peace, and it also requires

Fourmile Creek, along the Dome Rock Trail

Dome Rock, with the Sangre de Cristos in the background

you to wade the creek five times! Instead, turn right onto **Cabin Creek Trail**. You'll ascend through a gated barbed-wire fence and arrive in a meadow, where remnants of two cabins sit next to a pond where trout drift lazily. Continue on a beautiful stretch through forest and up a meadow to a four-way junction. A sharp left here takes you onto **4 Mile Overlook Trail** for an up-and-down walk along a ridge.

Where is the Dome? Craning your neck over each hump in anticipation, you have to settle for impressive views of Pikes Peak. Soon the Sawatch Range displays itself to the west, and the Sangre de Cristos appear through the trees to the southwest. Still, no sign of a dome! Then suddenly there "Old Baldy" is, so unmistakable it makes you laugh: a smooth curved globe of granite backed by a dramatic line of Sangre peaks.

Dome Rock is a striking example of the geological process called exfoliation. When its near-uniform granite was thrust up about 65 million years ago, it was covered with thousands of feet of softer sedimentary rock. This softer rock eroded, relieving pressure on the granite, whose outer sections then expanded and cracked into concentric layers like an onion.

From here the trail heads downhill along the ridge for another half mile. Should you continue? Yes—both for the accomplishment of reaching the trail's end, and for the lonely promontory, perched over the creek valley with Dome Rock and Pikes Peak still in view. It's a fine reward for going the distance.

From Denver. Take I-25 south to Exit 141, Colorado Springs, then US 24 west another 25 miles to Divide. Turn left onto CO 67 and drive 5.4 miles. Turn right on Four Mile Road (CR 61), proceed 2 miles, and turn right at the entrance to Dome Rock State Wildlife Area. There are two parking areas; the trail begins at the one farther north. *1 hour, 50 mins.*

100 Pancake Rocks

THIS FORESTED WALK ON THE SIDE OF PIKES PEAK LEADS TO SOME DELICIOUS ROCK formations and offers side trips to a waterfall and a onetime pasture for stolen horses.

At a Glance

DIFFICULTY	🚶🚶	**DISTANCE/TIME**	6 miles/2.5 hours
TRAIL CONDITIONS	🚶🚶🚶	**TRAILHEAD ELEVATION** **TOTAL HIKING GAIN**	9,700 feet 1,300 feet
CHILDREN	🚶🚶🚶	**FEATURES**	Forest, meadow, curious rock formations, waterfall, views
SCENERY	🚶🚶🚶	**BEST SEASON**	Early summer
PHOTO	🚶🚶🚶🚶	**OTHER USERS**	Bikes, horses, dogs
SOLITUDE	🚶🚶	**NOTES**	No toilets at trailhead
PROPERTY	Pike National Forest	**JURISDICTION**	U.S. Forest Service

Horsethief Falls Trail (FS 704) starts next to a closed railroad tunnel. Built in the mid-1890s, the tunnel served one of three lines to Cripple Creek, home of Colorado's last great gold rush. After abandonment, portions of the railbed were used for the highway, including this single-lane, timber-lined tunnel. After the monumental Eisenhower Tunnels were built on Interstate 70 in the 1970s, the passage here got the whimsical nickname "Little Ike." After voters legalized gambling at Cripple Creek in the 1990s, Little Ike became an unbearable bottleneck, and so the road was routed around it.

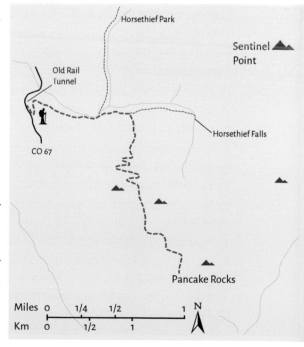

The trail is smooth and covered in the crumbled red granite that is characteristic of Pikes Peak trails. After making a switchback, you'll curve into a valley where Sentinel Point's rose-colored summit rises above the trees. At 12,527 feet it looks like the highest thing around, but it isn't; Pikes lies unseen beyond the hump. The trail

Sawatch Range, from Pancake Rocks Trail

eases along a willow bottom where, at 0.7 miles, Horsethief Park Trail branches left. Go straight instead into tall pines and aspens. In minutes another junction arrives: straight to Horsethief Falls, or right to the destination "Pancakes."

The ancient profession of horse thieving has a history in this valley. Native Americans stole horses from settlers (not that things weren't thieved from them as well), and immigrants stole from each other. Anglo-run horse thieving operations were established here in the 1870s and didn't really end until cars made horses obsolete in the 1910s. The thieves usually didn't steal from their neighbors; rather they swiped animals from places like Pueblo and Cañon City, and then hid them here to rest and rebrand them before driving them to lucrative markets in places like Denver.

The modest Horsethief Falls are an easy half mile away and make a good picnic spot on the way back. For now, turn right onto **Pancake Rocks Trail** (FS 704.A), and climb six switchbacks to a saddle where there's a bulbous rock wall on the right. Continue south along the hillside on mostly level trail with views of the distant Sawatch and Sangre de Cristo Ranges. Preliminary pancakes appear above-left as the trail descends. The path then bottoms out, steepens, and crosses another saddle to reach the unmistakable formations. Not overwhelming in scale, the pancakes are fun to investigate close up, and the setting is lovely. It would be interesting to see a time-lapse film made over the eons, to watch rain and wind whip the exposed granite into these breakfast-house creations.

Above and below, Pancake Rocks

The pretty setting is not isolated. The highway is visible below you, as is the gigantic scar of Cripple Creek's open-pit gold mine across the way. What you see is a small fraction of the largest present-day gold mining operation in Colorado where low-grade ore is heap-leached to extract less than a gram of gold per ton. Production has declined in the 2010s, and gold prices will dictate whether continued mining is feasible. Almost all of Cripple Creek's historic underground mines are now idle, although there's still gold down there. So far the veins have yielded about $30 billion in 2018 gold prices.

After visiting the falls on the way back, you can make another detour to Horsethief Park. The trail proceeds through meadow and willow bottom beneath a flank of Pikes Peak that is utterly vibrant in fall aspen season. In this hidden and bucolic valley, it's easy to imagine a herd of stolen steeds being fattened up for sale.

From Denver. Take I-25 south to Exit 141, then US 24 west another 25 miles to Divide. Turn left onto CO 67 south and continue 9.3 miles to the parking area for Horsethief Park Trailhead, on the left. *2 hours.*

101 Oil Creek Tunnel

Tucked into a high cirque on Pikes Peak are the fascinating remains of a failed gold mine. Your imagination might run wild here, but if not, the stunning scenery more than compensates.

At a Glance

DIFFICULTY	🚶🚶	DISTANCE/TIME	4.5 miles/2 hours
TRAIL CONDITIONS	🚶🚶🚶	TRAILHEAD ELEVATION TOTAL HIKING GAIN	10,900 feet 800 feet
CHILDREN	🚶🚶🚶🚶	FEATURES	High mountain traverse, Pikes Peak cliff views, historic mine site
SCENERY	🚶🚶🚶🚶🚶	BEST SEASON	Summer
PHOTO	🚶🚶🚶🚶🚶	OTHER USERS	Bikes, horses, dogs
SOLITUDE	🚶🚶🚶	NOTES	Fee required for Pikes Peak toll road, toilets at nearby Glen Cove tourist stop, thunderstorm exposure above tree line
PROPERTY	Pike National Forest	JURISDICTION	U.S. Forest Service

This unusual and unadvertised trail begins above timberline on Pikes Peak and heads downhill. From the trailhead, the first mile of **Elk Park Trail** (FS 652) is in clear view—a visible slant through orange dirt. Above and ahead of you, "America's Mountain" displays its vertigo-inducing north face in three successive waves culminating in the summit. Below is the bright green marsh-meadow of Elk Park, backed by an attractive knob that would be a notable mountain if it weren't dwarfed by its parent.

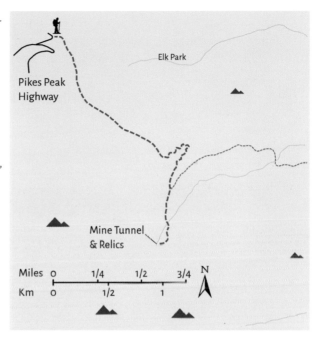

After the initial drop, the trail levels in some trees, then reenters scree to descend to a forested shoulder. The woods thicken as the trail descends steeply via switchbacks. Soaring cliffs grab the eyes, presenting an aspect and mood of Pikes that most people never see up close like this. What appears serene and majestic from a distance is intense and dizzying here, almost menacing. Aspens arrive before the trail reaches a junction, where an antiquated sign points right to Oil Creek Tunnel, a half mile away.

Remains of cabins appear, then the path widens into a handcart road as it nears an amphitheater of cliff walls. Soon you arrive at a jobsite where it seems the workers left on a coffee break that has lasted a hundred years. The wheel of a steam engine sticks out of the ground; pipes scatter in the creek. The old-style font on a rusted boiler nameplate evinces a bygone era. In the hillside, you'll see a barred-off tunnel portal.

It's an intriguing scene to say the least. This was one of just a handful of mines on the mountain that gave the 1859 gold rush its name. When folks painted "Pikes Peak or Bust" on their wagons, it was symbolic, because the riches actually lay farther west and north. But when gold was struck at nearby Cripple Creek in 1890, interest in Pikes revived; folks theorized the source of this gold was Pikes, after all. By this time a carriage road ran to the top of the peak for tourists, and around 1896 a mining group blazed a side road (now this trail) and began blasting here. Work proceeded for several years and the operation claimed several lives, includ-

ing that of 22-year-old Walter Johnson, who lost his head to a stick of dynamite. After 1,600 feet of fruitless digging, the backers lost hope and everyone walked away, once again prompting wags to say, "A gold mine is a hole in the ground with a liar standing next to it."

If you turn back here, you'll finish the day with a satisfying 4-mile hike. But if you'd like to keep going, turn right instead of left on Elk Park Trail, and continue downhill through the forest, where periodic clearings will give you shifting views of the cliffs. Keep right at the junction with Severy Creek Trail (now closed), and you'll soon reach a nice picnic spot alongside French Creek.

Back at the car, be sure to finish the drive to the top of Pikes Peak! After all, you've paid your admission. The best part comes right away in the set of thrilling switchbacks known as "The

Oil Creek Tunnel

Ws." In 2011 the last section of this road was finally paved, which means 70,000 tons of sediment no longer wash into adjacent wetlands, meadows, and forest each year. At the summit you can gift-shop galore and enjoy a hot snack. The restaurant is famous for its donuts, which fry nicely up here. Unlike the boiling point of water, the temperature of frying oil isn't much affected by the 14,114-foot altitude.

Pikes Peak from Elk Park Trailhead

From Denver. Take I-25 south to Exit 141, then US 24 west another 9.5 miles. Take the Cascade exit and turn left onto Fountain Avenue, continue 0.4 miles, then bear left onto Pikes Peak Highway. Continue through the fee station and up the toll road. Three quarters of a mile past the 13-mile marker, turn left onto an unmarked dirt road to reach the small parking area for the (unsigned) Elk Park Trailhead. *2 hours.*

Ridges of Pikes Peak from Elk Park Trail

The Author atop South Arapaho Peak

Acknowledgements

MY DEEP GRATITUDE GOES FIRST TO MY PARENTS, PAT AND SANDY JARVIS, WHO GOT ME hiking on the trails of the Pacific Northwest when I was a small child. This planted the seed, which sprouted at age 16 after I got my driver's license. I can still remember the day. It was a hot summer day. A buddy and I were sitting in inner tubes out on Lake Washington, asking ourselves, "What should we do?" The answer was, "Go hiking," of course! With my parents' blessing and their green 1970 Mustang convertible, we proceeded to spend many summers stomping *all over* Washington State's Cascade and Olympic mountains. I am deeply grateful to this buddy, Joe Cissna, who undertook all those early, formative, and often wild crazy adventures with me.

Our bibles in those days were the hiking guides published by the Seattle Mountaineers. One was called *101 Hikes in the North Cascades*, and to this day it retains a revered position on my shelf. I consider the authors, Ira Spring and Harvey Manning, to be my heroes, along with Helen Sherman (a neighbor of my grandmother), who created the lovely hand-drawn trail maps. With these books, my buddy and I went out and explored our world! Now that I've had the honor of writing a *101 Hikes* book of my own, it is my sincere hope that it will help people in a similar way that Ira, Harvey, and Helen's books profoundly helped me.

I wish to thank Mark Sedenquist of Imbrifex Books, not only for making this guidebook possible, but also for supplying the vision, critical advice, and key parameters I was able to run—I mean walk—with. I also wish to thank Nancy Zerbey, this book's editor, for her unfalteringly rigorous work hiking all of these trails with me, over and over again, virtually. And I would like to thank Sue Campbell for her wonderful book design.

Finally I wish to thank black licorice, Honeycrisp apples, wasabi dried peas, and a red Mazda 3 named Ruby.

CHOOSE YOUR PERFECT HIKE

EVERYONE BRINGS DIFFERENT INTERESTS AND ABILITIES TO THE TRAIL. HERE'S A ROUNDUP of five of the best hikes in several different categories to help you choose your perfect hike for what interests you today.

Easy for Children & Adults with Limited Mobility

Teen Favorites

Waterfalls, Streams & Wetlands

Wildflowers

Interesting Geology

Summer

Winter

Spring

Fall Foliage

Solitude & Remote Adventure

Strenuous

Bird-watching

Stargazing

Historical Interest

Moose or Mountain Goats

INDEX

U

T

V

W

Y

Z